# The Making of Nantucket

*Matthew Crosby at age 53, painted by William Swain, 1844.*

# The Making of Nantucket

Family Lives and Fortunes
in the Nineteenth Century

Everett U. Crosby

*Spinner Publications, Inc.*
New Bedford, Massachusetts

**Cover art:** *Capturing a Sperm Whale,* painted in 1835 by William Page (1811- 1885) from a sketch by Cornelius B. Hulsart (1795-1876), and engraved, colored, and printed by John Hill (1770-1850). An early depiction of the extraordinary labor and danger involved in whaling. Hulsart was well aware of the risks since he had lost an arm while on the whaleship *Superior* out of New London in 1830. Cover art was reproduced from a glass negative, edited to replicate original color, and manipulated to fit format.

Library of Congress Cataloging-in-Publication Data

Names: Crosby, Everett Uberto, 1932– author.
Title: The making of Nantucket : family lives and fortunes in the nineteenth century / Everett U. Crosby.
Description: New Bedford, MA : Spinner Publications, Inc., [2018] | Includes bibliographical references and index.
Identifiers: LCCN 2018000126 | ISBN 9780932027351 (pbk.)
Subjects: LCSH: Crosby, Matthew, 1791-1878. | Nantucket (Mass.)--History--19th century. | Ship captains--Massachusetts--Nantucket--Biography. | Shipowners--Massachusetts--Nantucket-Biography. | Merchants--Massachusetts--Nantucket--Biography. | Nantucket (Mass.)--Economic conditions--19th century. | Crosby family. | Nantucket (Mass.)--Biography.
Classification: LCC F72.N2 C78 2018 | DDC 974.4/97030922 [B] --dc23
LC record available at https://lccn.loc.gov/2018000126

*To Candace*

*History is the essence of innumerable Biographies.*

– Thomas Carlyle, 1830

# Contents

Preface . . . . . . . . . . . . . . . . . . . . . . . . . . . 4
Introduction . . . . . . . . . . . . . . . . . . . . . . . 7
1. Packet Captain . . . . . . . . . . . . . . . . . . . 31
2. Family Matters . . . . . . . . . . . . . . . . . . . 65
3. In the Counting House . . . . . . . . . . . . . 113
4. New Markets for New Wealth . . . . . . . . 141
5. Down Main Street . . . . . . . . . . . . . . . . 183

    Appendix I . . . . . . . . . . . . . . . . . . . . . 228
    Appendix II – Genealogical Charts . . . . 229
    Notes . . . . . . . . . . . . . . . . . . . . . . . . . 230
    Bibliography . . . . . . . . . . . . . . . . . . . 238
    Index . . . . . . . . . . . . . . . . . . . . . . . . . 244
    Illustration Credits . . . . . . . . . . . . . . . 250
    About the Author . . . . . . . . . . . . . . . . 250

# Tables

1. Whaleships in service, Nantucket & New Bedford, 1845–1860 . . . . . . . . . . 89
2. Whaleships leaving Nantucket and oil imported: 1815–1870 . . . . . . . . . . 115
3. Comparative returns of selected Nantucket whaleships, 1822-1851 . . . . . . . 121
4. Sailing schedule of the whaleship *Washington*, 1819–1849 . . . . . . . . . . . 123
5. Estimated losses in the Nantucket fire of 1838 . . . . . . . . . . . . . . . . . . 147
6. Matthew Crosby's investment portfolio, 1868 . . . . . . . . . . . . . . . . . . 172
7. Matthew Crosby's interest in selected whaleships . . . . . . . . . . . . . . . . 176
8. Average return of sperm oil landed by American ships, 1842–1847 . . . . . . 177
9. Cost of selected household staples, 1819–1820 & 1835 . . . . . . . . . . . . . . 191
10. Comparative grocery prices: Nantucket and the mainland, 1824 . . . . . . . 193

# MAP
## OF THE ISLAND OF
# NANTUCKET,
### Including
## TUCKERNUCK.
#### Surveyed by Wm. Mitchell.
### 1838.

E.W. Bouvé's drawing & Lithography. Graphic Court – Boston.

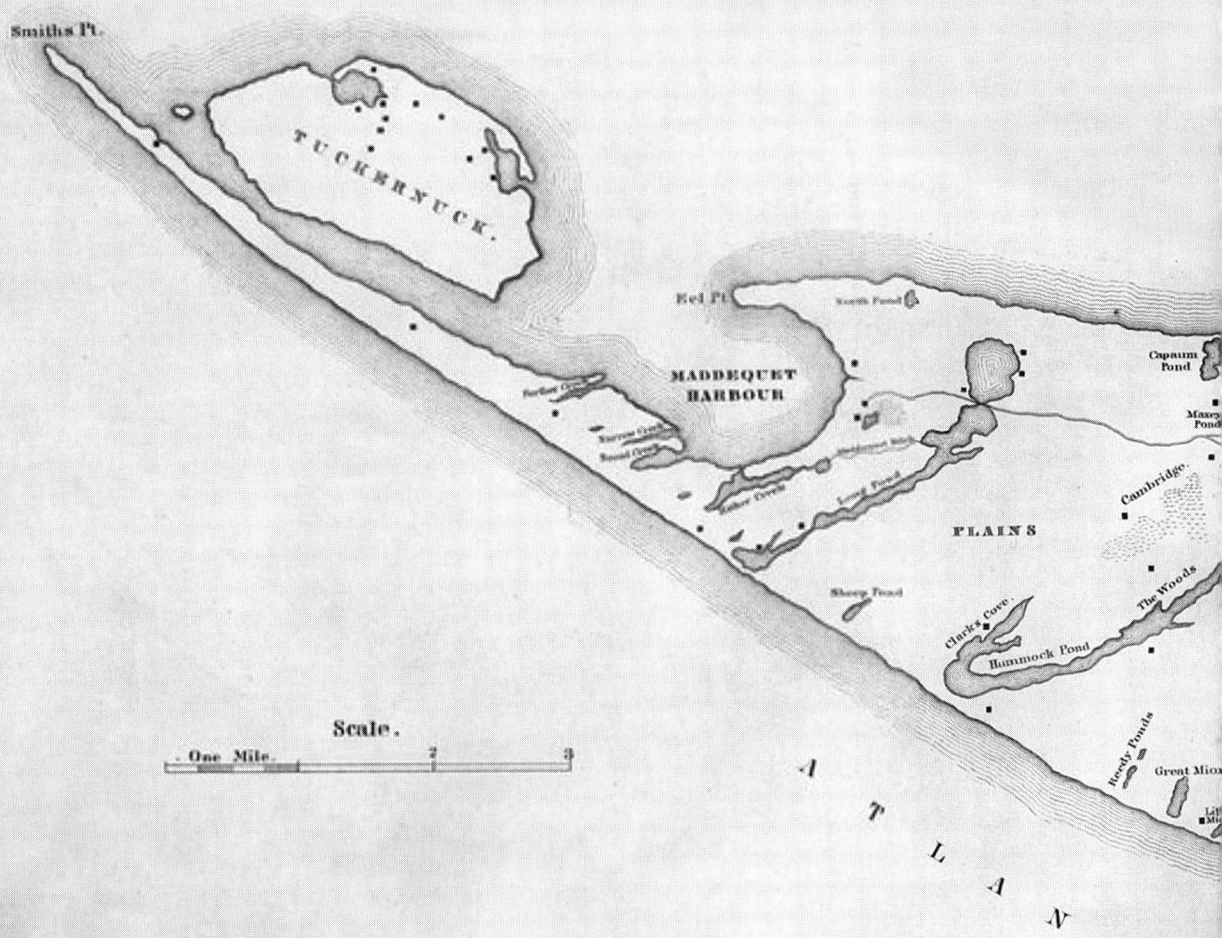

Scale.
One Mile.

Latitude of the Central part of the Town    41° 16′ 36″ North.
Longitude West of Greenwich    70° 06′ 06″ or 4 40 24.4 in time

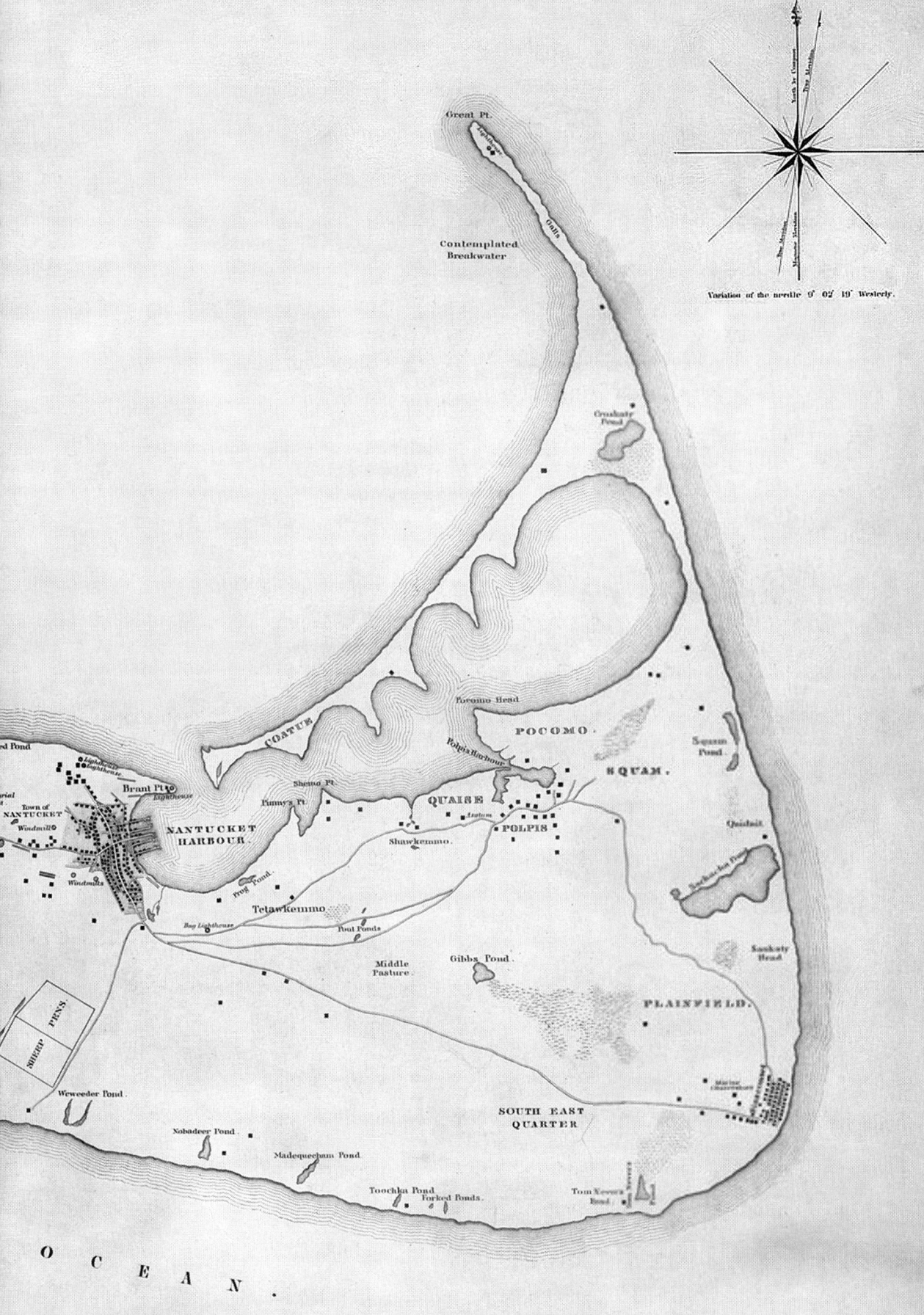

# Preface

The idea of writing a book about Nantucket in the nineteenth century began to take shape several years ago when I became interested in the striking achievement of a small town resourceful enough to have fashioned a fortune from the sea and then, having lost it, to have been able to reinvent itself as a burgeoning prosperous summer resort. Who were the citizens responsible for leading the way? What can be said about their daily lives and their relations with each other? Where do we find sufficient information to draw up a balance sheet of gains and losses? How was it possible, in spite of a multitude of adverse factors, to turn a severe economic depression into a productive source of new wealth?

To answer these questions meant looking at the material circumstances and the social life of the ruling class on the island before and after the mid-century crisis. In the manuscript collections of the Nantucket Historical Association, in the County deed books and property records, and in published accounts and newspaper articles, there is a good deal of material to be found concerning the small circle of the important families. In that tightly knit community, they are the key figures to study in any attempt to chronicle the events of those formative years. Coffin, Starbuck, Folger, Gardner, and Macy are the familiar names commonly encountered, but there were others, less well known now, but no less prominent then.

The list could easily be extended to include such influential ones as Barnard, Barrett, Bunker, Coleman, Mitchell, Pinkham, Swain, Worth, and Wyer. A search of the relevant documents also turned up not a few references to various members of the Crosby family. Naturally, I was first attracted by the name. But on closer reading, Matthew Crosby, a leading figure in the town, whose life from 1791 to 1878 spanned the larger part of the century in question, emerged from the manuscripts and the printed pages as a rewarding subject for a biographical study and the ideal centerpiece for an island history. As it turned out, this was a fortuitous discovery.

Although we have the last name in common and a shared ancestor from England in the early seventeenth century, our families descended along different lines. But the surprising amount of archival material relating to him has made it possible to reconstruct part of the island chronicle through his experiences. He appeared to be a personage too valuable to neglect. In this way, the reader may be brought directly into the life of the community, often quite vividly from day to day, which is far more difficult to accomplish with a second-hand summary and description. First the captain of a packet boat carrying freight and passengers between Nantucket and New York, then the owner of a fleet of whaleships and a respected businessman with investments at home and abroad, Matthew's career is a convenient mirror in which to see, and to explain, the successes and failures that shaped the lives of the people most concerned in bringing this small corner of New England into worldwide prominence.

The last point is worth emphasizing because, while renowned today chiefly as a popular summer resort, Nantucket occupied an important place in the early history of the young republic. Although living thirty miles at sea may have heightened the idea that they were a community unto themselves, the citizens of the island were, in fact, always closely linked to the mainland upon which their existence depended. Public debate on issues that exercised their neighbors in Boston, Philadelphia, and Washington affected them as well. In the nineteenth century, current questions, such as those relating to religious conformity, federal versus regional political authority, and the regulation of industry and trade, as well more immediate concerns involving better charts for the surrounding waters, or the pros and cons of neutrality in wartime, or the structure of hometown government, were up for daily discussion on the market square. The lives of Nantucket men and women, therefore, cannot be just an island story, inasmuch as the way they thought and what they did, although played out on a smaller stage, were to a large degree affected by issues shaping the greater national history.

For help in obtaining the needed documents, I am especially indebted to Louise Hussey, Jacqueline Haring, Elizabeth Oldham, and Ralph Marie Henke at the Nantucket Historical Association for their kind assistance, and to the officials at the Nantucket Registry of Deeds and Probate Records, as well as to the librarians and archivists at the Boston Public Library, Brown University Library, the Dedham Historical Society, the Connecticut Historical Society, the Baker Library at Harvard University, the Library of Congress, the National Archives, the New Bedford Historical Society, the New Bedford Registry of Deeds, the New York Historical Society, the New York Public Library, the San Diego Historical Society, and Alderman Library at the University of Virginia.

Notes have been added to provide references to the manuscript sources cited in the text and to the quoted material. Works found to have been particularly useful are listed in the bibliography. As far as possible, the illustrations have been selected from collections of photographs, paintings, and drawings that can be dated to those years of the nineteenth century with which this history is concerned. Early photographs, in particular, often lack modern-day precision and resolution, so that in some cases authenticity must be valued over clarity.

I also wish to record my thanks to Joseph Thomas and Jay Avila, as well as to Frances Karttunen, for their support of the project and their expert advice and wise counsel in the preparation of the manuscript.

# Introduction

*A stylized view of* The Town of Sherburne in the Island of Nantucket *attributed to Joseph Sansom (1767–1826) and engraved by Benjamin Tanner (1775–1848), circa 1815.*

Nantucket, "a mere hillock and elbow of sand," but whose inhabitants have "overrun and conquered the watery world like so many Alexanders," as Herman Melville put it in a famous line from *Moby-Dick*, has, indeed, had a history much larger than itself. From its early years as a haven for the outsider, followed by a stunning rise and fall as an important whaling port in the nineteenth century, only to be redeemed by a growing tourist trade in the twentieth, down to its present-day international eminence (and all the excess baggage that goes with it), the island has never failed to attract the visitor and charm the resident.

But as much as we today may deplore the power of the dollar to alter the landscape and social habits, it is worth remembering that the history of English settlement on Nantucket began as a commercial venture, and aside from some lean years in the mid-nineteenth century, the island has been a place for lucrative investment ever since.

In 1497, Henry VII licensed John Cabot and his sons "to discover lands, to subdue heathens and infidels, and to possess the territory in the king's name as his vassals," in what was then an easy combination of religious zeal and material profit. More than a century later, the charter of the Massachusetts Bay Colony, obtained from King Charles I in 1629, "for the glory of God and the honour of the king," confirmed a large part of present-day New England to a group of financial entrepreneurs. Soon after, in October 1641, Thomas Mayhew, an English merchant from Wiltshire with business in Watertown, Massachusetts, and his son, purchased a part of the crown grant that had been made to William Alexander, Earl of Stirling, a literary figure and a favorite of James I and Charles I. Their portion included Nantucket, Tuckernuck, Muskeget, Martha's Vineyard, and the Elizabeth Islands.

Because of the haphazard way of bestowing titles at the time, some of the rights to Maine and the islands had already been conveyed to Sir Ferdinando Gorges, a merchant mariner and a member of the Plymouth Colony. Under the circumstances, Mayhew thought it best to buy the Gorges interests as well. Several years later, Nantucket was sold again to nine investor-proprietors for thirty pounds and two beaver hats, so it has been told, with Mayhew retaining one-twentieth of the land, a parcel in Quaise, and bearing one-twentieth of the cost. Thus, there were ten purchasers, each of whom soon admitted another partner, so that by 1660, there were twenty principal owners, plus seven additional men who came over from the mainland.

The Wampanoag Indians, who in those years outnumbered the English, were initially compensated by payments to their sachems, and tentative arrangements were made for shared property rights. The so-called conquest of New England was deemed legitimate by the English because the natives, while living on and using the land, had made no improvements on it. What they were really interested in was not a particular acre here or there, but the benefits that all the land provided for hunting, trapping, fishing, herding, and planting. As so often happened elsewhere, they eventually lost out, and while many of the native place-names remained, the new settlers became permanently integrated into island history: Tristram Coffin from Devon, Thomas Macy from Wiltshire, Edward Starbuck from Derbyshire, Peter Folger from Norfolk, John Gardner from Dorset, and Christopher Hussey from Surrey.

Of the original buyers, only four remained on the island. Thus, it would seem that even though some of their children came to live there, a return on investment was the principal motivation for their business venture. Moreover, if "return on investment" were expanded to include a sense of spiritual well-being and peace of mind, then Nantucket had something to offer Thomas Macy.

Macy had run into trouble with the Massachusetts court by harboring Quakers and doubtless found that he could combine an interest in land with a refuge from Puritan collectivism and intolerance thirty miles at sea. So he appears in John Greenleaf Whittier's labored verses:

> Far round the bleak and stormy Cape
> The venturous Macy passed,
> And on Nantucket's naked isle
> Drew up his boat at last.
>
> And how, in log-built cabin
> They braved the rough sea-weather;
> And there, in peace and quietness,
> Went down life's vale together;
>
> How others drew around them,
> And how their fishing sped,
> Until to every wind of heaven,
> Nantucket's sails were spread.
>
> How pale Want alternated
> With Plenty's golden smile;
> Behold, is it not written
> In the annals of the isle? [1]

But, in truth, compared to the sufficiency and extent of agricultural communities on the mainland, it was not obvious that the sandy soil of Nantucket, interspersed with patches of loam, might support a flourishing economy. On an island twelve miles long and three miles wide, there were no great forests for an endless supply of timber, no extensive fields for cultivation, and sheep raising, while profitable, had limited room for expansion. Many necessities, such as bulk building materials, ironwork, kitchen staples, and any luxury goods desired, had to be transported by water at increased cost. Nantucketers, therefore, did what so many New Englanders had always done: they looked to the sea, first to cod fishing and then to whaling.

The early reports of whales being captured come from the middle of the seventeenth century. In those days they were killed and towed back to shore, where the blubber was cut off and boiled down to extract the oil. Emboldened by the success of this operation, which arose from the great number of whales in nearby waters, the men of the island put farther out to sea, stayed out for a longer time, and packed the blubber into barrels to be brought home.

Before long, much larger ships were launched. These could remain at sea for months at a time, so that the work of trying-out, that is to say, boiling down, was done on board, and assuming a profitable voyage, the men returned to port only when the hold was full.

Investment in whaling was risky and expensive, but it could produce significant returns. Oil was exported to the mainland and to London for the European market. Soon, factories were set up to process it and to turn the waxy substance from the head cavity of sperm whales, the so-called spermaceti, into high-grade candles. So it was that Nantucket emerged as a prosperous community of merchant mariners governed by a group of often closely related families who were wholly dependent on a broad infrastructure of shipmasters and crews, as well as blacksmiths, carpenters, caulkers, chandlers, coopers, riggers, rope makers, sail makers, and other skilled workers drawn from the native population and from off-island immigrants. The formidable effort demanded to make a living from whaling consumed the time and energy of most of the inhabitants. If they were not directly engaged in it, they were supporting those who were, and both men and women had important parts to play.

It was the success in this endeavor that drew the attention of the young Frenchman, Michel Guillaume Jean de Crèvecoeur (who, upon naturalization, took the pseudonym J. Hector St. John). Crèvecoeur's visit to the island in the 1760s convinced him to devote a third of his book, *Letters from an American Farmer* (London: 1782), to a description of Nantucket, including a map. It was, he wrote:

> A barren sand-bank insignificant in extent, inconvenient in its situation, deprived of materials for building, it seems to have been inhabited merely to prove what mankind can do when happily governed.[2]

A child of the romantic enlightenment, Crèvecoeur painted a portrait of "the American, this new man,"[3] to conform more to the image of what he hoped the new man would be by exploiting the gift of political freedom to prosper in the New World, than to the rather ordinary figure that he was. Probing deeper, he asked himself, and his reader, how it was possible for the people on Nantucket to flourish, live well, and sometimes to make considerable fortunes when they were deprived of almost every basic necessity? It was an enigma to be solved only by coming to the island to breathe the purity of the air and to observe the national genius at work. Here was the celebration of rural America and the contented souls, happily endowed with unwearied patience, perseverance, and moderation in all things,

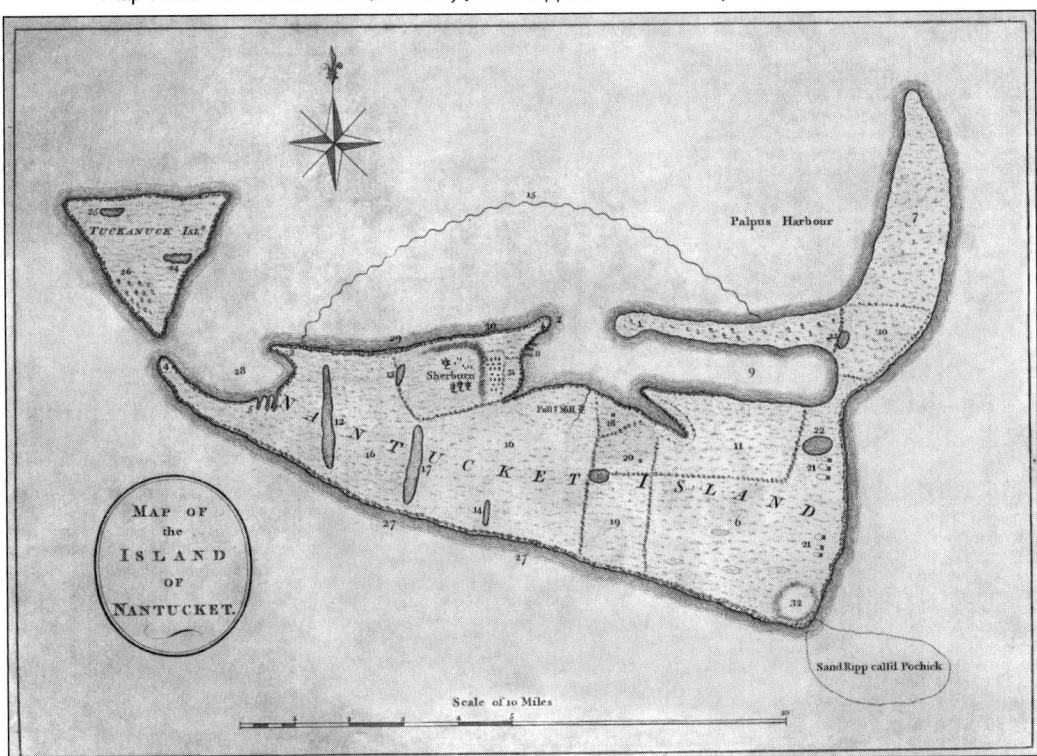

Map of the Island of Nantucket, *drawn by James Tupper, and included by Crèvecoeur in his book.*

who lived close to nature, unhindered by class distinctions, rules, religious conformity, or political oppression:

> After all, is it not better to be possessed of a single whaleboat, or a few sheep pastures, to live free and independent under the mildest governments, in a healthy climate, in a land of charity and benevolence, than to be wretched as so many are in Europe, possessing nothing but their industry, tossed from one rough wave to another, engaged either in the most servile labours for the smallest pittance, or fettered with the links of the most irksome dependence, even without the hopes of rising?[4]

There is certainly no doubt that the islanders had turned the environment to their advantage by the time the author came to see for himself. The population had grown to some 4,000 people, largely by immigration from the mainland, since the number of Indians, reduced by disease, had continued to decline to only a few hundred. The driving force behind the vigorous economy was not the successful cultivation of the fields and forests, but the precipitous growth of deep-sea sperm whaling fed by an international market eager for the use of the oil in lighting and industrial applications.

New ships were designed, built, and sent out on voyages of a year or more, and the skill of men from Nantucket in the business was becoming well known. A letter from London, dated 1776, by Dennis de Berdt, probably the son of the Dennis de Berdt who was the colonial agent for Massachusetts, to an unknown correspondent concerning whaling off the coast of Brazil, is clear on the point:

> Reports of good whaling induced merchants of Nantucket to send three vessels there in 1773…The next season 30 vessels were sent from Nantucket and parts adjacent…Last year upwards of 140 vessels came from different parts of N. America…The people of Nantucket and Cape Cod are so much better at taking the sperm whale that some of them would be necessary in every [British] ship. They proved their superiority in the Greenland fishing when they raised and struck a whale 15 minutes before the British boats came up, although they had started at the same time.[5]

Between the time of the visit of Crèvecoeur in the mid-1760s and publication of his book in 1782, it has been estimated that, with so many ships abroad, Nantucketers brought in more than 4,000 tons of oil annually which was worth almost 170,000 pounds sterling. In spite of the great dangers and uncertainties of the enterprise, they had found a gold mine in the sea. A sure sign of success was the attempt of John Hancock and his uncle, Thomas, of Boston to corner the market on whale oil in the 1760s and a counter move by Joseph Rotch and his son, William, to do the same on Nantucket. They were opposed, of course, by the small group of independent whalemen who were fearful of being crowded out with a subsequent loss of market share.[6]

But very soon, decisions by men in a position of authority in the capitals of London and Paris, but who were little-known to those they affected most, unleashed greater forces that would depress the market and have a numbing effect on the prosperity of the region for many years. In the struggle for empire by the European powers, the British defeat of the French in North America in 1763 had opened the way for the American colonists, with the aid of French, to defeat the British in 1781. But this chain of events, justly celebrated in the United States ever after, made it clear to the islanders that Nantucket was unlike other New England towns in that it had no vast stretch of adjacent inland to which it might expand and exploit. To increase the supply of goods to use and sell, it relied solely on trade, which by 1770 was carried on increasingly with England instead of through middlemen in Boston. The paradox was that the fisheries, especially cod fishing and whaling, were a national resource and served as the basis of American maritime power to confront threats from abroad.

It was reasonable, therefore, that as the storm clouds gathered, a large number of the citizens came to oppose a break with the mother country. They were, after all, vulnerable on their island with no way to protect themselves from attack, dependent on an open water route, and justified in their view by a strong strain of Quaker pacifism. So they settled down to an uncomfortable neutrality, suspected by the British of revolutionary sentiments, and by the patriots of subverting their cause by engaging in commerce with the enemy. In a summary passage in his *History of Nantucket*, written in 1835, Obed Macy, who was born in 1755 and was, therefore, a contemporary witness, relived the distress:

> The long expected period at length arrived: even before spring closed, the first blood was spilt in the battle of Lexington. The news of this action spread rapidly to every part of the colonies; in a few days it arrived at Nantucket. The countenances of the people here bespoke the anguish of their hearts. All business was immediately at a stand. Discouraged and powerless, they could do little else than meet together and bemoan their fate…Many were deeply concerned for the welfare of their husbands, children, or brothers, then at sea, on whom they depended for their subsistence and the comforts of life; many were anxious on account of their property, both at home and at sea, on which their dependence was placed. A common distress pervaded all hearts, which was in no way relieved by anticipations of the future.[7]

Within a short time, the merchants had to endure an embargo by the Crown on goods shipped abroad, and a little while later, another one imposed by the Continental Congress. British and American privateers roamed the nearby waters so that a serious concern was the loss of capital through the capture and destruction of the whaleships. Thus, were they caught between the Charybdis and Scylla of the maritime war, "between two dangers, either of which was difficult to avoid without encountering the other."[8] It was also the case that the market for whale oil in England was limited by high excise duties imposed to favor the home industry, which lowered the return on a single barrel by almost 40%. Further damage was incurred later in the commerce with France by the upheaval of the revolution in 1789.

By the end of the century, the strength of the fleet had dropped from about 150 ships in 1770 to not more than 50. To recover their investments by establishing a new base for trade, some of the leading men of the island toyed with the idea of transferring whaling operations to New York, or Nova Scotia, or even to England or France. A few families did choose to leave, but most appear to have remained, turning once again to the old-time pursuits of farming, fishing, and sheep-raising as their means of survival. Even though the grand idea envisioned by Jefferson and his like-minded colleagues to establish a peaceful and profitable world order based on trade, at least insofar as it benefited the United States, was found to be unworkable and too expensive for everyday use, by the end of hostilities in 1783, the practical-minded men of Nantucket were actively rebuilding their lucrative industry.

There followed a brief period of growth in the last decade of the eighteenth century. In 1791, the year in which Matthew Crosby was born, it should be noted, the first Nantucket whaleship rounded Cape Horn and entered the Pacific to open up a vast new territory of rich whaling grounds. But, by 1793, as a consequence of the French depression and disorder in Paris and the provinces, France and England were once again at loggerheads. In spite of President Washington's controversial resolve not to become engaged in another "European" war, and in spite of the proclamation of neutrality as public policy for America, there were blockades off the eastern American coast again. In an ironic twist, the Jeffersonian embargo act of 1807, which forbade trade with a foreign port, although not everywhere enforced,

Sperm Whaling: the Chase. *A lithograph from a drawing by Albert van Beest (1820–1860) and R. Swain Gifford (1840-1905), corrected by Benjamin Russell (1804-1885), and published by Charles Taber in New Bedford in 1859.*

nevertheless caused another serious loss of oil exports. Voices were raised in protest. "The times are too perilous," warned Senator Timothy Pickering in a letter to the Governor of Massachusetts in February 1808:

> to allow those who are placed in high and responsible positions of our country to be silent or reserved. The peace and safety of our country are suspended on a thread. The course we have pursued leads on to war, war with Great Britain, a war absolutely without necessity, a war whether disastrous or successful, must bring misery and ruin to the United States: misery by the destruction of our navigation and commerce (perhaps also of our fairest seaport towns and cities), the loss of markets for our produce, the want of foreign goods and manufactures, and the other evils incident to a state of war: ruin by the loss of our liberty and independence. For if with the aid of our arms Great Britain were subdued, from that moment (thought flattered perhaps with the name of allies), we should become the Provinces of France.[9]

The further conflict of 1812–1815, punctuated by fighting tempered with negotiations for a peaceful settlement, brought about another interruption of seaborne commerce in New England. Obed Macy, who was well aware of the serious effect that renewed hostilities would have on Nantucket, once again made a gloomy entry for June 24, 1812:

> The declaration of war with England had thrown the inhabitants into the utmost confusion in the line of business. The people are shipping off their property to the continent to save it from the grasp of the enemy and many families are moving from the islands.[10]

Some representative examples from the list of Nantucket vessels captured by British warships and lost to trade reveal the depth of the distress:

> Ship *Hope*, captured full of oil, sent to Barbadoes
> Ship *Ranger*, captured full of oil, sent to Bermudas
> Ship *Alligator*, captured full of oil, sent to St. Thomas
> Ship *Fame*, sent to England
> Ship *Manilla*, captured, sent to England full of oil
> Brig *Ocean*, captured and sent to Cape of Good Hope full of oil
> Brig *Leo*, captured in the West Indies
> Schooner *Mount Hope*, taken and burnt.[11]

To relieve the suffering on the island, a few intrepid captains continued to run a profitable, but dangerous, coastal commerce with supplies of food, fuel, timber, and hardware. But this was never enough, and people with the fewest means fared the worst. In May 1813, Macy was still full of concern:

The cry of the poor are [sic] daily increasing, not having business that will produce the means of subsistence. Great numbers of poor children are begging from door to door. One or two vessels have gone after corn and flour. Should they come short, the consequences would be shocking, as the needy could not receive the daily supply which they now have from the rich.[12]

Ultimately, the best course of action was deemed to be an agreement reached with the British authorities to allow the provisioning of the town in return for a second declaration of neutrality. This entailed the serious concession on the part of the islanders not to pay taxes to the federal government and the reluctant acceptance of a prohibition on whaling from the home port. In a turbulent period of conflicting loyalties, however, impassioned and resolute patriotism was not the natural sentiment for all Americans. It seemed especially ill-sorted for those who were in peril of their lives and who, moreover, had developed the habit peculiar to islanders of seeing themselves as a shade different from their fellow citizens on the mainland.

Nevertheless, bad times, like good times, could not endure forever. Upon the signing of the peace treaty in December 1815, there was again a gradual increase in the population of

Whaleship Adam *of London, circa 1817. A watercolor by an anonymous British seaman depicts the whaleship* Adam, *formerly known as the* Renown *of Nantucket, built in Duxbury, Massachusetts in 1794. She made several successful voyages to the Atlantic and the Pacific before being captured by the British during the War of 1812 and renamed.*

the island and an accompanying rise in wealth. New men with new ideas began to appear in industry and politics, and however much the established order might have resented their intrusion, room had to be made for them. Equally noteworthy was the determined effort by those with an invested interest in the whaling business to regain their economic power. Such perseverance was rewarded in the course of the middle years of the nineteenth century, which saw the peak of success and profits. So claimed a correspondent for the *Niles Register* in 1833:

> This interesting little island is said to be in a very prosperous state, and the value of some of the town lots has increased 50 per cent in the last five years. Its industry and enterprise extracts 'the oil of gladness and rejoicing' from the distant and deep ocean.[13]

Historically, this period of prosperity had important consequences for the fortunes of the island. High quality sperm and whale oil and spermaceti wax were still much in demand for use in lighting and industrial applications, and this led to further investment in an extended infrastructure of factories and warehouses. Larger whaleships were launched, and longer voyages, often for two, three, or four years, were undertaken. But there were concessions to be made. Greater wealth brought back in oil was offset by the rising cost of building, outfitting, and insuring the ships and paying the shares of captain and crew. Moreover, there was substantial capital literally afloat for a long time, constantly subject to loss by shipwreck, injury, death, piracy, and even mutiny. Investments could not turn a profit until enough whales were taken, the oil extracted, and the ship had returned to port. Although Nantucket merchants were able to finance well over a hundred ships between 1820 and 1840 and invest their money in new business and fine houses, there were signs that the fortunes made in deep-sea whaling were soon to reach a turning point.

Serious competition from the burgeoning port of New Bedford on the mainland, itself a town built on whale-oil money, but with a better harbor and inland connections, began to drain away the profits from the near-monopoly on the island. Coastal towns such as New London, Westport (Mass.), Stonington, and Sag Harbor also grew to be serious rivals with a combined fleet of several dozen active whaleships. Then, in 1836, 1838, and 1846, three major fires in Nantucket destroyed important sections of the downtown shops and warehouses, and the wharves vital to daily commerce.

Moreover, the sandbar at the entrance to the harbor proved to be an insurmountable difficulty for the easy passage of the heavily laden vessels. In spite of the temporary use of a novel contraption, called the "camels," to float the larger ships over the shallows, the problem was not solved until many years later. The invention of the camels was doomed to failure, however, not because it proved unable to lift the boats, but because, even in the late 1840s, there were fewer boats to lift. The costs of the operation, including frequent overhauls, remained much too high. A prophetic death notice sent from Edgartown appeared in the *Whalemen's Shipping List* in 1849:

*The town of Nantucket in 1834, surveyed by William Coffin Jr., and printed by Henry Clapp (1814-1875). This is the first detailed layout of the streets, residential and commercial buildings, and churches. Clearly depicted are the five wharves, three windmills, two ropewalks, and several fire cisterns placed at critical locations.*

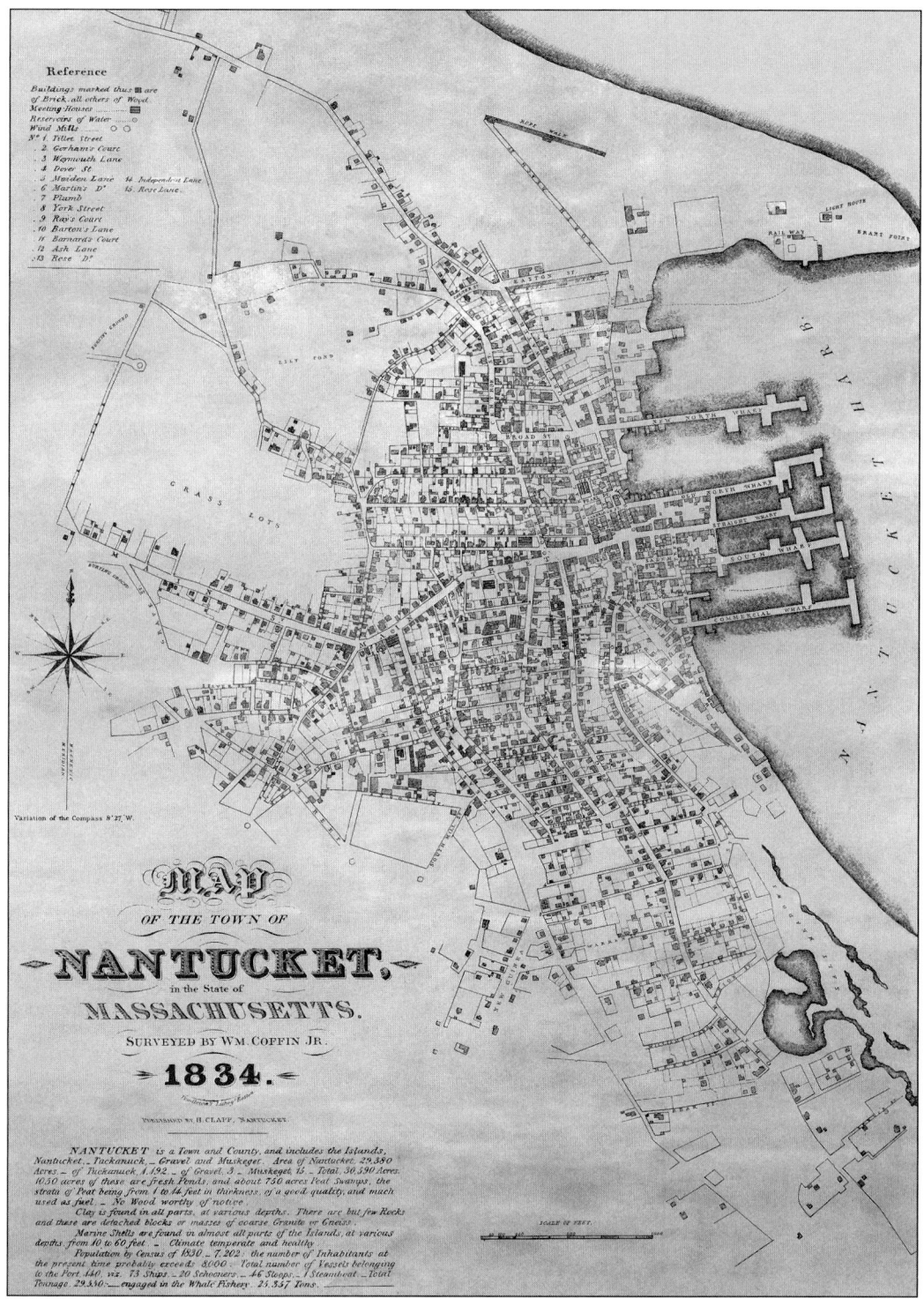

For a number of years past Nantucket ships arriving laden, and those sailing from that port, have been taken over the bar by the 'camels.' They [the camels] have been repaired several times, but are at present entirely used up, and will not again be put in order. Consequently when any of the Nantucket whalemen arrive, they will stop at this port and unload.[14]

There was, in fact, no satisfactory solution short of dredging the channel and building a jetty, or, as the above notice makes clear, off-loading the barrels of oil at another port. But in the darkening economic picture, neither option gathered sufficient support.

*A vessel in the camels under tow by the steamboat* Telegraph *in a drawing attributed to James W. Folger.*

Farther afield, the rediscovery and growing commercial availability of petroleum spelled the beginning of the end of the strong market for the more expensive whale oil. The former quickly appeared to be a satisfactory product which was easier to get out of the ground than the latter was to get out of the sea. A pair of ominous yet unrelated notices appeared on the same page of the Nantucket newspaper in December 1866. If read together, they point up the problem.

In column 1:
A well was struck on the Tarr farm, Oil Creek, Pennsylvania, about two weeks since, which is now flowing three hundred barrels of oil every twenty-four hours. The well is 591 feet deep, and is the largest producer in Pennsylvania.

In column 2:
New Bedford oil market for the week ending December 3. The market continues quiet for both sperm and whale oil. The transactions for the week include the following sales of sperm: 158 barrels prime and 80 barrels dark for manufacture on private terms; and resale of 300 barrels prime also for manufacture on private terms. We hear of no sales of whale.[15]

To aggravate these woes, more and more people now began to leave the island. From a high figure of about 9,000 inhabitants in 1840, there were to be counted only about 3,000 in 1875. This reduction in manpower was brought about by the exodus of young men in search of better jobs on the mainland, then by the siren call from the gold fields in the west, and finally by recruitment of some two hundred volunteers for the Union army in 1861–1865. Consequently, there was a noticeable difficulty in finding experienced crews for the

*The list of Nantucket vessels in the* Whalemen's Shipping List and Merchants' Transcript *for March 17, 1843, includes the Mariner, Navigator, and Washington, which belonged to Matthew Crosby.*

# Whalemen's Shipping List,
## AND MERCHANTS' TRANSCRIPT.

VOL. I.   NEW BEDFORD, FRIDAY MORNING, MARCH 17, 1843.   NO. 1.

| VESSELS NAMES | ton | MASTERS. | AGENTS. | SAILED. | WHERE BOUND | DATE AND PLACE OF LAST REPORT. | OIL. |
|---|---|---|---|---|---|---|---|
| Nantucket. | | | | | | | |
| Alex Coffin | 381 | Wyer | R Mitchell & Sons | Sept 8, 40 | Pacific | Oct 19, at Oahu | 1500 sp |
| Alpha | 345 | Congdon | Hudson & Barney | May 15, 42 | Pacific | June 11, at Fayal | 30 sp |
| American | 329 | Coffin | Danl Jones | Dec 1, 41 | Pacific | At Payta Nov 20 | 750 sp |
| Atlantic | 321 | Hoag | Danl Jones | May 13, 39 | Pacific | Oct 17, at Tahiti | 1500 sp |
| Aurora | 346 | Coffin | T & P Macy | May 12, 41 | Pacific | May, at Gallipagos Islands | 350 sp |
| Baltic | 402 | Gardner | Ino H Shaw | Aug 17, 39 | Pacific | Nov 18, lat 40 s lon 77 w | 1450 sp 60 wh |
| Barclay | 301 | Barney | Griffin Barney | Dec 10, 39 | Pacific | October 17, at Talcahuana | 1700 sp |
| Catawba | 335 | Pease | U G & H Coffin | Feb. 1, 40 | Pacific | In September, at Tombez | 1500 sp |
| Catharine | 384 | Hunter | Christopher Wyer | May 8, 39 | Pacific | August 7, at Payta | 900 sp |
| Chas & Henry | 336 | Coleman | C G & H Coffin | Dec 20, 40 | Pacific | July 1, on the equator, lon 121 16 | 300 sp |
| Charles Carroll | 376 | Andrews | W C Swain | May 29, 40 | Pacific | June, at Gallipagos Islands | 1800 sp |
| Chris. Mitchell | 387 | Keene | C Mitchell & Co | Oct 25, 41 | Pacific | May or June, at Gallipagos Islands | 100 sp |
| Clarkson | 390 | Chase | Jas Athearn | Sept 18, 42 | Pacific | Oct 27, at Cape de Verde | clean |
| Columbia | 329 | Joy | C G & H Coffin | Sept 4, 41 | Pacific | June 26, on off shore ground | 200 sp |
| Columbus | 314 | Gardner | R Mitchell & Sons | May 21, 39 | Pacific | Sept 21, a Payta | 1100 sp |
| Congress | 339 | Pitman | P H Folger | Aug 27, 39 | Pacific | July 2, at Payta | 1200 sp |
| Constitution | 318 | Ramsdell | C G & H Coffin | Sept 23, 42 | Pacific | | |
| Cyrus | 325 | Emmons | George Myrick jr | Nov 1, 40 | Pacific | August at Marquesas Islands | 1000 sp |
| David Paddock | 352 | Hussey | Daniel Jones | Oct 7, 41 | Pacific | Sept 13, at Tombez | 70 sp |
| D. Webster | 396 | | French & Coffin | In port | | | |
| Edward Cary | 359 | Tobey | Jos Athearn | Sept 26, 41 | Pacific | June 2, off New Holland | 200 sp |
| Eliz. Starbuck | 381 | Bigelow | Levi Satbuck | Aug 21, 41 | Pacific | Between Aug 21 and sept 10, Tahiti | 300 sp |
| Enterprise | 413 | Cannon | Gilbert Coffin | Dec 13, 40 | Pacific | July 29, at Tahiti | 750 sp |
| Foster | 317 | Congdon | R Mitchell & Sons | July 28, 41 | Pacific | April 25, at Maui | 200 sp |
| Franklin | 216 | Ray | James Athearn | Aug 11, 41 | Pacific | June 23, heard from | 150 sp |
| Fabius | 432 | Chase | G & M Starbuck & Co | July 17, 40 | Pacific | Sept 11, at Tombez | 1200 sp |
| Ganges | 315 | Pitman | David Joy | July 28, 41 | Pacific | May 3, lat 5 18 lon 115 17 | 250 sp |
| Harvest | 360 | Gardner | Edward Field | Sept 17, 40 | Pacific | July, on Japan | 600 sp |
| Henry | 346 | Brown | Daniel Jones | June 1, 40 | Pacific | Spoke no date &c 27 mos out | 1100 sp |
| Henry Clay | 335 | Sayer | Christ'r Wyer | Dec 17, 39 | Pacific | Spoke no date &c 32¼ mos out | 2100 sp |
| Henry Astor | 375 | Pinkham | Wm R Easson | Jan 24, 40 | Pacific | Sept 22, at Marquesas Islands | 1300 sp |
| Hero | 313 | Chase | Joseph Starbuck | Sept 29, 41 | Pacific | August 5, heard from at sea | 85 sp |
| Howard | 364 | Bunker | Timothy Hussey | Nov 1, 41 | Pacific | April 8, at Maui | 60 sp |
| James Loper | 318 | Cathcart | Levi Starbuck | Oct 30, 42 | Pacific | | |
| Japan | 332 | Riddell | Barker & Athearn | Sept 17, 41 | Pacific | Aug 3, lat 6 46' lon 118 15 | 350 sp |
| John Adams | 296 | Stockman | David Joy | Aug 31, 41 | Pacific | May 9, at Payta | 50 sp |
| Kingston | 312 | Rawson | Frederick Hussey | June 12, 40 | Pacific | June 24, at Payta | 700 sp |
| Levi Starbuck | 376 | Nye | Levi Starbuck | May 27, 41 | Pacific | On off shore no date | 300 sp |
| Lexington | 399 | Weeks | F C Sanford | Aug 29, 40 | Pacific | August 12, on the equator | 1150 sp |
| Lydia | 3.3 | Cathcart | James Athearn | Sept 2, 40 | Pacific | August 10, at Tahiti | 950 sp |
| Mariner | 318 | Palmer | Matthew Crosby | Oct 6, 40 | Pacific | July, spoken at sea | 900 sp |
| Mary Mitchell | 354 | McCleave | Aaron Mitchell | Aug 25, 42 | Pacific | Dec 15, lat 45 16 lon 53 20 W | 150 sp |
| Mary | 369 | Coffin | Daniel Jones | Sept 10, 39 | Pacific | June, at Gallipagos Islands | 1250 sp |
| Marin | 365 | Fisher | Barret & Upton | May 11, 42 | Pacific | Spoke no date &c 5 mos out | 130 sp |
| Martha | 279 | Baxter | Wm R Easton | July 29, 41 | Pacific | August 5, at Callao | 500 sp |
| Mount Vernon | 383 | Imbert | Ino H Shaw | Oct 1, 39 | Pacific | April, on off shore ground | 1500 sp |
| Massachusetts | 360 | Nickerson | Geo C Gardner | Aug 26, 41 | Pacific | June 3, off New Holland | 250 bbls |
| Montano | 365 | Chase | Barker & Athearn | Oct 24, 41 | Pacific | June 8, off Payta | clean |
| Monticello | 368 | Coggeshall | Ino H Shaw | Aug 2, 41 | Pacific | May, heard from at sea | 250 bbls |
| Nantucket | 351 | Gardner | H G O Dunham | June 16, 41 | Pacific | September, at Tombez | 700 bbls |
| Napoleon | 356 | Fisher | Barret & Upton | Oct 21, 42 | Pacific | Nov 28 on Abrolhos banks | clean |
| Narraganset | 395 | Coffin | Christ'r Wyer | Nov. 7, 41 | Pacific | Dec 11 in lat 4 S, lon 104 W | 1000 sp |
| Navigator | 333 | Fisher | Matthew Crosby | Aug 12, 41 | Pacific | July 19, lat 0 31 lon 117 14 | 830 bbls |
| Obed Mitchell | 355 | Coffin | Aaron Mitchell | Sept 4, 41 | Pacific | July 26, at Tahiti | 400 sp |
| Ocean | 319 | Parker | T & P Macy | Oct 18, 40 | Pacific | Spoke in Sept | 900 sp |
| Ohio | 333 | Smith | Christ'r Wyer | July 13, 41 | Pacific | July 3, at New Nantucket | 600 sp |
| Omega | 355 | Haggerty | Joseph Starbuck | Sept 8, 40 | Pacific | Aug 21 to Sept 10, at Tahiti | 800 sp |
| Ontario | 354 | Gibbs | Barret & Upton | In port | | | |
| Orion | 354 | Nichols | Frederick Hussey | July 5, 41 | Pacific | June 27, lat 26 lon 122½ | 300 sp |
| Penobscot | 13c | Carr | A W Starbuck | Sep t26, 41 | Pacific | At St Catherines Jan 1 | 100 sp |
| Peruvian | 93 | Arthur | Wm B Coffin | July 30, 40 | Pacific | October, at Oahu | 1300 sp |
| Phoenix | 323 | Hamblin | T & P Macy | June 21, 40 | Pacific | At Payta Nov 27 | 1550 sp |
| Peru, bark | 259 | | David Joy | In port | | | |
| Phebe | 379 | Harris | C Mitchell & Co | Sept 19, 42 | Pacific | October 8, at Fayal | clean |
| Planter | 340 | | Gilbert Coffin | In Port | | | |
| Ploughboy | 391 | Brown | V Hussey & Bro | June 27, 39 | Pacific | July 1, at Talcahuana | 750 sp 600 wh |
| Potomac | 356 | Hussey | T & P Macy | Nov 14, 41 | Pacific | July, at Nooaheva | 350 sp |
| President | 293 | Brock | Joseph Starbuck | Dec. 27, 42 | Pacific | | |
| Rambler | 318 | McCleave | F C Sanford | In port | Pacific | | |
| Rich'd Mitchell | 356 | Gardner | R Mitchell & Sons | July 17, 39 | Pacific | About sept 1, at Tahiti | 1150 sp |
| Rose | 345 | Swain | Simeon Starbuck | Feb. 6, 40 | Pacific | Aug 1, lat 14 S, lon 76, | 90 sp |
| Sarah | 195 | Upham | Geo B Elkins | July 14, 39 | Pacific | Oct or Nov Off Oahu | not stated |
| Spartan | 333 | Coffin | Daniel Jones | Oct 16, 39 | Pacific | At Talcahuana Oct 27 | 1500 sp |
| Statira | 346 | Folger | Samuel B Tuck | Nov. 9, 39 | Pacific | At Tahiti Oct 17, | 2500 sp |
| Susan | 348 | Russell | Aaron Mitchell | Dec 11, 41 | Pacific | Aug 12, on Equator, lon 128 W | 80 bbls |
| Three Brothers | 394 | Mitchell | G & M Starbuck & Co | July 12, 41 | Pacific | July at sea | 550 bbls |
| Thule | 286 | Coleman | Saml B Tuck | June 27, 42 | Pacific | Aug 2, at Cape De Verde | clean |
| Tyleston, brig | 111 | Brown | David Thain | Oct 2, 42 | Atlantic | Dec, off Rio Janeiro | clean |
| United States | 306 | Worth | Barret & Upton | Nov 14, 41 | Pacific | July 8, lat 14, lon 118 20 | 75 sp |
| Walter Scott | 339 | Bunker | Barret & Upton | Oct 31, 40 | Pacific | Oct 19, at Oahu | 950 sp |
| Washington | 302 | Bailey | Matthew Crosby | May 14, 40 | Pacific | Spoke no date &c 27 mos out | 950 sp |
| Young Hero | 340 | Alley | Joseph Starbuck | April 17, 42 | Pacific | May 16, at Cape De Verde | clean |
| Young Eagle | 377 | Austin | Simeon Starbuck | Aug 20, 40 | Pacific | Aug, on Japan | 1900 sp |
| Zenas Coffin | 338 | Bailey | C G & H Coffin | July 12, 40 | Pacific | Aug 17, at Callao | 2500 sp |
| Zone | 365 | Hiller | James Athearn | May 19, 39 | Pacific | May 20, at Payta | 1700 bbls |

whaleships. Unskilled labor in the towns now was paid better than unskilled labor aboard ship. The work was also safer, the hours were shorter, room and board might be more acceptable, it was easier to change jobs, and a set wage was known beforehand.

Furthermore, high volume industrial manufacturing was shifting permanently to the big cities. The products of two large cotton mills, it was reported in 1873, equaled very nearly the aggregate value of the imports of the fishery each year.[16] The last local boats to depart on a whaling voyage were the barks *Bohio* and *R. L. Barstow* in 1868, and the brig *Eunice H. Adams* and the bark *Oak* in 1869. The last one to arrive with a sizeable cargo of sperm oil was the bark *Amy* in 1870, and that was the year, you could say, that marked the end of whaling on Nantucket.

Yet what might be bad in one respect might often be good in another, and it did not go unnoticed in the popular press that for the whales, this unexpected reprieve was worthy of celebration. Fewer whaleships, it was thought, meant brighter prospects for the creatures of the sea. The apparent certainty of this conclusion was confirmed in a popular cartoon printed in *Vanity Fair* on April 20, 1861, which bore the title: *Grand Ball given by the Whales in Honor of the Discovery of Oil Wells in Pennsylvania*. Pictured was a group of sperm whales dressed in formal attire enjoying themselves drinking and dancing to mark the happy occasion. Posters were hung around the room with clever messages to remind them of their good fortune: "Oils well that ends well;" "We wail no more for our blubber;" and appropriate for the year in question, "The oil wells of our native land, may they never secede."

But locally it was hard to see the humor, and the serious drop in profits threw a pall over the citizens that could not be disguised. After a tour of the island in the 1870s, Samuel Adams Drake, the well-known writer on colonial America and the history of New England, was particularly struck by the lack of activity:

> But what, in a place of its size, is most remarkable is the almost total absence of movement. It impressed me, the time I was there, as uninhabited. There were no troops of joyous children by day, nor throngs of promenaders by night; all was listless and still. Here, indeed, was the town, but where were the people? I was not at all surprised when accosted by one who, like me, wandered and wondered, with the question, 'Does anybody live in Nantucket'?

R.R. Minturn, who came as a first-time visitor in 1873, had the same impression:

> Returning from my stroll early in the afternoon, I was surprised at the almost death-like stillness of the town. As I turned into the main street, but a single person was in sight; every one seemed to be asleep, and I imagined that the houses blinked drowsily as I passed.[17]

While it could be argued that these remarks were occasioned by the obvious contrast that a newcomer might notice between the atmosphere of the busy city and the slow-paced life of the village, there is sufficient evidence to show that the people of Nantucket had momentarily lost their driving force and were struggling to find an answer for the future. Yet, the established social structure had not been fundamentally changed. Whether they are viewed positively as a force for social stability, or negatively as an inbred merchant monopoly, a handful of families and their near relations still led all the others by wealth and prominence. For more than half a century they had prospered and, in turn, had helped to support the majority of the islanders. By constant attention to the details of the business at hand, by mastering the most efficient means to turn catching whales into a prosperous industry, and by a redoubtable capacity to persevere in the face of an array of disheartening crises, they succeeded in building a small maritime empire.

For those who had lived through the golden years of the middle period, amid the noisy bustle and clatter of the streets and wharves, the constant loading and unloading of ships in the harbor, where every nook and cranny, it seemed, exuded the unmistakable odor of oil, pitch, and tar, and where the press of population had grown to more than 9,000, the spreading somber silence of the island must have seemed an unsettling change for the worse.

*Lily Street, circa 1870, looking east.*

Some attempts were made to find new investments. Silk production was tried in 1836 but failed a few years later. A straw factory was set up in 1852, and shoe manufacturing was resumed in 1859, but neither of them turned a sufficient profit.

At the same time, broadening relations with the mainland and Europe forced the islanders onto a larger stage with significant challenges that threatened the stability of the community. Far from Crèvecoeur's "land of charity and benevolence," life on the island revealed many wayward currents that worked against the collective endeavor, raised deep-seated animosities, and divided the citizens. These opposing forces were noticeable at an early date.

The dissension generated with regard to the question of neutrality during the war with England is one example. The notorious robbery of the Nantucket bank only a few months after it opened in 1795 was another crisis that exposed deep rifts of a personal nature between those accused and their accusers. This was apparent to Josiah Quincy, later the mayor of Boston and president of Harvard, who made a journey to the island in 1801:

> In the evening, Mr. William Hammatt and Mr. Josiah Barker, to whom we had letters from Mr. Coffin, called and invited us to a party they had made up for us to the east end of the island. Our landlord and his wife, who were, I found, companions for the best on the island, were invited. Very early in conversation with these gentlemen, I discovered the passions which the famous Nantucket Bank prosecution, for its robbery, had planted in the island, and which will never cease to rankle under the bosoms of the present generation of inhabitants. They were both, as also Capt. Hussey, friends of the accused, and spoke with an honest and becoming indignation of the injurious charges made against the most worthy men of the island, and which, by the villainy of some and the weakness of others, through perjury and artifice, had nearly effected their conviction and ruin.[18]

Other sores of discontent were exposed, as citizens found that they had competing interests which demanded resolution. On the spiritual side, the Quakers on Nantucket were affected by a split between the reformist groups and the mainline members who were taken to task for engaging in business and holding political office to the detriment of their avowed religious ideals. On the material side, the habit of mutual aid and benefit, to whatever extent it had existed, was wrought asunder by a long-standing controversy over rights to the common lands. Should the hundreds of acres on the island, which for so long had been untitled and available for general use, now be divided into separate parcels individually owned? The simmering dispute came to head with the successful legal suit brought by the Mitchell family in 1813 to withdraw over 2,000 acres for themselves. Others soon followed their lead.

But Nantucket had latent assets, held in abeyance, as it were, by the single-minded purpose of so many people determined to make a profit in whaling. By mid-century, when it was obvious that new sources of income had to be found, the natural advantages of the island as an attractive summer watering place gradually came to be recognized. That it was thirty miles off the coast lent a shimmer of excitement and adventure to those making the crossing and, once they were landed, the distance traveled lent them a refreshing sense of detachment from their cares and problems amid the hurly-burly of the mainland. Nantucket was close to the Gulf Stream, which provided an agreeable climate for bathing and boating; there was a protected harbor on the north side, while a short distance to the south, along a stunning stretch of pristine beach, the great breakers of the Atlantic boomed and crashed on the shore.

But of even greater importance, for there were other attractive watering places up and down the coast, was the town itself, a mostly untouched architectural treasure unique in the collage of notable private houses and public buildings nestled together in an unexpected harmonious whole. Unlike restored and rebuilt villages elsewhere, Nantucket was not "new old;" nor was it "fake old;" it was "real old."

*Centre Street, circa 1870. In the background is the house at no. 53 in the Greek Revival style with a square cupola.*

The inhabitants came to realize what an exceptional gift they had to offer and they slowly roused themselves to prove that they could move forward into modern times and begin to provide those services required by the traveling public. In this chapter of the island story, whales give way to tourists, not always easily, not always in good humor, not always with the best interests of the island in mind, but steadily and inexorably, nonetheless. A new industry was created which undoubtedly preserved the island from desolation and abandonment, but in the course of time, threatened to destroy its greatest attractions..

*Cliff Road at Easton Street, known as North Shore Hill, circa 1870.*

The promotion of the island as a health resort was already being advertised in the 1830s, but growth was slowed by the Civil War, by the need to build a satisfactory infrastructure to accommodate the visitors, and, indeed, by the effort to convince the well-to-do in the cities that they should spend the time and the money to take a summer vacation in so remote a place. Nantucket at mid-century had few paved streets, fewer sidewalks, no public water supply, no public sewage, no gas-lighting of the streets (until 1854), and no scheduled public transportation. In this regard, however, it was probably not much different from many other small towns that sought to cater to a leisured public. Moreover,

standards of comfort and health in the nineteenth century, it is well to recall, were not those of the twenty-first.

Although visitors to the island during the years of depression in the 1860s and 1870s naturally took note of the rundown aspect of the place, what was of greater significance for the future was their appreciation of its extraordinary past and its historic remains, upon which they often remarked. The opening lines of "A Summer in New England" by D. H. Strother, published in *Harper's New Monthly Magazine* in November 1860, is an early example:

> On entering the harbor of Nantucket one is impressed on every hand by the signs of decadence. A few battered and dismantled hulks of whale ships sleep alongside the lethargic old wharves; quiet, listless-seeming people saunter about with an aimless air very uncommon in New England; grass-grown streets and dingy warehouses all combine to complete the picture of departed glory. No, not of departed glory, I mean, simply of decadent commercial prosperity; for the fame of Nantucket is historic and the glory of having given birth to the boldest and most enterprising mariners that ever furrowed the seas is hers, imperishable and forever.[19]

Another piece by Henry M. Baird in *Scribner's Monthly* for August 1873 reveals much the same sentiments:

> Let no traveler visit [the renowned whaling port of Nantucket] with the expectation of witnessing the marks of a flourishing trade, such as its enterprising citizens pursued while the various species of whale abounded in the neighborhood of our Atlantic coasts, or even after those monsters of the deep had been driven into the distant Pacific. Of the great fleet of ships which dotted every sea, scarcely a vestige remains. Two vessels were, indeed, still abroad at the time of our visit, but they had met with poor success, and were more likely to be sold than to return with cargoes of the precious oil. The solitary brig "Amy" lay rotting at the wharf, waiting for some purchaser to take her away and turn her to some more profitable use. But if Nantucket has few attractions to offer such as arise from present prosperity, there is scarcely a seaboard town in America so quaint and so interesting on account of the reminiscences of the past which one constantly meets in every ramble.[20]

Even if he were concerned mainly with a description of the island next door, the author of the *Visitor's Guide to Martha's Vineyard*, published in 1876, could also find light in darkness:

> Nantucket. None should miss visiting this quaint old town, with its old business blocks, houses, and wharves, long since gone to decay. There is something sad about the old place, yet one is charmed with the curious sights and customs of the few inhabitants remaining.[21]

Edward K. Godfrey, a businessman on the island, who in 1882 wrote the first comprehensive pocket guide to Nantucket comprising 365 pages of history, geography, notices of famous people, resources, and practical information, along with two maps, was eager to promote the potential wealth he saw lying around him. He appears to have been impatient with the natives who, to his mind, were too hesitant to take advantage of a good investment:

> That there remains very little of that spirit which incited our ancestors to brave the ice and sleet of the frozen North, or drift, day after day, under a blazing tropical sun, in their perilous for those oleaginous monsters of the deep, bringing to the island millions upon millions of wealth, and making the town the greatest whaling mart of the world, is evidenced by the dilapidated condition of the streets, the nearly total destruction of the wharves, and the general apathy shown in any needed improvement. Nations or people, to be successful, must be producers as well as consumers, and Nantucket island has wonderful resources for production, if her people see fit to utilize them for agriculture, or other purposes… 'Yet a little more slumber, a little more folding of the hands in sleep,' and Nantucket will become so dead that the last trump will fail to awaken her.[22]

To encourage a change in the lagging state of affairs he, with other interested parties, launched the Nantucket Improvement and Industrial Association. A circular was issued which was, in effect, a call to the inhabitants to exploit the resources of the island to promote its attractions in the hope that more visitors would come and spend more money. He need not have worried too much, but little did he realize the extraordinary dimensions that the island renaissance would assume.

One sign of interest in the exploitation of the land was an expected rise in property values. Very soon developers from off-island, as well as some prominent natives, were laying out clusters of house lots north, south, east, and west across the island. The Nantucket Surf-Side Company, led by Henry Coffin, George W. Macy, and Alfred Swain, drew up a plan for 480 lots along more than a mile of Atlantic oceanfront between Weeweder Pond on the west and Nobadeer Pond on the east. A proposal by S. D. Tourtellot of Worcester, Massachusetts, for dozens of new houses in Madaket in 1873 was greeted with enthusiastic approval by the editors of the *Inquirer and Mirror*. Two years later, W. and J. Veazie from Boston attempted a development at Miacomet; in 1876, Henry Coffin was again involved in scheme called "Sherburn Bluffs" on the Cliff; the oddly named "Sunset Heights" on the east coast near Siasconset was sponsored by Charles Robinson and F. A. Ellis; and there was even a minor land boom on Coatue.[23]

As it turned out, most of these projects were too ambitious for the resources at hand and languished soon after they were drawn up. But other proposals had greater success and more lasting value. Several new hotels were built; a summer steamboat service was scheduled; retail stores appeared in the old buildings once used by coopers, sail makers, rope makers, riggers, and blacksmiths; piped water was supplied to the town; a railroad, of all things, was constructed, first to Surfside, and then to Siasconset; and the noted American artist, Eastman Johnson, drawn by the sea, the light, and the unspoiled landscape, set up a studio on the Cliff.

Nantucket in a word, had been "rediscovered." It would constantly be "rediscovered" in an unusual and fortuitous relationship whereby the island, which owed its later attraction not only to its geography and climate, but in large measure to the prosperity of the former whaling era, now arose resplendent upon the grave thereof. The secret of its success was the way in which the past was preserved in a living community, first by chance (islanders after 1850 were too few and too poor to tear down and rebuild much of anything), and then by law (but precariously late, beginning with modest zoning regulations only in the 1950s).

*A plan of the proposed real estate development at Surfside on the South Shore in 1873 with 480 closely-packed house lots and the new roads to connect them.*

But beyond the summary statements and general facts, to know the history of a place is not only to read about it, but also to make an effort to see and to hear the people who lived there and made it what it was.

In this regard, an account of the life of Matthew Crosby is another window opened to a richly-colored past. In his case, as in a "looking glass for the times," to quote Peter Folger in 1676, we can see the early attraction of maritime enterprise for a young man at the beginning of his career, the added benefits of a propitious marriage, the vicissitudes of the whaling industry, in which impressive profits were too often tempered by substantial losses, the fundamental importance of close family relations, and the constant concern with the vagaries of local politics and business practices; in short, something of the long life of a well-known and respected citizen in a small close-knit community.[24] His history is the history of Nantucket as he knew it and lived it day by day for eighty-seven years during the first and greatest period of its growth and prosperity. To reconstruct a part of it is to draw into sharper focus the unique development of the island by providing answers to the questions historians like to ask: who was he, what did he do, why did he do it, and why is that important?

*Orange Street, circa 1870, looking southeast.*

# 1. Packet Captain

*Nantucket, circa 1815, from the Shimmo shore. "What wonder, then, that these Nantucketers, born on a beach, should take to the sea for a livelihood!"* – Herman Melville, *Moby-Dick*. Painting attributed to Thomas Birch (1779-1851).

WHEN MATTHEW CROSBY was born on March 31, 1791, the new American nation was eight years old, George Washington was president, the first ten amendments were soon to be voted as part of the Constitution, Nantucket town was still called Sherburn (or sometimes Sherborn), the census of the previous year recorded 4,620 persons living on the island, and if you wanted to cross to the mainland, it might take a day or a week, depending on the weather. In the same year, Walter Folger, a native son much admired for his scientific and engineering work, wrote up a description of the town, in which he noted that:

> The inhabitants are for the most part a robust and enterprising people, mostly seamen and mechanicks. The seamen are the most expert whalemen in the world, for a proof of which one need only consider the efforts that France and England have been making to draw them away for the purpose of conducting their fisheries… The inhabitants are mostly ingenious in using mechanical tools. It is no strange thing to see the same man occupy the station

of a merchant, at other times that of a husbandman, of a blacksmith, or of a cooper, or a number of other occupations. The women are thought to be handsome. They make good wives, tender mothers, kind and obliging neighbors. The inhabitants live together like one great family, not in one house, but in friendship. They not only know their nearest neighbors, but each one knows all the rest. If you wish to see any man, you need but ask the first inhabitant you meet, and he will be able to conduct you to his residence, to tell what occupation he is of, and any other particulars you may wish to know.[1]

This cheerful portrait perhaps unintentionally points up the limited choice of vocations, the inherent pressure to conform to accepted standards, the forced acceptance of private lives made public, and the pride in collective difference, which are the familiar characteristics of small-town society. But the passage is worth citing because the positive qualities singled out by Folger: the shared development of expert knowledge, mutual help, dedication to work, thrift, and simplicity of daily life, were habits which, aside from being inherent in the Quaker ethic that had dominated religious thought for many years, were fundamental to the development of the character of Matthew and his family and friends.

Dependent on the sea around them and, therefore, on each other, Nantucketers were by nature practical, energetic, industrious, persevering, and courageous, clever with tools and ships, and, for the most part, assiduous in making an effort to keep income in excess of expenses. With little time, or desire in their isolated island existence for excursions into the world of fantasy, their way of life was justified by the results they achieved when business was good, but which served as a reservoir of hope when it was not.

Matthew is worth attention, not because he showed forth as a man of outstanding talent in any particular regard, but rather because he is a good representative of the Nantucket ruling class in the most productive period of its early history. During this time, his steady personal success and contributions to the welfare of the society in which he grew up, in spite of numerous disappointments, were in many ways similar to the accomplishments of his merchant friends. Greater income allowed increased expenses for personal comfort, for a wider range of investments, for the improvement of social services, and for an ambitious building program, all within the island tradition of understated luxury.

As is the case with many of the Crosby families in New England, and even with regard to those branches that later migrated west to become famous in Minneapolis and Hollywood, the ancestry of Matthew can be traced to Simon Crosby (1608–1639) from Yorkshire, who married Anne Brigham and arrived in Boston with his family aboard the *Susan and Ellen* in July 1635.

Simon's descendants, in direct order, were his son, Thomas (1634–circa 1702), who was born in England and graduated from Harvard in 1653, and Thomas's son, another Simon (1665–circa 1718), the husband of Mary Nickerson. Simon and Mary, in turn, had at least five sons, three of whom, Nathaniel, John, and Daniel produced family lines of importance, but our interest lies with John (circa 1701–1750) and his son, Sylvanus (1747–1817), the father of Matthew.

After three generations on the mainland, John Crosby appears to have been the first to settle in Nantucket, notwithstanding the fact that his wife, Sarah Luce, came from Martha's Vineyard. There was, therefore, a link established with the neighboring island

*Nantucket waterfront from the beach near Easton Street, circa 1870.*

that may explain why John's son, Sylvanus, is listed in the public records as having married Huldah Pease in Edgartown on October 25, 1770. The Pease family was widely represented there and she and her husband and four of their young children, Anna, Sylvanus, Huldah, and Mary, ages three to ten, were on the Vineyard when they were baptized together in Edgartown on October 14, 1781. Nevertheless, it was about this time that the family moved to Nantucket to occupy the John Morris house on Pearl Street (now India Street), where Matthew was born ten years later. In that same year, Huldah's uncle, William Butler, died and left his property on Lily Street to her. It was there that Sylvanus subsequently had a new house built. It was natural, then, that when the daughters married, they chose Nantucket men. Anna became the wife of Sylvanus Ewer, Huldah of Benjamin Whippey, Mary of Owen Wyer, and Betsy of John Clisby. Matthew, the only surviving son, also remained on Nantucket and, as we shall see, married into a powerful line of the widespread and important Coffin family.

Sylvanus Crosby appears in the First Census of the United States, taken in 1790, as the "head of a family in Sherburn on Nantucket island, with two males under sixteen years of age, and five females."[2] At that time, his occupation was listed as "mariner," which designation did not preclude listing him and his wife as owners of property between Straight Wharf and North Wharf. He acquired more land in 1798 from Richard Gardner, and a parcel on No-Headed Hill (now upper Centre Street) from Joseph Coleman of New York City in 1803, as well as a share of the common and undivided land from John Butler of Farmington, Massachusetts in 1807.[3]

Like many men who had settled on the island with money to spare, Sylvanus tried to balance losses from the sea with investments in real estate. But even more interesting than the predictable fulfillment of his obligations as husband and citizen, is the likelihood that he was the "Silvanus Crosby" who was second mate on the whaleship *Asia* (Elijah Coffin, captain) on a voyage to Africa and Australia from 1791 to 1794, and who wrote a narrative, partly log and partly journal, of his time at sea.

The *Asia*, outfitted to hunt for whales and seals, and in the company of her sister ship, *Alliance* (Bartlett Coffin, captain) sailed across the Atlantic to the Canary Islands, then down the west coast of Africa, around the Cape of Good Hope, over to Australia, back to Madagascar, south to the remote Kerguélen Islands, around the Cape again, up to the West Indies, where important repairs were made, and then home to Nantucket in about twenty-eight months.[4]

In a recent commentary on the manuscript, Silvanus, the mate, is assumed by the editor, Rod Dickson, to be Sylvanus (both spellings of the name occur), the father of Matthew Crosby. Although the identification is nowhere made certain, this appears to be a reasonable assumption.[5] It would doubtless be based on the chronology (Sylvanus would have been forty-four years old in 1791, experienced and able to manage on board); on his occupation as "mariner" (he was still in the packet trade during the War of 1812); and on a note in which he mentions the death of his sister, although not her name or the year (we know that he had two, Sarah and Mary).

Another possibility worth mentioning, although it has a weaker claim, is that the author of the log was Silvanus Jr., the son of Sylvanus, and a brother of Matthew, who was born in 1773, which would have made him eighteen in 1791, old enough to serve as second mate on a whaling voyage.

There are also the verses of a love song about the girl left behind (the ubiquitous "Molly") copied into the log, which seem more suited to the thoughts of a teenager than to those of Sylvanus, Sr., who had been married for twenty-one years and had seven children. The timing also makes it possible for the younger Crosby to be the author of the log, since he has been reported to have died on November 25, 1794, nine months after the *Asia* returned. Although he is known to have had four sisters, all of whom died after he did, there may well have been an unrecorded infant death. At the beginning of the account, the author fitted his name into a commonplace prayer in verse, which makes clear that he is from the island, but unfortunately, he gives no other particulars:

> Silvanus Crosby His Remark Book and his hand in the year of our Lord 1791 & 92 & 93 Silvanus Crosby is My Name and English is my Nation Nantucket is My Dwelling Place and Christ is My Salvation When I AM Dead and in my grave and All My Bones are Rotton this you see Remember Me and Dont Let Me Be for gotton Silvanus his Name and Hand.

In any case, the fact that a Silvanus Crosby, mariner, of Nantucket, wrote up this record of the years 1791–1794 on the *Asia*, which hailed from the island, and the most likely man with this name at the time was the father of Matthew, lends enough significance to the narrative for us to give it more than passing mention. It is, moreover, a remarkable first-hand account of daily life aboard a whaleship. Who today can say he knows what it meant to cast off the last lines from home, to contend for weeks, or months, or years with the hazards of wind and water, and to wager on a safe return? A few excerpts from the narrative of the *Asia* will bring the present-day reader as close as he will want to come to the reality of the work that lay behind the whaling fortunes. We catch a glimpse of the constant, and often dangerous task of adjusting sails and rigging in good weather and bad; of the long and arduous labor involved in finding, killing, towing, and cutting up a whale to extract the oil; of attacks by hostile natives when anchored in foreign ports; of the threat from British, French, and Spanish privateers which might be encountered at any time; of the perils of sailing in an old ship prone to leaks and rot; of the sudden ravages of disease on board, and, in this case, even of an early instance of group inoculation against smallpox.

The narrative also reveals that no more than an elementary education was needed to become a successful whaleman. Silvanus inserts no punctuation, makes random use of upper and lower case letters, and spells the words the way he has heard them pronounced. But this was in no way unusual in an era before compulsory schooling and the tyranny of the dictionary. Indeed, in the short sketch which Matthew wrote concerning his own school days, which amounted to lessons from half-a-dozen instructors from 1798 to 1806, he admitted that in a hurry to get into trade, and through no fault of his parents, he had spent little time with his books.

It is worth remembering that Nantucket had to wait until 1818 for a vote by the town authorities to consider the establishment of a public school and to set in motion a reform of the educational system for island children. Until then, instruction generally amounted to basic reading, writing, and arithmetic taught hit-or-miss by private tutors in their homes. On the other hand, organized schools may have made instruction more regular, but not always more satisfactory. A later letter from Matthew's son, Francis, mentions seven different schools he tried out from 1846 to 1856, including one off-island, near Boston, most of which proved to be inadequate. This seems a dismal record, but it is difficult to know whether the fault lay chiefly with the teachers or with the student.

But to return to the logbook. The *Asia* left the wharf in Nantucket harbor on September 30, 1791, crossed the sandbar, and anchored in the chord of the bay to begin the work of loading water, wood, and other provisions from a lighter that had been drawn alongside. Here is an early reference to the problem of the shoaling at the harbor entrance, which would bedevil the growth of trade on Nantucket at great cost in time and money. In the case of the *Asia*, much effort was spent in ferrying supplies from shore to ship. It took about a week, including a delay caused by a sudden storm, before they were ready to set sail "towards the coast of New Holland" by which place-name then in use, Sylvanus probably meant Australia.

The portions of the text reproduced here are transcribed exactly as the author wrote them. Comments follow the entries to explain certain nautical phrases and to suggest corrected readings.

> Remarks on Saturday October the 15 Day 1791 first Part of this 24 hours Begins with Strong Breeze and fair Run under reef topsails Last part Moderate Breeze and Cloudy Shok out reafs and Set hole Sail Brock up Betwict tacks and fited out cuting gere wind at NNW So Eands this Day. (p. 3)

["Shok out reef," to reef was to reduce part of the surface of a sail spread to the wind by tying it down; to "shake out a reef" was to untie it. To "tack" was, and is, to change the direction of the ship when sailing to windward. The "cuting gere" referred to the heavy block and tackle, knives, spades, hooks, and chains needed to carve up the whale into small pieces that could then be boiled down to extract the oil].

Remarks on Sunday April the 29 Day 1792 first Part of this 24 hours Begins with fine weather at 4 PM our cabbin Boy went up to help furl the Mizzen topsale and gut up as far as the top and went to Make a grab at the top Mist his hold and Come Down By the Lump wich will Prove his fatte But we are in hopes of his Recoveerry Middle part we still Lying at ancor In Sharks Bay Latter Part fine weather our Boy is no Better So Eands this 24 hours all hands Employed A Bout the rigin Still Lying at ancor in Sharks Bay. (p. 44)

[The "Mizzen topsail" referred to the sail, in second place from the deck, set on the mizzen, or aftermost, mast. The cabin boy, who remained "censless with convultion fits" for several days, finally recovered, and the last we hear of him, he was walking about the deck. Sharks Bay, now Shark Bay, is off the western coast of Australia, north of Perth].

Remarks on Saturday May the 5 Day 1792 first part of this 24 hours Begins with fine weather wind at SE by S our Consort Saw wales and put of after them our Captain Struck one But She drawed her Iron and went of at 6 PM The Boat came on Board hove tow under Maintopsale Middle Part wind and varable Latter Part Made Sale with the S By E Stearing N our Consort came on Board to Dine our Boy no Better But Verry Low So Eands this 24 hours (p. 46)

[The "Consort" was the sister ship, *Alliance*, which sailed with the *Asia* for most of the voyage. In the second line above, "put of" means "put off." "Drawed her iron," meant that the harpoon was thrown with too little force and the whale escaped. For "went of," read "went off." The "main topsale," was the sail in second place from the deck set on the center mast].

Remarks on Thursday August the 30 day first part of this 24 hours Begin with fine weather wind at ESE saw 5 Boats Coming of on Board of us just Before they gut up with us they went on Shore and went in to the Woods and Blowed of there guns of and Blowed there horns as Quick As our Captains Saw that it was git under way as fast as posable our Captain on Board our Consort o they put of from the Shore thinking to have us the Allance But one anker down She Slipt her Cable the Asia Being Mored She Run A verry great resk of Being taking But She Slipt her Best Bower and wayed her Small anker now by this time the Boats is not far of our Captain hald Mr Starbuck not to Be Sacrefised By them But to Come with the Boats But The Asia Made Sale as Fast as posable then they hove up thare Chase they ware not more then A Musket Shot of At 11 AM our Captain came on Board and told us that we run of our Lives for they ware the Chance looking at them with Spye glases So Ends this 24 hours. (p. 72)

["She Slipt her Cable" meant that the heavy anchor rope was let go. The "Best Bower" refers to the larger of two anchors that held the ship by her bows. "Hald" is "hailed." Sylvanus gives the latitude and longitude for the days in question, so it appears that the attack took

> *Remarks on Thursday, August 30, 1792.*

place off the island of Ste. Marie, now Nosy Boraha, just south of Antogil Bay on the east coast of Madagascar].

> Remarks on Saturday October the 6 Day 1792 first part of this 24 hours Begins with fine weather and Still Warping up at 8 PM gut our Ship up to the Landing Place and made fast to the Anker on Shore and gut A Little Supper and then turned in Latter part fine weather gut our Cabolls on Shore and Moreed our Ship Solled at 10 AM the Doctor came of and Nockolated Both our Cruse for the Small Pox is so Breef that it is Emposable to keep Clear from it it is So Breef that 129 died in one Day there is one Ship Along Side of us that has got 2 or 3 Down with it. (p. 79)

["Warping" was a way of moving a ship in stages by means of ropes fastened to some fixed point. "Solled" is "solid." "Breef" is "brief," in the older sense of "rife, common, prevalent." Inoculation against smallpox was just beginning to be accepted. In a well-known instance, George Washington ordered his troops to be inoculated in 1777. But Edward Jenner did not develop an effective vaccine from cowpox until 1796].

> Remarks on Fryday December the 6 Day 1793 first Part of this 24 hours Begins with fine weather and Calm At PM A Small Breeze of Shore We Employed trimming our Sails to the Breeze Still runing Down Saw Monserat to Leeward Middle Part fine Weather and A fine Breeze Still running Dow the Islands For St Eustatia Island Saw Antigua and Redondo Island And Saba Island We Saw Sevrel Vessels one Large English Frigget At 8 AM She took Chase to us and fired 2 guns At us And We hove too and She Came up with Us and Spake Us and Came on Board and took our Captain and Carred him on Board of the frigget and they Streamed A hawser on Board of Us in order to tow Us in tow Sta Christophers Island to See if they Could Dow any thing with us So Ends

> this 24 hours all well as to helth and the frigget Still towing us And Beating up to windward for St Christophers. (p. 169)

["Trimming sails" means changing the position of the sails to catch the wind. "Running down" is sailing before the wind. "Leeward" is the side opposite to the side on which the wind blows. "Streamed a hawser" means they heaved over a heavy rope. "Beating to windward" is sailing to windward by tacking].

> Remarks on Monday December the 23 Day 1793 first Part Of this 24 hours Begins with fine weather and a Small wind Breeze to the NNE Cours NW By N Braised up By the…and took in our Studing Sails our Consort A head of us Middle Part fine weather and calm Latter part fine weather And a fresh Traide at 6 am Set the fore topmast and Studing Sail At 10 am took him in Again our Captain Employed A Blacksmithing A riging the pump Spears our Ship leaks Verry Bad Cours the same NW By N So Ends this 24 hours. (pp. 174–175)

[For "braised up," read "braced up," which means having trimmed the sail by changing the position of the yard-arm to which it is attached so that it lies in a more fore and aft position. "Studing sails" were supplementary sails set out on booms from the side of the ship for use in light winds. "A fresh Traide" refers to the Trade Winds which blow from the east toward the Equator in a permanent belt around the earth].

In fact, the ship continued to leak, so that on New Year's Day in 1794, the captain put into port on the island of Hispaniola (which includes Haiti and what is now the Dominican Republic) for repairs. It remained there for most of the month, while the crew spent their time cleaning the decks, drying the sails, visiting with other vessels, and going ashore. Sylvanus brought his story to an end at that point, but the *Asia*, still not whole but sufficiently seaworthy, set sail again and returned to Nantucket in February.

Soon after he reached the island, Sylvanus was caught up in the misery of the war with Britain in 1812. Although well along in years, he had enough experience and incentive to reenter the exceedingly risky packet trade between Nantucket and New York. A brief excerpt from Obed Macy's *Journal* for April 16, 1813, will illustrate the perils:

> Our coasts have become so infested with British ships of war and their cruisers that it is dangerous to pass to and from any port on the continent. Our vessels have wholly stopt' going to Boston, or any place eastward, and also to any port the southward of New York, and even to any place this side, it is very hazardous. Sil(vanus) Crosby arrived today from York [sic] with provisions. Off with [sic] Rhode island fell in with a fleet of British ships and small vessels who have been cruising between Gay Head and Point Judith for some time, who take every coaster they can fall in with. Fortunately for Crosby, he escaped by running among the rocks at Bretons reef.[6]

Brenton Reef is a cluster of rocks just off the southern end of Newport Neck, and the passage was most likely badly charted and too uncertain for the British frigates to follow him in. Nevertheless, Sylvanus was enough concerned about a loss of income and a serious shortage of provisions during the blockade to add his name to the petition of June 1814, addressed to the British naval commander, pleading neutrality in the war in order to relieve the suffering on the island.[7]

When he died on a Sunday evening in December 1817, he left his estate, real and personal, to his wife, Huldah. Should she remarry, all the assets were to be divided equally among his four surviving children, Huldah (named for her mother), Mary, Betsey, and Matthew. As far as we know, she lived as a widow until her death in July 1833.[8]

At the time his father died, Matthew Crosby was a young man of twenty-six and already thoroughly experienced in a life at sea. It was common and expected for young boys to be sent off to work at an early age, so that when he was about fifteen Matthew was serving part-time as a cabin boy on a large coastal schooner. He was also apprenticed to Joseph G. Coleman as a shoemaker; but by his own admission, he found that trade far less to his liking than sailing with his father on business trips to New York, Long Island, and Boston in the sloop *Sally*. He soon joined him in the packet trade, and two years later, showed that he knew enough to become a pilot under Captain Joseph West on a vessel running from Nantucket to New York. Shortly thereafter, he and his brother-in-law, Owen Wyer, took charge of the sloop *Rose* on the same route.

Moving goods by water, especially those of great bulk and weight, had always been cheaper, and often faster, than moving them overland. Before the construction of the railroad and the paved highway, New England coastal towns, such as Portland, Portsmouth, Boston, New Bedford, Newport, Providence, and New Haven, developed a flourishing seaborne commerce that extended from eastern Canada all the way to New Orleans and the West Indies. In those days, the term "packet" referred to any vessel large or small, whether ship, brig, schooner, or sloop, although usually the latter two, that carried freight and passengers. They are to be distinguished from the later and more famous transatlantic "packets," like those of the Black Ball and Red Star lines, which ran twice a week between New York, Liverpool, and London at fixed times.

The earlier packets, nevertheless, also had an advertised sailing schedule, and besides passengers, the mail, and the latest news, they supplied an astonishing variety of goods to the growing towns. Itemized accounts of cargo included lumber, shingles, nails, staves for barrels, empty oil casks, posts for fences and gates, cordage, hides, furs, canvas for sails, cotton and wool cloth, calico, coal, firewood, stone, lime, lead, paint, tar, whale oil and candles, soap, wire, hardware, dry goods, glass, china, salt, coffee, tea, wine, rum, molasses, potatoes, beef, pork, fish, tobacco, spices, and, on occasion, chickens, ducks, cows, pigs, sheep, horses, and mules. For the inhabitants of the island, who produced very little of what they needed, the packet service was the means of support upon which their livelihood and, indeed, their lives, depended. Matthew numbered many of the leading families, including Coffins, Barneys, Bunkers, Pinkhams, and Gardners, among his customers.

In the case of younger men, who were used to handling boats and were skilled in navigation, coastal trading was an attractive and lucrative business in which to begin a career. Even in wartime, there was a never-ending market eager to buy and sell. Moreover, the United States Navigation Act of March 1, 1817, which recognized the importance of the coastal trade by forbidding foreign vessels to transport goods from one American port to another, largely guaranteed a monopoly to the natives.

But if there was money to be made, it was always a hazardous, and often dangerous, occupation. Arthur H. Gardner's catalogue of *Wrecks Around Nantucket*, first published in 1877, and in which he acknowledged the help of "Captain Matthew Crosby," lists a succession of disasters at sea from 1810 to 1820, the years of Matthew's apprenticeship.[9] Many of them involved the coastal traders:

> In 1816: December 16th, schooner "Susannah," Damon, with a cargo of potatoes and other vegetables, came ashore off Squam Pond and went to pieces.
>
> In 1817: June 15th, sloop "Mary" of Sag Harbor, Capt. Jonah Rogers, was wrecked on Nantucket Shoals. The crew were saved, but the vessel and cargo were totally lost.
>
> In 1819: October 10th, the mail packet, which left here for Falmouth, had proceeded as far as the Horse Shoe Shoal, wind SSE, when she was struck by a squall of wind, hail, thunder and lightning from the northward. The mast was struck by lightning and shivered to pieces, the bowsprit injured, and several on board knocked down and stunned. They let go the sails and run before the gale, expecting every moment to founder, but got back here all right.
>
> 1823: January 6th, schooner "Solon," Johnson, from Fredericksburg, Va., with a cargo of 750 barrels of flour, went ashore at Smith's Point in a heavy gale, but was gotten off next day after discharging about 250 barrels.
>
> 1825: December 13th, sloop "Ranger," Small, from Portland to Newport, came ashore on the northwest side of Great Point and bilged. The cabin boy was drowned in attempting to reach land. The remainder of the crew were saved in an exhausted condition.

In addition to the familiar and expected forces of nature, those brave enough to run the naval blockade during the War of 1812 faced the risk of capture and the loss of vessel and cargo, as we have seen in the narrow escape of Sylvanus. Matthew, like his father, sailed in all seasons and in all weather, enemy ships and privateers present or not, and he, also, was lucky to have survived. By this time he had command of the sloop *New Packet*, in which he made frequent round trips between Nantucket and New York on behalf of several island merchants. At this stage of his career, he was known as "Captain Crosby," a title that he retained for the rest of his life.

In an open letter to his children written just before he died, Matthew recalled how he "…packeted through the war of 1812 to 1815, running the gauntlets of the enemy; twice taken by the enemy and ran away from them without loss."[10] Late in the war, he benefited from the favorable response of the British authorities to the petition of the islanders, the one signed by his father, to remain neutral in return for protection from the official naval forces and the privateers. There exists the copy of a permit, among several issued at the time by Sir Henry Hotham, the officer in charge of maritime affairs on the east coast from New England down to Delaware, which names Matthew's boat:

> Having by the direction of Vice Admiral The Honb'le Sir Alexander Cochrane K.B. Commander in Chief, etc., etc., stipulated with the Magistrates and Selectmen of the Island of Nantucket for the neutrality of that island, and in consideration thereof, granted permission to the inhabitants to import Fuel for their use from Buzzard Bay, these are to require and direct the Commanders of His Majesty's Ships and Vessels, and of the private Armed Vessels of His Subjects, not to molest nor interrupt the Sloop New Packet of about Thirty Nine Tons Burthen, carrying no Guns, nor other arms of any kind, while she is employed on that service and navigated by Inhabitants of Nantucket. Given under my hand and seal on board His Majesty's Ship Superb, off New London, 28th August, 1814.[11]

At that time, Matthew recorded that he was "laying up $3,000 a year," but he had to give up the business, probably around 1821, because of ill health. Nevertheless, as he said, he had secured:

> the best of customers in New York…supplying them with oil and for over 10 years never lost one cent by a bad sale. I had valuable friends in N.Y. giving me all the credit I wanted to buy ships, or anything I wanted.[12]

This early turn of fortune led to an interest in several other vessels, including the sloop *Patriot*, partly owned by Zenas Coffin, and the sloops *Amy, Nancy, Success,* and *Fame*. A later editorial piece in the *Inquirer and Mirror*, written in 1868 to complain about the recent commercial isolation and the new economic disadvantage suffered by Nantucket compared with the mainland, largely because of the lack of fast railroad connections, drew attention to the earlier days of prosperity when everyone was equally dependent on ships and sails and horses and wagons:

> but now we are still further removed from the great centres than when we depended on the good sloop *Experiment*, and other vessels of her class for communication with

the hub, or laid plans for a fortnight's absence, taking passage in the good sloop *Patriot*, Crosby master, for New York. What times those were! How the wife and mother used to bake and roast and boil, for two or three days beforehand, so that the voyager to those far-off ports might have substantial provision for a long passage, in addition to the ordinary salted beef, hard biscuit, and milkless coffee of vessel fare. To those not in a hurry, and not seasick, how pleasant it used to be, to make harbors in the various ports of Newport, New London, Saybrook, or Huntington.[13]

New York Evening Post, *May 31, 1813.*

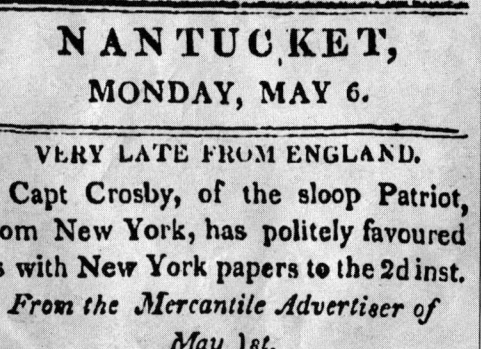

Nantucket Gazette, *May 6, 1816.*

New York Evening Post, *July 14, 1817.*

A partial schedule of the *Patriot* after the war can be reconstructed using the shipping lists and Matthew's own account books and diaries. From May to December in 1816 and June to December in 1817, for example, two or three round-trips from Nantucket to New York were recorded each month. The time it took to make the run varied, of course, with the season and the weather. It could be as short as twenty-five hours, which occurred exceptionally on July 22, 1816, or more usually, as long as four or five days, with a turn around time of a week or more in port.

A preferred route, because it was shorter and better protected from the open ocean, was from Nantucket, north of Martha's Vineyard, down the Vineyard Sound south of the Elizabeth Islands or through one of the passages at Woods Hole or Quicks Hole into Buzzards Bay on the north side; then north of Block Island, on into Long Island Sound by the Race, around Riker's Island, through the Hell Gate, and down the East River to berth at one of the dozens of slips that had been built out on the east side of Manhattan.

John Lambert, a popular English travel author with an eye for detail, who was on a visit in 1807, just before the embargo act took effect, wrote up a vivid description of the waterfront that captures the furious daily activity:

When I arrived in New York in November, the port was filled with shipping and the wharfs were crowded with commodities of every description. Bales of cotton, wool, and merchandize, barrels of pot ash, rice, flour, and salt provisions, hogsheads of sugar, chests of tea, puncheons of rum and pipes of wine, boxes, cases, packs and packages of all sizes and denominations, were strewed upon the wharfs and landing places, or upon the decks of the shipping. All was noise and bustle. The carters were driving in every direction, and the sailors upon the wharfs and on board the vessels were moving their ponderous burthens from place to place…[14]

At that time, mariners were still awaiting a satisfactory chart of the approaches to the port of New York. The British Des Barres charts and views from the *Atlantic Neptune* (1779–1784) were an obvious improvement over previous attempts and better for their purpose than the well-known Ratzer map of the city printed in 1770. By the end of the century, Edmund Blunt published *The American Coast Pilot*, with sailing directions and a chart of Long Island Sound by John Cahoone and Nicoll Fosdick. Between 1813 and 1817, Ephraim Chesebrough and John Purdy issued two more charts, and the survey by William Damerum

*William Damerum Map, 1815. This early map of Long Island Sound, from surveys by William Damerum and engraved by Peter Maverick Jr. (1780-1831), was made during the time Matthew Crosby was engaged in the packet trade.*

came out in 1815. But the measured Commissioners' Plan by John Randel, which showed mainly the East River, was not published until 1821, and the better Hassler chart of the harbor only became available in 1845. Moreover, work to remove the heavy rocks from the Hell Gate channel was still going on in 1873.[15]

Nevertheless, Matthew was certainly familiar by this time with the winds and tides and currents and shoals, and probably relied less on the printed charts, which were soon out of date, than on his own experience. For company and security, he often sailed with other packet boat captains, such as Starbuck in the *Factor*, Ray in the *Omega*, and Robinson in the *Sophronia*, which were bound for Providence or New York.

Although the records of his debits and credits are not always complete, and sometimes appear to be inaccurately copied, the coastal trade was clearly a financial success for Matthew. In spite of the annual costs of insurance, wharfage, pilotage, entry and clearance fees, the expenses of loading and unloading, the maintenance of the vessel (caulking, scouring, varnishing, and blacksmithing), wages for the crew, "for a boy to mind the boat" (when docked), he made a considerable profit. Matthew ran the *New Packet* and other sloops from 1812 to 1815, and then took command of the *Patriot* for a few more years. His estimate of $3,000 a year may have been fairly near the mark. According to his own calculation, he had a balance on hand of roughly $2,500 in 1816, which had been increased to about $12,000 by the beginning of 1820. Converted into dollar-values, $2,500 would represent something like $41,000 today, and the $12,000 close to $235,000.[16]

Whether the source of these funds was from shipping alone, or whether other income was combined with them, is not clear. Nor can it be certain from Matthew's accounts how much was net profit. He continually had loans outstanding which had to be paid off, as well as notes due him which in some cases were never honored, and running expenses for the boat. But the estimates, even if approximate, point to a flourishing business.

For a less determined man, the onset of an armed conflict with Great Britain in June 1812 might have been the warning sign to remain at home and to wait out the loss of work and revenue as best he could. But Matthew, like so many of his friends, seemed born to seafaring; and trade, the lifeline to the island, was too important to give up. Incidents involving American, British, and French vessels had recently occurred often enough to have become an accepted part of the risk for any captain and his crew, so that his decision to continue to sail the waters of Long Island Sound was in no way surprising. Moreover, as we have seen, the New England states had generally opposed "Mr. Madison's war," and Nantucket, in particular, was early committed to a declaration of neutrality. Packeting, if it adhered to the rules, was still permitted by the competing powers. Matthew was just twenty-one years old, and we would know very little about these momentous years were it not for the chance survival of a now-damaged ledger book in which he used the blank pages to write up a short history of the part he played in the wartime coastal trade.[17]

It seems safe to say that Matthew's firsthand account is a reliable record of the events as they happened and as he lived them, and not an embellished version of what he thought might have happened. It is written in a direct, matter-of-fact, and unadorned style typical of his letters and memoranda, and most of the events he describes, and the people involved in them, can be documented from other sources. The geography in and around Long Island Sound is accurately laid out and the dates correspond to the accepted chronology of the war.

Although there is no indication as to when Matthew wrote the manuscript, he mentions so many people and places that would have been difficult for him to remember afterward that it must have been part of a journal he kept in some form while he was ferrying freight and passengers. This is the more likely because now and again names and dates were later filled in above and below the line. A few dates were also changed, two extended passages were interrupted and then continued further on, and occasional comments were made about events when the outcome was known, all of which suggest that the editing was done on a second reading, but not on a later copy.

The beginning pages of the financial accounts have been cut out, but the book bears the date "4 October, 1833," and the section of bills paid was for 1839. At the end of the journal, Matthew noted that the sloop *Patriot* was purchased in January 1816, and sold in 1820, so that perhaps sometime between 1820 and 1839 he was at work on the final version. As was the case with the log of the *Asia* kept by his father, Matthew's prose, although written in an even and flowing cursive hand, has its share of inconsistencies in grammar, syntax, and spelling. But except for a few passages that have been emended to clarify certain words and phrases for easier comprehension by the modern reader, the excerpts printed here have been left largely as he wrote them in order to preserve the flavor of the original.

With regard to the imposed conditions with which Matthew had to contend, the British blockade, as already noted, was the ever-present threat. It was designed not only to cripple American trade with French ports, but also to dissuade the politicians in Washington from undertaking an assault on the Canadian frontier and to prevent them from extending a military presence in Spanish Florida and into the Indian territories to the west. This action, made more effective by the large number of naval vessels available, had an uneven, but generally depressing, effect on American shipping and economic life. A decision to counter it by the embargo of 1807 caused more damage to mercantile New England than to British shipping, and thereby increased resistance to the war in that part of the country. A second attempt in December 1813, and put in place by Draconian means, also proved ineffective. It was, however, a disaster for Nantucket, and was repealed in less than a year.

Moreover, after the defeat and abdication of Napoleon in April 1814, the British were free to commit more men and ships to the Atlantic theater, considerably expanding the scale of their naval operations. Alexander Cochrane, the Royal Navy commander, ordered an "attack and destroy" campaign on the eastern seaboard to discourage support for the American army and, it would seem, since he forbade whaling, to entice the islanders to set up their business in Nova Scotia under his control. The British fleet was further strengthened, which gave the blockade runners more to worry about. British troops occupied part of the coast of Maine, while another force attacked New Orleans. As every student knows, Washington was burned, Baltimore threatened, and Fort McHenry was bombed and shelled "in the dawn's early light" before the contending powers staggered to a round of peace treaties, concessions, and compromises beginning in December 1814.

But the journal makes clear that, while His Majesty's ships and crews were always referred to as "the enemy," opportunities existed for cooperation and profit among the belligerents. The British were well aware that access to American markets was crucial in order to supply their troops in Spain and Portugal, the West Indies, and Canada. Local merchants, for their part, depended on the free movement of goods abroad to make a living, while the government collected import and export taxes to fill the treasury. Licenses and passports issued by both the American and British commands allowed ships to sail on a restricted basis; claims of neutral status preserved some rights of free trade; and plain goodwill among the captains of vessels, tempered with bribes and concessions, often prevailed over official rules and regulations.

That Matthew succeeded where others failed, despite the constant dangers he faced, was due to a good deal of luck. But absolutely essential was his expert skill in handling a boat, and in this regard, he was in the true Nantucket tradition. Sea-faring brought out in his character those qualities of energy, resourcefulness, and perseverance, combined with no little courage, which were clearly apparent at an early age.

The value of Matthew's account can be seen on the first page, where he brings us at once into the uncertainty and anxiety felt by all the businessmen on Nantucket, so vulnerable thirty miles from the mainland, when he writes that, as soon as war was declared, his crew "loaded up with candle stock for Gideon Gardner which was carried to Providence to be placed out of reach of the enemy." There follows a description of that escape from hostile pursuers off Brenton Reef in April 1813, already given brief mention by Obed Macy in his reference to Sylvanus Crosby. Matthew had accompanied his father and his version provides some dramatic detail:

> I left N.Y. in sloop *New Packet,* my father with me. In returning, came near being taken by a smack which was in possession of the enemy in Long Island Sound. We lay in Stonington for several days. The *Ramillies 74* and *Orpheus* coming in off Stonington every day, sending in their barge several times at night. The Stonington people, being on their guard, drove them off. The two gunboats lying there under Commander

[William] Coit, he not having men enough, wanted we should come on board & help keep off the barge which was expected to come in every night. The chance of our getting home in safety appearing so small, a Capt.

> The sloop New Packet, Crosby, cut out of Tarpaulen Cove, on Wednesday night last, by the privateer brig John Sherbroke, has been retaken by the captain and owner on board, and arrived at Newport.

*Poulson's American Daily Advertiser, Philadelphia, April 8, 1813.*

Howland and ourselves concluded to haul up our vessels, he being bound to New Bedford, and go home by land. Being on shore in the afternoon, we saw a fleet of vessels come out of New London bound east. Amongst them, was a sloop belonging [to] and commanded by Capt. David Joy who, we presumed, had a licence. We concluded to go out and take our chance after them. We came down off Point Judith at 7 p.m. The wind at WNW strong. Capt. Howland came near us and we concluded to steer for Sakonnet Rocks, as we heard there was a seventy-four off New Port. After talking a short time, we were surprised by a cannon shot from the *Liverpool Packet* that was lying under bare poles under our lea. The moon had now risen. We immediately hauled by the wind in order to run our vessel on shore if we could not escape. The sea was heavy & she [the *Liverpool Packet*] nearly within musket shot fired her long guns thirteen times, her shot passing all around and over us. We kept in and found we were near Brentons Reef off New Port light. Saw a sloop on the weather beam after us. We thought we could not escape at this time. The packet, discovering the reef, tacked off shore. I immediately put our helm up and passed to leeward of him, being nearly on the reef, Brentons. We put our square sail on and out sailed and escaped him. The sloop [next] after us was Capt. David Joy, which the packet had taken and was after us. The packet had taken fourteen sail before she saw us and had the prisoners on board, amongst them Peter G. Fosdick, Daniel Chase, & others. Before we left Stonington, we had made arrangements to have our tiller ropes rigged to steer below. [But] when we came within shot of the packet, every man wanted to be on deck and take his chance of being shot in order to escape him, if possible. We escaped and soon afterward struck a reef in the Bay and came near losing our vessel. Arrived home safe with a number of passengers.

The *Ramillies* and the *Orpheus* were heavily armed British frigates rated, at the time, by the number of guns they carried: the first with seventy-four (and often referred to simply as a "74" because it was the most common warship in service) and the second with thirty-six. With several other vessels, they were brought in to reinforce the blockade in the Sound. Captain William Coit was a well-known American shipmaster who had already seen action in the War of the Revolution but, in this case, was handicapped by the lack of an experienced crew. Although the *Liverpool Packet* had been built for the trans-Atlantic run from Liverpool to Halifax, at the beginning of the war she was converted to a British privateer and subsequently caused a good deal of damage to American shipping. The "long gun" was a type of long-range cannon, so-called to distinguish it from the lighter and more usual short-range "carronade" manufactured by the Carronade Ironworks in Falkirk, Scotland.

Matthew must have continued to carry goods and passengers back and forth, but his next entry was for June 1813. He again sailed to New York and met the American frigates *United States* (44 guns), commanded by Stephen Decatur, and *Macedonian* (38 guns), and the sloop-of-war *Hornet*, which were coming back through the Hell Gate headed eastward down the Sound. In October 1812, Decatur had engaged and damaged the *Macedonian*, then a British warship, off the Azores and brought it back to New London as a prize vessel. Instead of the HMS *Macedonian,* it became the USS *Macedonian* and Decatur had taken her to New York for repairs. On his return trip to Nantucket, Matthew encountered the ships one more time:

> When we came home, we saw our frigates and *Hornet* chased into New London by Commander Hardy in the *Ramillies* seventy-four and *Orpheus* frigate. Saw them exchange one shot each. They had a very narrow escape. When we passed our frigate inside of the Gull light, the 74 was in full chase of the *Hornet* which was about two miles to leeward of our frigate. Commander Decatur, as we were informed by a pilot that was on board, was preparing both frigates and men for boarding the 74 if she came up with the *Hornet*. At last the *Hornet*, by lightening, throwing over guns, spare stores, etc., came through the Race before the 74 came up with her. The *Orpheus* frigate, being far to leeward, the 74 waited for her to come up before she attempted to come through the Race. As soon as she came up, they came into the Sound after our frigates. They, the *United States* and the *Macedonian*, bore up and passed into New London harbor after exchanging one shot or compliment each. A very narrow escape. We, being in sight all the time, went into Stonington.

From other accounts, we know that the *Macedonian* and, perhaps, the *Hornet* grounded on the passage into New London, and then, having reached a safe haven, were kept bottled up there by the British frigates for the rest of the war.

Late in 1813, Matthew had charge of the sloop *New Packet* and made three trips to New Bedford before sailing again to New York:

> I went to New York loaded with oil, candles, sugar, etc. In going out of Stonington with a pilot we came in sight of the [British] fleet of ships off New London. We came down off Groton Long Point. The wind died away, and the tide against us, came near being captured by the tender of the admiral called *Good Intent*. She came beating down with the tide. There was no chance for us to escape. I kept steady for him, hoisted up

our topsail. The admiral, watching our maneuvers, recalled the tender for fear, as we supposed, [that] we were prepared to blow them up, as was done a few days before by the schooner *Eagle* which was sent from New York for the purpose, by which the enemy lost thirty or forty men and officers. Owing to this cause, no doubt, we escaped. We went into New London, Commanders Decatur, Jones, Biddle with their vessels laying up the river, kept in by thirteen sail British men-of-war laying off the harbor. Owing to vessels leaving the harbour every night carrying provisions and news to the enemy, Commander Decatur laid an embargo on all vessels in port, detaining us several days, there being about forty sail of us bound to New York. Several Nantucket vessels, say Barzillai Cottle, Silas Coleman, William Robinson, Hezekiah Coleman, and ourselves.

After laying several days, I concluded to go up to the frigate and try & get a pass to go out. Went on board the *United States* with B. Cottle, S. Gelston, S. Coleman. Found the Comd. was on shore about one mile off. Whilst on board, I saw twenty-two men flogged at the gun for getting in liquor while rowing guard the night previous. I went on shore, met the commander coming down on horseback in the rain. Stopt and made known our business. He invited us to go back nearly one mile to his quarters where we saw his wife. He informed us that in consequence of vessels leaving the harbor, the enemy had received information & knew what was going on on board his ship as well as he did, and he visited her every day at 2 p.m. He had, therefore, laid on the embargo to stop all communication. We told him we knew it was all true. We had ourselves seen vessels leave the enemy every morning whilst we lay down river. We said to him it was a hard case for us to be stopt there by the fault of others. Persuaded him to let us pass for this time. He said he was satisfied we were not going to give information & he was as anxious to escape and get out with his fleet as we were. He gave us the pass and all the vessels in the harbor.

We made several attempts to get out. Our militia, being stationed near the mouth of the harbor, fired upon us. [They] made us come on shore to show our pass which put the enemy upon the look-out, hearing their muskets, and prevented our getting out for some time. At last came on a NE storm. We left in company with the fleet. We took the lead. It being very dark and stormy, we did not fear their barges. They had a guard ship laying directly in the channel within gun shot of New London light house. We saw his light [and] ran for him until we heard them cry "all's well" three times. They never saw us. We escaped up sound and arrived at New York the next day after being chased by an American barge under English colours which took Capt. Cottle and came near running us on shore. Thinking we had English licence, he was in hopes to trap us. When we returned from New York, came down off Saybrook in the evening. Met a fleet of vessels coming out. Could not speak them. Went on shore to inquire where the fleet lay. Was informed they were near in off New London and that the vessels that had gone out were bound east. Thought it a favorable time to escape them. We went immediately out, saw the 74 lights.

At daylight, were chased by two frigates which were coming in from off Block Island, this being a fleet of vessels bound west. We escaped and they chased several vessels on shore and captured several. The *Lily* of Nantucket ran on shore [at] the same time. This day the mail packet, Capt. Childs, was taken by the brig *Borer* off Long Shoal. We arrived at Woods Hole same day. Left in morning and, when daylight came, we had passed the *Borer* with the mail packet with her laying off Squash Meadow Shoal. Had a narrow escape. Samuel Gelston, who came out after us, was captured and had to ransom his vessel. We arrived home safe after a hard cruise.

Groton Long Point is just to the east of New London and opposite Fishers Island. The *Good Intent* was an American schooner that had been captured by the British and was being used to ferry men and provisions from ship to ship and from ship to shore. Long Shoal lay to the west of Cross Rip and Squash Meadow Shoal was off Martha's Vineyard between East Chop and Cape Poge. The incident of the schooner *Eagle* and the British commander's fear that his tender would be blown up can be traced to an Act of Congress of March 3, 1813:

That during the present war with Great Britain it shall be lawful for any person or persons to burn, sink, or destroy, any British armed vessel of war, except vessels coming as cartels or flags of truce; and for that purpose to use torpedoes, submarine instruments, or any other destructive machine whatever; and a bounty of one half the value of the armed vessel so burnt, sunk, or destroyed, and also one half the value of her guns, tackle, and apparel, shall be paid out of the treasury of the United States to such person or persons who shall effect the same, otherwise than by the armed or commissioned vessels of the United States.

The practical consequence of this order was felt on June 25, 1813, when the *Eagle* was abandoned by her crew off New London and taken in tow by a British pinnace. As the men were tying her alongside a captured sloop, there was a tremendous explosion that killed an officer and ten seamen. It was thought, probably correctly, that the intent was to blow up the *HMS Ramillies* and Captain Hardy. The incident elicited a letter from Admiral Sir John B. Warren, the commander of the British naval forces in North America, to the Admiralty complaining of the death of the men:

> …by a Diabolical and Cowardly contrivance of the Enemy. Indeed, the Dayly attempts practiced by Commodore Decatur and the americans [sic] against that valuable officer Sir Thos. Hardy and the Ships under his orders now Blockading the Enemy's Frigates in the Port of New London, by means of Torpedoes, Fire Vessels, and other Infernal Machines, are beyond conception.[18]

Fireships, to take one example, were still part of the British naval forces in the early nineteenth century and had recently been employed against the French. If the Americans reciprocated, however, it was deemed a heinous offense. It all depended on whose ox was gored.

A winter expedition to Providence in December 1813 provided Matthew with an opportunity to see Commodore Oliver H. Perry, recently returned from his victory on Lake Erie, and some of his family. He was also invited by Commander John Rodgers for breakfast aboard the frigate *President* in order to advise him about the depth of the water in certain parts of the Sound. Apparently, the pilot he employed, a man named Silvanus Dagget, who belonged to a well-known family of ship-pilots operating out of Nantucket and the Vineyard, while knowledgeable, was given to drink and could not always be depended upon, whereas Matthew by this time enjoyed a reputation as a skillful captain. With but a short stay on Nantucket, he was off again in January of 1814 on a voyage that turned into an endurance test of unexpected challenges:

> I went to Newport after a load of oil from the ship[s] *Lydia* and *Criterion*. After getting there, was stopt by our government laying on an embargo on all coasters, boats, etc. for a time. I left our vessel in the care of Gilbert Chase of New Port, took our packs on our backs, and started at night to walk home as far as we could, myself, Owen Wyer, and Joseph Rawson. In crossing on to the toll house at Howland Ferry Bridge, Wyer gave out several times, being nearly perished with cold. At last we succeeded in getting him to the house nearly frozen. The next morning hired a horse & waggon, & man to take us to New Bedford. Arrived there at dark, met about twenty men going down to Clarks Cove to take two boat[s] which a man by the name of Smith said he had laying there and would take them to Woods Hole for one dollar each. We joined them. When we came to the Cove, we found an old whale boat. Smith, with eight of us, left in her, leaking badly, calculating to land on West Island that night and the next day go on to Woods Hole.
>
> We got out into New Bedford river. We found so much ice, could not get near West Island and started for Woods Hole where we arrived after a hard pull at 2 o'clock p.m., all of us very much exhausted. After getting a hot supper, fearing if the Mail Packet was at Falmouth that she might leave before morning, concluded to walk down there that

night. We got to Falmouth at day light. No packet, she being frozen up at Nantucket. Zenas Gardner, F. W. Mitchell, Paul West rowed around the bay that night. The next day we hired the mail boat to go to Nantucket. Agreed to pay fifteen dollars and return her in safety.

We started after dinner, came down off Cape Poge. It came on cold, the ice making all over us. We concluded to get into Edgartown which we were fortunate in doing, as the night was very cold, our harbor closed with ice. We found in Edgartown the boats were not permitted to leave the harbour and it was necessary for us to keep out of sight, or we should be put under bond not to leave the harbour. We agreed with a pilot to take us down to Waqua. At two o'clock a.m. left and got to Waqua and walked the beach until daybreak. It then came on to snow, wind at NW. We left believing it would clear off. In going through the rip, a sea filled our boat one third full [of] water, wetting our trunks and us badly. We sailed & rowed & made Muskeget before it stopt snowing. It then came on clear & cold. We got our boat nearly to Brant Point light house and hauled her on the beach. All of us glad to get there. Nearly perished. When I got home my clothes were all frozen down in my trunk which was wet in the bottom of the boat. The Packet went out in a day or two, carried our boat, and returned with the passengers.

*The landscape of the Howland Ferry Bridge, which posed such a challenge to Matthew and his friends during their expedition in January 1814. In those days, however, they crossed the Sakonnet River by a much older bridge, which was subsequently destroyed and later rebuilt several times.*

Matthew was the victim of Madison's embargo of December 1813, already commented upon, which in its broad sweep discomfited United States nationals as well as the British. As to the other stopping points, Howland's Ferry Bridge, later known as the Stone Bridge, allowed passage over the Sakonnet River between Portsmouth and Tiverton, Rhode Island, just south of Fall River. Clarks Cove is an inlet between New Bedford and South Dartmouth, while West Island lay farther to the east off the southern tip of Fairhaven. The "New Bedford river" refers to the outer harbor or the mouth of the Acushnet River. Cape Poge, on the northern side of Chappaquiddick Island, and Waqua (Wasque Point), at the southern end, were the last landmarks before coming in sight of Muskeget and Nantucket. It was a "hard pull" to Woods Hole because the men were obliged to row the whaleboat rather than sail across. Afterward, another packet returned the hired passengers and the mail packet to Falmouth.

By March 1814, Matthew was ready to embark again for Newport to collect the boat he had left there, as well as to recover the sloop *Earl*, now moored in a creek near the Howland Ferry Bridge. He sailed with a crew that included his father, as well as Raymond Castino, a man from Nantucket who had property in Westport, Massachusetts, and Jacob Barney, captain and part owner of the sloop *Earl*. Barney had probably thought that a safe place because he had a cargo of valuable head-matter, the oil and waxy substance from the sperm whale's head used in candle-making, and the risk of having it seized during the embargo was too great.

They landed at Ponegansett (Apponegansett) in Dartmouth and spent the night at a place called Squire Slocum's. Matthew writes that the next day they walked through the snow to reach the *Earl*, a distance of at least ten or twelve miles. The boat they came in was evidently returned to Nantucket by the men who had been left with her. Sylvanus Crosby and Jacob Barney and their crew then got on board the *Earl* to prepare for sailing, while Matthew and some others walked down to Newport to retrieve his own vessel. They came back up to the bridge, and Matthew, ever ready to pursue his business interests, went up to Somerset, just above Fall River, to purchase oil brought in by the ships *President* and *Lima* and to have it stored there for his father-in-law, Zenas Coffin. Upon returning to the Howland Bridge, they found that the *Earl* had left for Nantucket the day before. When they came down toward Woods Hole, however, they were surprised to see the sloop aground in the channel. They also spied a brig anchored a little distance away in Tarpaulin Cove on the south side of Naushon Island, a place long used as a safe anchorage by British vessels. It could only mean that the enemy had taken the *Earl* in hand:

> We lay by waiting for her [the *Earl*] to get off, which she did in a short time. We then came on after her. She headed up sound and came to anchor. Our fears were correct, she was then in possession of the enemy. We were hailed from the shore to get back

if we could, which we attempted, but the tide being against us, did not succeed. Were then hailed to run on shore, as they had dispatched a sail boat from the *Earl* down for us. The sloop *Two Friends*, laying on Grassy Island, burned at the time [and] I thought I would rather take my chance to get by or be taken. The boat came down, met us off Parker's Point, only one man in sight. When she came near enough, five men with muskets sprang up, pointed at us, and ordered me to put down the helm. I did not mind them, put the helm hard up, and lay down on deck until their shot had passed. Then stood up, keeping my eye on them and kept the vessel head for the wharf before they could load and fire again. We were on shore, our rigging cut away and unrove [and] carried up and buried under the salt works, to keep them from making sail on her if they came in. They dare[d] not venture to come. They lay there all night a little to the south of the harbor. That night Daniel Russell came in with a number of passengers.

In the morning discovered a schooner at anchor off Nobska. It proved a neutral, commanded by Simon Gardner, the barge alongside. She lay there all day, expecting we should come out, expecting to capture us. We saw the barge and kept quiet until she left the schooner and went up to the Cove after detaining the schooner two nights and days. They, the *Nimrod*, then manned all their barges and came down to take us out. We saw them coming, got under way and cleared them and arrived home safe. The inhabitants of Woods Hole informed us they had been threatened by the *Nimrod* to destroy their town if they fired on their barges. They said they could not protect us if the barge came in. We got five muskets with powder and ball and Moses Davis of Woods Hole requested us if they came in at night to give him a call. He had two

*The geography of Matthew Crosby's excursion to the mainland during the winter of 1814.*

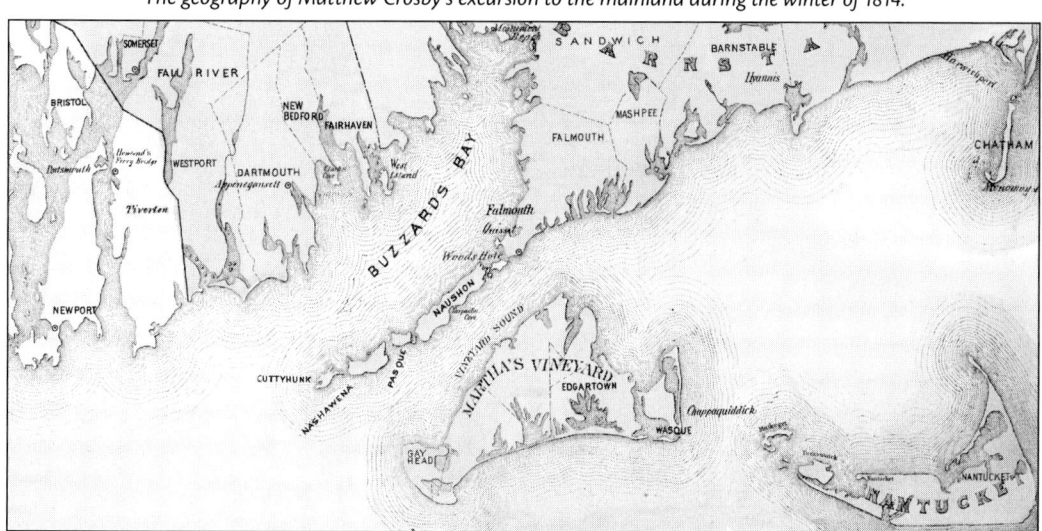

muskets and would do all he could to assist us. They did not make the attempt to come in and we were glad of it. After we ar[rived] home, Peter Chase & Charles W. Cartwright went to the Cove, ransomed the *Earl*, released my father & the crew, they paying about five thousand dollars. The cargo being valued at over twelve thousand, she arrived home safe. Father Coffin owned considerable part of the cargo. Silas Coleman came in to Woods Hole whilst we lay there, which made us strong.

*A page from Matthew Crosby's journal (see pp. 55-56 for the text).*

Such were the perils of packeting in wartime when every sail sighted raised an alarm and no port was a guarantee of safety. Matthew apparently made the quick decision to run for it in order to avoid the fate of the sloop *Two Friends*, which had struck on Grassy Island, a partially submerged reef at the entrance to Woods Hole Harbor, and had been burned. But if this was the same sloop named *Two Friends* that later was rowed with an armed force from Falmouth to Tarpaulin Cove in October 1814 and captured the British privateer *Retaliation*, the damage to the hull cannot have been very great. As to the attack off Parker's Point, Matthew may also have relied on the fact that it took as long as half a minute to reload a musket and that aiming at a distance from a moving boat was extremely uncertain. Nobska Point lies just south of Wood Hole, and Parker's Point, now Juniper Point, is on the eastern entrance to the harbor. The *Nimrod* was a new and heavily armed British bark that appeared off Cape Cod late in 1813.

New Bedford Mercury, April 8, 1814.

But blockade or not, business could not be allowed to idle. As we can see from this description, whale oil was still being traded on the market, provisions had to be delivered to the island, and passengers transported. So, in June 1814, Matthew took the mail packet to New Bedford and returned to Somerset, and to Greenwich, R.I., with his uncle, Gilbert Coffin, to put the oil stored there into proper barrels. On the way back, they were held up by a report that the British frigate *Nymph* and her barge were lying off Nantucket bar. It was all in a day's work to find an acquaintance in New Bedford and hire him and his sailboat for the trip to the island, to elude the barge, and to arrive home safe and sound.

Afterward, Matthew and his father, with a few others, went out fishing in the sloop *Maria* belonging to Peter Paddack. What better way for these hardy seamen to bring their labors to an end than to go out again for a few pleasant hours on the water?

Two of the later entries in the journal are of particular interest for what they reveal about the day-to-day relations between the British invaders and the American defenders, not least with regard to the licenses issued for free passage, and for the references to the personal concessions offered by both sides during a long period of contention and close contact. The narrative was continued in August 1814:

> Licences were granted from the British to several vessels to run to Philadelphia, New York, and a number to bring wood from Buzzards Bay. Captain Childs [in] the Mail Packet, as a wood-man, obtained one of the licences. Childs, being a Falmouth man, I took charge of the vessel and licence, Childs acting as pilot. In going off first trip, was taken by a barge off Holmes Hole from the *Pactolus* frigate and carried up to her at Tarpaulin Cove. After they had examined our licence, I asked the officer if we were at liberty to proceed on. He said we must lay until morning, then come to the frigate as the captain wished to talk with us, as the officers were on shore having a dance at Withingtons. We were fearful if we lay there all night, he would say, there lays the Mail Packet, and we should lose our mail and vessel. Having a lady passenger very much frightened, we hauled up our anchor in hopes we should drift out. Finding we should go on the Point, we made sail and escaped. We made a number of trips. [Later] we ran on shore to the east of Falmouth with thirty passengers on board. Lay all night without any light on board, all of it by the carelessness of Childs.
>
> I then left him and went to New York in sloop *Amy*, having a licence, Charles H. Robinson and myself equally interested. Made several trips. In November, returning from New York, the fleet laying near-in off New London, we did not wish to be boarded as we intended stopping at Stonington and they would have the run of us. We took the inshore passage in hopes they would not notice us. The *Endymion* frigate, being the nearest in shore, commenced and fired five shot[s] at us which fell short. She then ceased and passed signals with Admiral Hotham in the *Superb* 74 laying near. She was then ordered to commence firing again at us. She fired a long time, only one shot coming near us. Finding we were determined to pass him, he manned three barges, went down to the admiral, they manned four more and veered astern of the 74 to try and stop us as we passed her. The wind increasing, they gave up and we passed in safety. They then got the *Dispatch* sloop-of-war under way and went out though the Race. We went nearly into Stonington, believing we could reach New Port before dark. We kept on along shore, the *Dispatch* off Block Island. When we came by Point Judith, they discovered us and made sail in chase. Fearing she had the run of us off New London, we did not like to have him board us. We ran for Seconnet Rocks, got there at dark, he in full chase. We ran down toward Westport off a reef called Cestawso Ledge. We were fearful we should strike it and he coming up with all sail now within gun shot, we concluded to luff to and let him come on board, which he did in a few minutes. They blamed us very much for making them chase. We told him we wanted to get in before night, etc. They then asked when we passed New London. We told

him a lie that we passed in the night. He was very inquisitive. We evaded. At last he left us. We went down to Tarpaulin Cove. Being well acquainted with the lieutenant and purser that came on board, we got off nicely. In going into the Cove, saw the *Paledeus* sloop-of-war laying there. She ordered us to send a boat on board. Charles Robinson went with the licence which was fortunate as the same sloop-of-war afterward recaptured our vessel from the privateer *Lunenberg*. Arrived home safe.

> **MARINE DIARY.**
>
> **PORT OF NEW-BEDFORD.**
>
> The British brig Nimrod, of 18 guns, Capt. Mitchell, has been lying for several days past in Tarpaulin Cove.—We have not heard of any captures made by the Nimrod. Her barges, we are informed, have been several times to Wood's-Hole, and some shot have been exchanged between them and the militia on shore; but we have not heard of any lives being lost on either side.—On Sunday they set fire to a small sloop (the Two Friends) belonging to Nantucket, ashore at Grassy Island; but the fire was extinguished.

New Bedford Mercury, *January 21, 1814.*

Holmes Hole is now Vineyard Haven, and the *Pactolus*, a 44-gun frigate stationed off New London along with the *Ramillies*, the *Dispatch*, and the *Terror*, took part in the bombardment of Stonington for several days in this same month of August 1814. A Mrs. Withington and her three daughters lived in a house at Tarpaulin Cove, which they used as a tavern and a place of entertainment for British officers.[19] The *HMS Endymion*, 40 guns, with several other frigates, was engaged in the famous attack on Pettipaug (now Essex), Connecticut in April 1814, during which a large number of American privateers were destroyed. Less than a year later, she was instrumental in attacking and capturing the *USS President*, under Stephen Decatur, when he attempted to run the blockade. The drama of the *Lunenberg* is related in an entry dated December 1814, after Matthew again set sail for New York:

> Simeon Gardner coming on board as passenger. Off New Port it commenced snowing and we were about going in when Gardner informed me he had dispatches on board from Admiral [Alexander] Cochrane from Bermuda to Admiral [Henry] Hotham of New London. Fearing to go in to New London with our licence and dispatches, we blamed Gardner very much, but were obliged to go on. The *Paledeus* sloop-of-war being in chase of us and a number of vessels bound west, he boarded us first which gave several vessels a chance to run on shore, which they did. We came up with the sloop *Paragon* of Wareham who hove to. We told him to run on shore. He did not and was taken by the *Paledeus* and sunk off Block Island, cargo of iron ore. We went into Stonington in chase of other vessels which saw us boarded. They were conversing about us and we, fearing we should be searched in the morning, we got under way at three o'clock in a snow storm and at daylight anchored under the stern of the *Superb 74*, Com. Hotham. He invited Gardner to come on board, which he did with his dispatches, etc.

He detained us several hours. Gardner came on board with a plenty of doubloons in his pocket. When we arrived at New York, he wanted us to stop to the 74 on our return. He wanted to carry some furniture, etc. to the admiral. We refused ever stopping again unless we were obliged to. He threatened to have our licence taken away, etc. The *Experiment*, laying in New York, took the articles on board with Gardner. When we passed, we saw the *Experiment* laying along side the 74 discharging furniture, etc., etc. When we came down off Block Island, discovered a schooner coming out from under the island. Did not try to get away. Kept on, which rather frightened him. He came abeam of us. Fired three musket shots, one of which came near hitting me at the helm. I then ran off to go near enough to talk with him. He got both cannons loaded and was about firing into us as we luffed-to and he ordered me on board. He said by our maneuvers he thought we were manned and intended boarding him, that he did not intend to be taken as the *Retaliation* was by one of our vessels in Tarpaulin Cove. When I first went on board I thought I was on board an American privateer. He said he was the privateer *Lunenberg*, Chamberlain master, being from Lunenberg, Nova Scotia. I had seen the sailing master who was acting as pilot not long before and told him he was not an Englishman. He then said he was at Nantucket within a short time, that his name was Gorham. His father moved to Lunenberg before the war. He had gone down there and came up pilot and sailing master of this privateer. The captain['s] name was Champlain [sic]. After finding their stories agreed, I informed the captain I had a British licence. The captain looked at my licence, said it

*Tarpaulin Cove, Naushon Island, circa 1860, in a painting by William A. Wall (1801-1885). The harbor became a hideaway for British warships, as well as a haven used by American whalers and merchantmen.*

was good for nothing, and refused to give us up. I remonstrated to no purpose. The officers were all for manning us for Halifax, which they did, taking Robinson and refusing to let me go with him. After manning her off, they landed me on Block Island. It so happened that the next day after we were taken, they fell in with the same sloop-of-war, the *Paledeus,* that had boarded us in Tarpaulin Cove. He took the vessel away [Matthew's vessel], gave her up to Robinson, towed her in off Point Judith. There fell in with Samuel Gelston, who had a licence. Gelston furnished Robinson with a man, Edward Swain, and arrived home safe, one week before I got home, which was about the twenty-second of January [1815]. [The *Experiment*] was captured at the same time we were by the same privateer [the *Lunenberg*], the crew all landed on Block Island except Simeon Gardner, who went to Halifax in her. After the peace, they went to Halifax and brought her home, having to pay about two thousand dollars, as I understood, for her. In February, peace was proclaimed and we had no further use for a British licence.

New Bedford Mercury, July 29, 1814.

    Doubloons, Spanish gold pieces worth about five shillings each, were in circulation by the British and the Americans. In fact, they were often the preferred currency at a time when there was doubt about the value of paper money. But Matthew may be using the term only to suggest that Gardner was well paid for his trouble. Simeon Gardner is obviously of some interest, but he is difficult to identify among the acquaintances in Matthew's circle. There were at least two men of that name who fit the time frame, both older than Matthew, who were born in Nantucket, but went to live in Nova Scotia, where, for more than half a century the British government had encouraged settlement to increase its revenue from whaling and shipping. Gardner's easy relations with the British naval authorities reflect the privileged position of neutral Nantucket in spite of the tighter restrictions put into place at the beginning of 1814.

Matthew had married Lydia Coffin in February 1813 in the early days of the war, and their first son, William, was born in November, so what the reader might expect to find in this narrative is some reference to his family life, to the anguish of a young wife left alone, or to Matthew's concern for those at home during these unsettled years. But, as is clear from his diaries and letters, he was not one to dwell on domestic affairs. Business was business, and that was the foundation of his success and where his interest lay. We are left to wonder about the emotional cost attendant on all involved when the husband was away at sea in wartime.

Matthew not only left us this stirring account, but he also may have illustrated it. Among the family papers in the collections of the Nantucket Historical Association is a hand-drawn pencil sketch of the eastern part of Long Island Sound from Sag Harbor

*Part of the sketch of Long Island Sound by Matthew Crosby, extending west from Fishers Island to Black Point. He has drawn in some the navigational hazards, a few prominent landmarks, and several British naval vessels active during the War of 1812.*

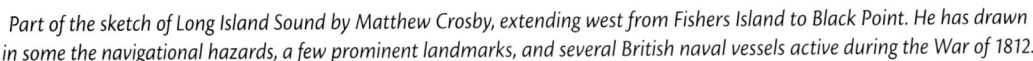

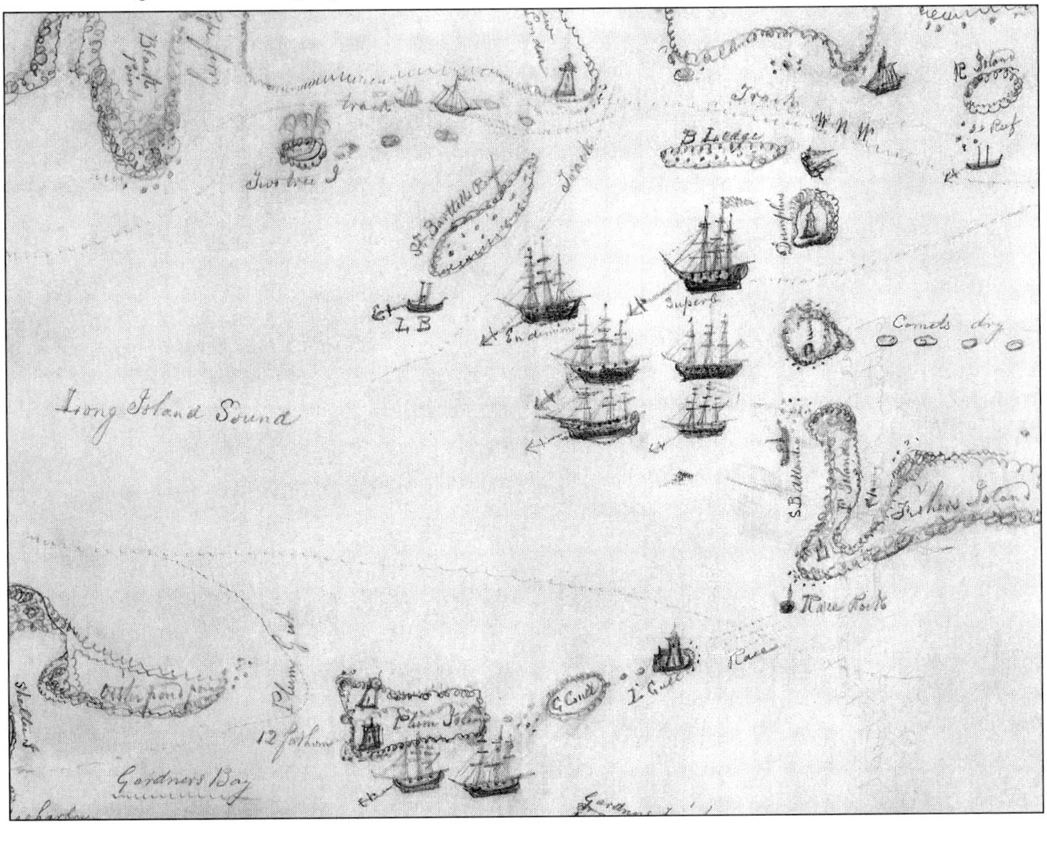

to Watch Hill which is attributed to him.[20] Indeed, it looks very much like his work, since many of the places he knew and which figured in the journal, such as New London, Stonington, Groton Long Point, Plum Island, Fishers Island, and the Race, are named on the sketch. Moreover, there are little pictures of the British fleet gathered off New London, including the *Endymion*, which opened fire on him; Hotham's flagship, the *Superb*, involved in the episode with Simeon Gardner; and the *Dispatch*, which boarded him off Sakonnet Point. As a mariner, he was also concerned to include some of the more important reefs and shoals encountered on the passage to New York, as well as prominent lighthouses and lightships, and coastal towns.

Like the journal, the sketch is undated, but one clue may be the drawing of a ship on the rocks off the southwestern end of Fishers Island which is labeled "S.B. Atlantic." The obvious reference is to the steamboat *Atlantic* which was wrecked in a heavy gale at that very spot on November 26, 1846, with the loss of the captain and many crew and passengers. It was a major disaster which received a good deal of publicity. Matthew must certainly have heard about it, and since it occurred in his old shipping lanes, it is likely that he would have added it to the sketch. If it was not a later addition, then a mid-century date for the document is plausible and reasonably close to the time-frame proposed for the journal.

*A chart of the islands by Joseph F.W. Des Barres (1721–1824), which was included in his monumental four-volume atlas,* The Atlantic Neptune, *circa 1776.*

# 2. Family Matters

*The built-up waterfront along Old North Wharf, showing New North Wharf (Steamboat Wharf), Brant Point, and the tip of Coatue. The photograph was probably taken from the Unitarian Church tower around 1870.*

Family matters are important because families matter. As we have seen, a loosely-connected but influential group of islanders traditionally filled the political offices, managed the growth of the whaling industry, dominated the social life, and generally promoted their own interests. Since marriage can be said to have represented another kind of investment in the social and economic life of the island, the lives of Matthew's wives, children, and other close relations need to be considered for what they reveal about the customs, circumstances, and conventions that shaped the outlook and the fortunes of the Nantucket well-to-do.

Although there are insufficient data on which to base precise figures, it is generally thought that the average life expectancy for white males and females in the United States around 1850 was thirty-five to forty years. For Nantucket, isolated to some extent from widespread contagion and known for a healthful climate, and in spite of the occupational hazards of whaling, these figures might be increased by another five or ten years. Still, the most productive period of life began and faded sooner than is the case today. It is not surprising, therefore, that most of the sons and daughters married for the first time when they were in their twenties. The men went to work to make a living and the women stayed home to manage the household and to have babies. For the encouragement of early marriage and more offspring, they might have looked to Benjamin Franklin, who knew something about it, and to his prescription "to marry in the morning, settle the children by noon, and retire in peace and leisure in the evening."[1]

Due partly to the effort to counter the high rate of infant mortality, and partly to the lack of effective birth control, it was not uncommon in this period for a young wife to have six or seven live births, although by the end of the century this number had dropped by half. The children who survived and grew to maturity then repeated the cycle, as we have seen in the case of Sylvanus and his son. Few of Matthew's sons and daughters remained single, and those of his first wife married into families they had known for some time. In a small community with limited options, it was wise to follow established custom. If, in preserving the familiar social connections, a sound financial basis was achieved, so much the better for present approval and future stability.

To gain perspective on this history, we can take the line back as far as Matthew's parents, who were married in 1770 when Sylvanus was twenty-three years old and Huldah just twenty. In the course of two decades, as already noted, they became well established as property-owners and raised a family of three boys and four girls. The oldest son, named after his father, never married and is said to have died young at Cape Nichols. If this is taken as a reference to Nickol Bay on the shore of Western Australia, it suggests that he had shipped out on a whaling voyage. His younger brother, William, born in 1782, fell victim to a yellow fever epidemic in New York when he was only seventeen.

The disease had raged up and down the east coast for several years, striking Philadelphia particularly hard in 1793, New Bedford in 1801, Philadelphia again and New York in 1799 and 1803. The dire effects were widespread and well known to the public. When Obed Macy was writing his history of Nantucket, he noted the occurrences and repeated the general view that the sickness had been brought to the cities by immigrants from Santo Domingo who were fleeing to escape a slave revolt.[2] The actual carriers were mosquitoes which swarmed about the swampy coastal lowlands during the warm-weather seasons. The deaths of Sylvanus Jr. and William before their time and before either of their parents, left only Matthew, the third and youngest son, to carry on the family name.

As to the four daughters, Anna, the eldest, died at twenty-six without issue, just one year after her marriage to Sylvanus Ewer, a shipbuilder on Nantucket. He later turned to investments in whaleships and in three more wives, two of whom died before he did, leaving one son, Peter Folger Ewer. It was Peter who would make a name for himself as the architect of the "camels," that floating dry dock mentioned previously and used for a short while to bring vessels over the harbor bar.

Huldah, the second born, and her mother's namesake, was the wife of Benjamin Whippey Jr. His father and his uncles, James and Zebulon, were well known and successful whaleship captains. In this tradition, Benjamin served as master of the *Brothers* during the momentous years of 1811 and 1812. As it turned out, this was one of the ships that had been commanded by Zenas Coffin in 1796. When Benjamin died childless in 1837 at the age of sixty-two, it was Matthew, the most successful of the siblings, who was called in to draw up an inventory of the estate, which included a loan he had made to Benjamin.

The third daughter was Mary, sometimes called Polly, who married Owen Wyer in 1799 and had two sons. Like Zenas Coffin and Sylvanus Crosby, Wyer, who came from a family heavily involved in seafaring, was a packet boat captain on the Nantucket to New York run and, as we have seen, Matthew's companion on several voyages. A younger relative, named Samuel, later had charge of the *Alexander Coffin*, the *Enterprise*, and the *Young Hero* in the years from 1840 to 1855. When he retired from the strenuous life of active service, he settled down as the owner of his own whaleship, the *Sea Ranger*, which was one of vessels in which Matthew Crosby had bought an interest. But it was soon to operate out of New Bedford, rather than Nantucket, a move that signals the shift in whaling activity to the mainland that occurred after mid-century.[3]

The children of Mary and Owen were William, who later moved to Ravenna, Ohio, to join a little settlement of Nantucket families already established there, and Charles, whose own son, Henry, became better known than any of them owing to his collection of photographs documenting daily life on the island from about 1885. Although highly valued today, many of his scenes were apparently retouched to make them appear more attractive.

The perils of a mariner's life were again brought home to the family of the youngest daughter, Betsey, who had married John Clisby in 1806 and who found herself a widow with an infant child less than two years later. Her husband was reported as another unfortunate "lost at sea," along with Jesse Bunker, captain of the ship *Commerce*.[4]

Matthew Crosby, born in 1791, grew up therefore with hardly an acquaintance of his two brothers and his sister Anna, all of whom died before 1800. Of the three surviving sisters, Mary lived to 1837, and Huldah and Betsey died within six months of each other in 1853. Although the latter two remained on the island and were buried with their parents and their sister Anna in the Old North Cemetery, there is very little information about their relationship with Matthew. Perhaps he was particularly close to his sister Mary, and her husband, Owen Wyer, since he left a bequest of $100 to their son, William C. Wyer, the only nephew remembered in his will.

If Matthew had, as he says, "the best of customers in New York," who assured him of substantial profits, he also had the best of friends in Nantucket who gave him timely advice and financial help early in his career. Of these benefactors, the most significant was the coaster captain-turned-whaling merchant, Zenas Coffin. He looms large in the history of the island, and his family and career are well worth further study.[5] But here, at least, we can show his importance through his relationship with Matthew.

Zenas was the son of Micajah Coffin, himself a mariner and merchant, as well as a public figure in the Massachusetts House of Representatives for more than twenty years. Not surprisingly, Zenas began his business life as a sailing master and an owner of ships.[6] In the course of time, he amassed a fortune consisting of investments in whaleships, whale oil (which he was able to store and then sell when prices rose), real estate, banks, and other corporations. At his death in 1828, his estate was assessed at about $380,000 (or about $9,000,000, in present-day dollars). Although there were substantial debts to be paid and several allowances to widows of his friends in the whaling business to be made, it was said to have been the largest fortune ever seen on the island up to that time. Indeed, money made money, and by the time of the second accounting of the estate in April 1835, through a general rise in prices and the sale of various assets, the gross amount had increased to about $400,000.[7] Yet, with Zenas, it was not all business, since he evidently had a strong sense of social responsibility that was manifested in his contributions to neglected causes. A notice inserted in the *Inquirer* at the time of his death, described him as:

> …an eminent merchant. In him we have lost one in whom were combined charity and benevolence in a high degree. He has done more, perhaps, for this town than any other man ever did, or ever will do. It was by his interest that the wretched poor were raised from a situation almost on a level with the brute creation to comfort and cleanliness, and we may almost say, to happiness. It was he that roused the inhabitants to petition for something to render the dangerous shoals round our harbor more secure to the life and property of the mariner. In fact, the whole tenour of his life has been of the greatest benefit to our citizens, and their loss will be deeply felt.[8]

A generous compliment to a generous man, but oddly inconsistent with an editorial in the same newspaper a month later, which blamed the evident decline of the island on the migration of wealthy businessmen to other towns, leaving too little capital for investment in the community. Zenas made his mark, but fell ill and passed away, while still in his prime, at sixty-four years of age. (His father, Micajah, on the other hand, by an unusual convergence of lives, had died aged ninety-three just a year before).

Zenas left behind his widow, Abial, two sons, Charles G. (1801–1882) and Henry (1807–1900), and three daughters, Eunice (1788–1843), Lydia (1793–1823), and Mary (1799–1827).[9] All of them would have important connections with the Crosby family, and the extensive real estate holdings which Zenas had acquired would be sold and resold among his heirs for a long time to come.

As we have seen, Zenas had been doing business with Matthew in the packet trade for several years. The latter was allowed an interest in the *New Packet* and in the *Patriot*, both Coffin vessels, and he carried consignments for Zenas and others on his trips up and down the coast.

Given the propensity for early marriages and for family members of the Nantucket oligarchy to marry among themselves, it is not remarkable that it was twenty-year-old Lydia Coffin who caught the eye of young Matthew Crosby. They were joined together in a civil ceremony on February 4, 1813. Apparently, neither one nor the other considered it mandatory to "stand up in meeting," as the Society of Friends required, and to be blessed by divine grace. Lydia, whose parents were members, and, who, herself, had been received into the Meeting soon after her birth in 1793, was, therefore, "disowned." Matthew, it seems, had never declared his adherence to the rules of the communion. The formal judgment was made on February 25, 1813:

> Preparative meeting informs that Lydia Crosby, daughter of Zenas Coffin, has married contrary to the Order of Friends, she having been previously labor'd with on the account; therefore, it is the judgment of this meeting, with the concurrence of the men's, to deny unity with her. Elizabeth Barney and Phebe Hussey are appointed to inform her thereof and report at next mo. meeting.
>
> And further, from the men's side: This meeting concurs with the women's in disowning Lydia Crosby, daughter of Zenas Coffin, for marrying a man not a member of our society, notwithstanding she was precautioned.[10]

In spite of these wholesale censures, the consequences were minimal. For Lydia, there was no question that her husband came first, and her determination to go through with the marriage in opposition to the critics doubtless weakened the impact of their disapproval. Indeed, victory of a sort was conceded in January 1822, when she was formally restored. Moreover, in a period when the force of orthodox Quakerism, with its uncompromising structure and strict discipline, was losing its attraction for members of the younger generation on the island, no one was inclined to contest publicly a marriage, which act would have raised a challenge to the well-respected Coffin family.

At the time, many Quakers were disowned for various offenses other than marrying outside the Meeting. Lax attendance, defaulting on debt, engaging in politics, going to war, dancing in public, or wearing buckles on your shoes were all causes for reprimands and, if they went unheeded, for expulsion. It would seem that the force of the punishment, as is so often the case, was blunted by the frequency of its use and by the fact that it often involved well-placed members of society, including Joseph Starbuck, William Rotch Jr., Thomas

Macy, Nathaniel Barney, and even Maria Mitchell "because her mind was not set on religious subjects."

So it was that Matthew prospered to an even greater extent through his new relations. During the next ten years, Lydia gave birth to a son, William Henry Crosby, then to a child who died within a year, and afterward to three daughters, Mary C., Ann G., and Lydia. All of the latter survived the perils of childhood, grew up, and married, although only Mary and Lydia had children of their own.

Then, suddenly, on Sunday morning, the 13th of July in 1823, tragedy struck the family with the death of Matthew's wife, then only thirty years old. The cause is unknown, but given the spacing of the births of the other children in 1813, 1814, 1816, 1818, and 1820, and with no mention of a previous illness, it is quite possible that her death was due to complications of childbirth, as was all too common at the time. For Matthew, it was a heavy loss, and the fact that he was left with the care of four minors, ranging in age from three to ten, must certainly have influenced his decision to marry soon again.

Elizabeth Barnard, who would become the second Mrs. Crosby, was born about 1800, the descendant of a line of Nantucketers that included Macys, Coffins, Gardners, and Inotts. When quite young, and living on the island, she had married a man named Caleb Powell from Poughkeepsie, New York. But in similar circumstances to those of Matthew, whose wife had died when he was thirty-two, Elizabeth was left a widow in her early twenties with a daughter to raise. When she married Matthew in 1824 or 1825, it was the beginning of a union that lasted for more than fifty years, and which brought him a new and larger family, including his stepdaughter, Phebe Powell. But, once again the custom of the Quakers, was violated. Matthew and Elizabeth were joined together outside the meeting by the magistrate, Benjamin Gardner, and eventually Elizabeth and Phebe were also disowned.[11]

*Portrait of Elizabeth Barnard Crosby painted by William Swain in 1845.*

The children of Matthew and Elizabeth who were born between 1826 and 1841 and reached adulthood were Martha, Matthew Jr., Sylvanus, Elizabeth B., Judith C., Susan B., Charles C., Emma, and Francis L. These are the ones we know, but there is some uncertainty about the total number of children Matthew had with his two wives. In one of his last letters, written in April 1875 to his old friend Thomas Gardner, he counted seventeen, of whom four had died.[12] But four by Lydia and nine by Elizabeth add up only to thirteen. Including Judith, the only grown child known to us predeceased Matthew, as one of the four who died, there must have been three others who died in infancy. As mentioned earlier, there is notice of a child born to Lydia who died around 1815 when less than a year old, and another of Elizabeth (named Amelia in some records, but identified as a male child in others), who died around 1844. The total, however, is still off by one. Could Matthew, in old age, have counted one too many? Or did he ignore deaths at birth as sorrows which were too common in the age to record? Or might he have included Phebe, his stepdaughter, in the total? One or another of these answers seems possible, but perhaps it is of no great consequence for this narrative of his life and times.[13]

A second misfortune for Matthew, after the loss of Lydia, came with the death of Zenas Coffin on July 8, 1828. Although he had been extraordinarily successful in the whaling business, he was, according to Matthew, negligent in keeping track of his investments and producing up-to-date accounts. A good deal, he noted in a letter, was done by "gess work."[14] It was a style of business that his son-in-law found worrisome.

He had every reason to be concerned, since Zenas had evidently promised certain payments and reimbursements to him, including outlays for piloting and the purchase of ships, which were never made during his lifetime. In a memorandum written when Zenas was quite ill and a month before he died, Matthew recounted a conversation he had had with him one evening when the two were walking on the waterfront near the candle factory. According to this version, Matthew, and Zenas's son, Charles G. Coffin, were to settle his estate after his death "satisfactory to every person." In the meantime, Matthew and Charles were to have half his ships, half of the supply of spermaceti, half of the stock of sperm-oil candles, and half the profit when sold. Zenas, if still living, was to take the other half. Matthew, of course, raised the question of the interests of Zenas's other son and his married daughters, and the fact that such a distribution would be impossible without a will. No more, it seems, was said about the matter.

Indeed, when Zenas died soon thereafter, no will was found; a state of affairs which limited the clear distribution of his estate. Such inattention was unfortunate, and Matthew was drawn to complain that:

> Had he lived a few days longer and made his will I have no doubt I should have received from his estate, clear of what I got for my children, more than fifty-thousand dollars which he actually gave me by word of mouth…[15]

But this was no more than hearsay evidence and little could be made of it. Yet, the fact that Matthew still felt strongly enough about the matter to write down the particulars fifty years later suggests that it had remained an unresolved issue in his memory of their relationship.

As it turned out, Abial, the widow of Zenas, refused to deal with the legal problems associated with her husband's death and, instead, wrote to Isaac Coffin, the judge of probate and the half-brother of Zenas' father, to appoint her two sons, Charles G. Coffin and Henry Coffin, and her three sons-in-law, Thomas Macy, husband of Eunice; Henry Swift, husband of Mary; and Matthew Crosby, husband of Lydia, as joint administrators. The necessary bonds were posted, the public announcements made, and the beneficiaries notified.

The estate was held in common and it remained in family hands. The important whale oil and candle business was taken over by his sons as the Charles G. & Henry Coffin, Company. Thomas Macy represented the interests of his wife and infant daughter, Mary. Henry Swift acted as guardian for the benefit of his daughters Sarah, six years old, and Mary, two years old, since their mother, also named Mary, had died in 1827. Matthew did the same for his children by Lydia: William, fifteen years old; Mary, twelve; Ann, ten; and Lydia, eight. It was understood that, where appropriate, the income would be used to support the minor grandchildren.

At a meeting of the heirs in November 1828, and again in December, at the family Mansion House on the corner of Pine and Summer Streets, an allocation of the major assets was made. The remaining whaleships owned by Zenas, which alone were worth close to $200,000, were divided among them. The *Zenas Coffin* went to Abial, his widow; the *Constitution* to Charles; the *Lydia* to Henry; the *Independence* to Henry Swift; the *Phoenix* to Eunice Coffin Macy; and the *Washington* to Matthew Crosby, although it was omitted from the inventory. Matthew also acquired the old house that Zenas had purchased from Benjamin Gardner, and which was then occupied by Josiah Hussey; the Sarah Clasby house and land near South Wharf, lately occupied by John Green; part of the brick store on South Wharf bought from Shulbael Barnard; a one-fifth share in the wharf; and land known as the Cato lot. Shortly afterward, he bought the remaining interest in the sloop *Patriot,* which had served him so well in the packet trade.[16]

*The Zenas Coffin house on the corner of Pine and Summer Streets.*

If Matthew was provoked on account of promises made, but not fulfilled, by his father-in-law, he may have gained some satisfaction from a deal arranged for Zenas's son, Charles G. Coffin. After Matthew had bought an interest in the whaleship *American*, Zenas evidently was impressed enough to wish that it had been bought for him. Matthew did not want to lose the ship, but because he held it in fractions, they agreed on a sale whereby Charles G. Coffin, the elder son of Zenas, was to have one fifth. Over the years, Matthew estimated that the *American* made over $9,000 for him and, he supposed, the same amount for Charles, but, as he wrote in his last letter to his own children, and it is easy to imagine a sense of satisfaction in being the anonymous benefactor to a son of Zenas, "I dont [sic] think he knowes [sic] by whose means he got one fifth of the *American*."[17]

With an estate the size of Zenas's, it was inevitable that there would be further disagreements over the settlement. When he died in 1828, he was sixty-four years old and his widow, Abial, who would live another twenty-eight years, was sixty-three. At her request, their sons, Charles G. and Henry Coffin, took over the property, including her share, which amounted to $83,062, paid her bills, and used the bulk of the money in their business interest-free. They drew up an account in 1844 showing a balance of $35,193, which was approved by Abial, and another account in 1851 with a balance of $29,043, which was likewise approved. When she died in 1856, her property amounted to $33,347, of which $32,132 consisted of two promissory notes from her sons whereby they agreed to pay over the sums outstanding at a convenient time.

This state of affairs prompted a lawsuit in March 1857 by Valentine Hussey Jr., who had married Mary Macy, a daughter of Thomas and Eunice Macy and was, therefore, a granddaughter of Zenas. Presumably, he had her interests, as well as his own, in mind. Hussey was joined by Matthew Crosby; his son, William H. Crosby; and his daughters, Mary C. Coffin, Ann C. Macy, and Lydia C. Burnell, all heirs of Zenas Coffin. The executors were charged with violating their trust by withholding funds for their own use and by failing to account for subsequent income. A petition was filed for their removal.[18] Just a month prior to this action, Matthew, William H. Crosby, and Thomas Macy, had written a letter to Charles G. and Henry Coffin proposing a settlement of their differences out of court. Aside from his family relationships, Matthew had had business dealings with the Coffin firm for some time. Moreover, it was in his nature to try for a peaceful solution rather than jump immediately to a lawsuit and the wording of the letter, written in his hand, makes this clear:

> Respected Kinsmen,
>
> The undersigned representatives of all the heirs of Abial Coffin (yourselves excepted) believing as they do that there is a mistake in the appraisement of the estate of the said Abial Coffin, as returned into the Probate Court, and having failed in our endeavers of procuring an interview with you on the subject and being sincerely desirous of terminating all differences to it in a harmonious and amicable manner, agreeable to the principles of right and justice, hereby propose to you to refer all matters touching the

amount and value of said estate subject to distribution to the determination of arbitrators mutually chosen whose award shall be final.[19]

The answer of the Coffins was that there was "perfect harmony among the administrators when the estate closed in 1835," and it was agreed that all the books and records relating to the estate were to be placed in a trunk deposited in a vault of the Pacific Bank that could not be removed without permission of all concerned. When, upon receipt of the letter, the Coffins went to inspect the documents, the trunk was gone. They accused Thomas Macy, and asked for the return of the trunk, but he refused to meet their demands. The case then went before the judge of probate, where the suit was rejected on the grounds that the executors had, in fact, complied with the law and that it had been Abial's intention to allow her sons to manage her money for many years. On appeal, the decision was upheld and the case was dismissed.

In that small and close island community, Matthew must have had good reason to accuse his relatives and business partners before taking action against them. But without further details, we are obliged to accept the official ruling. As executor of the Zenas Coffin estate on behalf of his wife, Lydia, an accusation in court that funds had been misused was certainly unpleasant news for him. Moreover, one of the issues in the suit concerned the ship *Washington*, which had subsequently passed into Matthew's hands and was, therefore, out of contention. But it was alleged that at the time of Zenas's death that his share of the cargo of oil, worth almost $14,000, had not been credited to his widow's account, or ever paid to her. Misdirected profits from the whaling ventures may have been at the bottom of the aggravation felt by Hussey and the other heirs. Such was the effect of this great fortune, that questions were still being asked half a century later. For it was in 1896 that Matthew Crosby Jr., on the death of William H. Crosby, wrote to his uncle, Henry Coffin (the son of Zenas and the last living executor of his estate) to determine the most efficient and least expensive way to have his portion paid to him.

The lives of Matthew's own children by his two wives, Lydia and Elizabeth, over a period of almost thirty years, bring us into the next generation and provide a more intimate picture of the changing social life of the ruling class. Lydia's first child, William Henry Crosby, was born in 1813 and, in what may be seen as an effort to give him a broader and better education than Matthew had received, was sent off to the Friends School in Providence, Rhode Island, for several years. On his return, he went into the whale oil and candle business with his father and began to invest in land on Commercial Wharf and in several of the more important whaling vessels, including the *Washington*, the *Peruvian*, the *Mariner*, the *American*, and the *Navigator*, in which Matthew had shares.

It was no surprise that an important connection with another well-known whaling family was formed when William married Elizabeth Pinkham in 1835. She was the second of five daughters of Seth Pinkham who, like many of his contemporaries, had made a success of his ventures at sea in command of the *Dauphin* in 1815 and the *Galen* in 1820, and, like them, had retired to settle on the island.[20] But unlike some of them, he soon faced serious financial losses which persuaded him to embark once more in 1841 in command of the whaler *Henry Astor*. The logbook, now lost, was evidently known in the 1890s to Harry B. Turner, the editor and publisher of the *Inquirer and Mirror*, who used it to give a brief account of the tumultuous voyage punctuated by a mutiny on board, a fight with cannibals, the loss of two boats smashed by whales, a serious leak in the ship after a storm, the death of Captain Pinkham in Pernambuco (now Recife) on the west coast of Brazil, the death of the first mate, Henry Smith, killed by a whale, and the difficult return of the ship to Nantucket under command of the second mate, Henry Colesworthy.

These were certainly not the usual incidents of a whaling voyage, but the *Henry Astor* nevertheless arrived with a full cargo of over 3,000 barrels of oil consigned to William R. Easton, the father-in-law of Matthew's son, Charles.[21]

One other example, which points up the fact that you could not go far on the island without running into someone you knew, is a letter sent by Seth Pinkham to Barker Burnell, the father-in-law of Matthew's daughter, Lydia, who was then serving in the U.S. Congress. In the letter, written when he was at sea off the coast of Peru in June 1841, Pinkham, who appears literate, thoughtful, and astute concerning marine affairs, urged Burnell to support federal legislation in favor of the production of accurate charts of the dangerous waters around the Pacific islands where the whaleships operated.[22]

Matthew's other children by his first wife were his three daughters, Mary, Ann, and Lydia. They all married into well-known island families, which once again illustrates the close relations that existed among that small and select group. When Mary, the oldest child, became the wife of Benjamin F. Coffin, she reestablished the important line with Zenas Coffin. Isaiah, the brother of Zenas, had married a Folger, and from that union was born Jared Coffin, whose son, Benjamin, became the husband of Mary Crosby. Both Mary and Benjamin, therefore, were the great-grandchildren of old Micajah.

Mary, in fact, had married well. The name Jared Coffin is known to visitors to the island because one of the better hotels in town, originally built as his private residence but later sold and called the *Ocean House*, once again bears his name. But what they probably do not know is that behind the impressive brick structure was a fortune amassed from investments in whaling. From 1820 to 1845, he had varied interests in at least a dozen ships, including the *Montano*, the *Catharine*, the *Planter*, the *Ohio*, the *Daniel Webster*, the *Reaper*, the *Ann*, and the *Sarah*, which in those years brought in over a million gallons of sperm oil alone at an average price of $.77 a gallon. If shipowners were making something like 50–75% of the gross value, then even Jared's fractional shares of the oil after the usual deductions produced a substantial return. Add to that the profits from whale oil and

*A photograph of Jared Coffin by Frank M. Taft in 1865.*

*The Jared Coffin residence on Broad Street transformed into the Ocean House Hotel, circa 1865.*

bone, and his gains were even greater. He had previously built another brick behemoth on Pleasant Street, now known as *Moors End*, before he gave it all up and moved to the mainland in 1846.

Mary's husband, Benjamin (not to be confused with another prominent Benjamin F. Coffin, the captain of the whaleships *Reaper* and *Thomas* who was lost at sea around 1830), inherited one-seventh of his father's estate in 1860. He began to earn a living as an outfitter to whaleships, then as an investor, and eventually as a partner in the firm of French & Coffin. Backed by Coffin funds, he built a large house on Main Street at number 98 on the corner of Pleasant Street within a year of his marriage to Mary in 1835.

A point of interest here with regard to family relations is that for a long time a Friends Meeting House, called the South Meeting House, had occupied the lot. It is clearly marked on the William Coffin town map of 1834. This was sold and torn down at a time when members of the religious community were embroiled in a serious quarrel over the nature of their commitment and purpose and, consequently, a decision by one group was made to move to a new site on Fair Street. The old property was bought by Charles G. and Henry Coffin, the sons of Zenas, who used the lumber for their warehouse and candle factory on Commercial Wharf.

But Benjamin soon experienced the ups and downs of business life on the island. With a reported loss of $32,000 by French & Coffin in the fire of 1838, and the growing signs of decline in the whaling industry, he evidently thought he could do better elsewhere. In 1849, he joined dozens of other men from Nantucket in the gold-rush mania and shipped out

Portrait of Benjamin F. Coffin
painted by William Swain, circa 1835.

Portrait of Mary Crosby, wife of Benjamin F. Coffin,
painted by James T. Hathaway, circa 1845.

to California. Before he left, however, he sold his new dwelling house to his father-in-law, Matthew Crosby, for $3,500 and his share in the *Washington* for $3,000. Perhaps this was a way to raise some cash for his new venture while keeping the assets in his wife's family for her use. Matthew, in fact, paid the taxes on the property for the next several years.

It was well that Benjamin thought to make these arrangements, since he failed to make a fortune in the West and later returned to the island. In February 1870, Matthew sold the house back to Mary for $2,100. Although she gained on the exchange, it was still a business deal. In January 1871, she sent her father the money needed "to pay the expenses of transferring the house and the insurance on the 16th of February last." It should be said that Benjamin's behavior was less odd than it might seem. In the whaling era of the 1840s, men and women were used to long absences from home and the sudden reversals of fortune that occurred with frightening frequency and, in his case, there may also have been other domestic difficulties with which to cope. Mary died in 1878, three months after her father. Benjamin retired from active business and lived until 1889, content to serve as town assessor, registrar, and commissioner of insolvency. He made his daughter, Marianna, executor of his will and left her the bulk of his estate, including the mansion house on Main Street. To his sons, Jared and William Seabury, who were then living in Brooklyn, he left just $5.00 each, a distribution hard to explain except on the grounds of a family estrangement.[23]

Matthew, for his part, seems to have kept up with his relatives, as well as with current events in the world beyond Nantucket until his death. Among his papers there is an interesting letter addressed to his "respected grandson" dated February 13, 1867.[24] No name is given in the salutation, but it is likely to have been Jared Coffin, the younger, or William Seabury, since he added a postscript that "Mary Anna [sic] and babes getting along nicely." These would have been Marianna's children: Henry, born in 1864, and Mary, born in 1867. Matthew's letter is a reply to one written to him concerning a petition he and his grandson sent to an insurance company urging that "all interested in navigation must see the necessity of steamers having a jib, if no other sail."[25]

To put sails on a steamboat? This proposal was not as bizarre as it sounds and in 1867 it was surely related to the ongoing public debate of iron boats against wooden boats and steam power against wind power. The transition from the old and proven use of sailing vessels to the new, and at times uncertain, use of steamboats was inevitably slow and cautious. Even in the more recent past, we still heard it said that "Mr. and Mrs. So-and-So sailed to Europe on the *Queen Mary*," without any sense of incongruity. Although the writing was on the wall, a large portion of shipping, well into the 1860s and 1870s, was still by sail, or by a combination of sail and steam, and many a motion was made in public debates to build vessels which made use of both sources of power. When the famous *Savannah* crossed the Atlantic from Georgia to Liverpool in 1819, for example, she relied mainly on her sails and used a steam engine connected to side wheels for only a few hours. The double-hulled iron ship, *Great Eastern*, which crossed the other way from Southampton to New York in 1860, was built not only with five engines but with six masts fully-rigged.

In fact, regulations of the United States Department of Commerce and Labor published in 1907 provided for "steam vessels under sail." Wind was cheaper than coal or wood and adjustments had been made to sails and rigging to furnish more power and better steering. They also were useful when the boilers broke down or the fuel supply ran out. On the other hand, steamboats, although more expensive to build and run, were faster, and a shorter crossing time meant less cost in provisions for crew and passengers, and, it was alleged, less risk of illness to those on board.

While this was the way of the future, Matthew Crosby had cut his teeth on sailing packets and made his fortune by square-rigged whaleships. With a generally conservative view of the world, as we know was his habit, he was naturally hesitant to commit himself all at once to such a momentous change. Yet, the fact that he urged at the least a jib, which by itself could hardly provide enough canvas to drive the ship but perhaps enough to steer it, suggests a reluctant concession to a changing world.

Matthew and Lydia's second daughter, Ann, married George C. Macy in 1839, and the couple moved to a house at 39 India Street. At the time, George was associated in business with his father, Gorham Macy, an established commission merchant and auctioneer. Although these were the years when the island economy was in full growth, the Macy firm, which acted in competition with a number of other family concerns as middlemen for the distribution and sale of a variety of goods including provisions such as corn, wheat, sugar, beef, butter, cheese, coffee, tea, chocolate, and tobacco, as well as furniture, dry goods, books, and even houses, ships, and bank shares, was rumored to be in financial distress. It was said by Asa Bunker, the local agent for a credit agency, of whom we shall hear more, that part of the money which came with Ann Crosby, estimated at several thousand dollars, had to be used to pay off creditors, and even then, George Macy was obliged to borrow from his father-in-law, Matthew.[26]

Apparently, the condition of his finances continued to be unstable, because in June 1858 Matthew sold a small parcel of land on Pine Street to his daughter for her "sole use free of interference or control by her husband and free from creditors of George C. Macy."[27] The causes of Macy's financial difficulties and the degree to which they compromised his standing are not clear, but it was a crowded market for that kind of commercial undertaking with narrow margins for profit. The company, in fact, was a kind of later department store, but without the multi-storied building, and still subject to a delicate balance of orders and sales. Success demanded constant supervision, enlightened management, sound business skills, and a determination to persevere.

*Pine Street looking north from the corner of Lyon Street, 1860s.*

Indeed, George Macy was an exact contemporary of Rowland Hussey Macy, another Nantucket boy, but from a different Macy line, who had dutifully shipped aboard a whaler when a teenager, but aware of the declining local economy, was disinclined to follow his father in the industry and sought a career on the mainland. After a series of failures as a salesman in Boston, and as another disappointed investor in the California gold fields, in 1858 he opened a dry goods and clothing store on Sixth Avenue and Fourteenth Street in New York City where at last his talents and industry were richly rewarded. A century and a half later the modern version of Macy's, still open to the public and self-billed as the "largest store in the world," is rarely given its place as a symbol of the momentous forces that were to change forever the lives of the families on the island.

With the marriage of Lydia Crosby, the last child of Matthew by his first wife, to Barker Burnell Jr. in 1840, the first winds of scandal rocked the family boat. Young Barker's father was a distinguished member of the Massachusetts General Court, as the state legislative body was then known, where he served in the House and the Senate from 1821 to 1838. In 1841 he was elected to the United States House of Representatives but died two years later. Inspired by Edmund Burke's speech to Parliament in favor of the American whaling industry given in March 1775, John Quincy Adams, then in the House and a visitor to Nantucket, linked Burnell's character to his island upbringing in a glowing testimonial:

> He was a native of Nantucket, a small island of the ocean appended to the State of Massachusetts, long renowned as the mother of a race of men for unblemished integrity, for perilous enterprise, for energy of exertion, and hardiness of endurance, unsurpassed by any other portion of the dwellers upon this terraqueous globe… The islanders of Nantucket, our contemporaries, have not degenerated from the virtues of their fathers, and of that race of men Mr. Burnell was the worthy representative on this floor.[28]

In keeping with the customary token of respect for the dead, the members of the Senate were asked to wear a mourning band of crape upon the left arm for thirty days. Isaac C. Bates, speaking in the Senate, recalled Burnell's honesty and integrity in a similar fashion:

> He died in the Christian's faith and in the Christian's hope. He left a widow, a lady with whom it is the happiness of some of us to have been acquainted, and a son of much promise.[29]

Clearly, Barker Burnell was a gifted statesman of high standing, and great hopes were attached to his family. Indeed, Barker Jr. appeared to have a bright future before him. Born into a successful family and married into another, he entered the banking business on the island as a very young man. His character and ability were soon recognized and he was promoted to cashier of the Manufacturers and Mechanics Bank, the most important position in the daily running of that institution which had been founded just a few years earlier. The esteem in which the father was held and the high expectations for the son are important to keep in mind because, on the one hand, these views make clear that Lydia, as well as her father, had every reason to think the match a desirable one, while on the other hand, they force us to realize the enormity of the deception that would occur. The impeccable reputation of the father rendered the scandal that tainted the character of the son even more shocking and inexplicable.

*Portrait of Barker Burnell Jr., painted by William Swain circa 1845.*

Like many well-to-do Nantucket men, Barker Jr. invested in farming and in whaleships. Even at his young age, he had interests in some major vessels, including the *Peruvian*, the *Washington*, the *Henry Astor*, the *Franklin*, the *Ganges*, the *Orion*, the *Henry Clay*, the *Navigator*, the *Foster*, the *Nantucket*, the *Enterprise*, and the *Mount Vernon*. To process the oil, he entered into partnership with Abraham Wing, a businessman from Sandwich who had married a Nantucket girl, to run a small factory. He also owned property left to him by his father and funds amounting to $23,000 from his wife's inheritance (which originally came from Zenas Coffin).

This privileged position mandated a proper residence, but eschewing Main Street, he bought a house at 48 Orange Street with a cupola on top and a grand view of the harbor. He was written up by the obliging Asa Bunker as a man "surrounded by wealth and his friends are very influential…No person stands higher in public estimation than Barker Burnell…"[30] In December 1845, he resigned his position at the bank, and early in the new year, following in his father's footsteps, he was elected a state senator and moved to Boston. Then, suddenly and without warning to the Nantucket public, or to friends or family, disaster struck and ruined his reputation, his career, and his life on the island. The ensuing drama is worth recounting for several reasons, not least because it involved important family members. It was one of the more sensational banking scandals to hit Nantucket and it was important enough to be taken up by the mainland newspapers. A number of prominent citizens were affected, Matthew Crosby was called as a witness, and a pair of well-known attorneys took the case for the prosecution and for the defense. The result, unfortunately, was an inconclusive trial with many important questions left unanswered. The whole affair raised the double problem of how to deal with incompetent management of a large business at the local level and how to see that justice was done in a very small, tightly knit, and protective community.

It should be said at the outset that banks on Nantucket had had a checkered history. Their difficulties, of course, were not specific to the island; a review of the beginnings of the First and Second United States National Banks in the years 1811 and 1817, for example, will demonstrate the problems. But from the time of the first foundation, there was never a question that they were needed. The increased prosperity from whaling in the late eighteenth century prompted several islanders to consider ways in which to provide easier access to credit in order to finance their undertakings at a reasonable cost. It was thought to be cheaper, safer, and more stable to borrow from an institution with fixed capital than from relatives and friends, and on this sensible idea, the first Nantucket Bank was incorporated in June 1795. The plan was good, but the execution was wanting, and many risks were left unidentified. Two weeks later, as noted earlier, the bank was robbed of over $20,000. The money was never recovered, and the shock of the incident remained in the collective island memory. Yet the merchants knew the value of what they wanted and forged ahead.

More successful was the Pacific Bank, named for the source of most of the wealth of the island by the nineteenth century. It was chartered in 1804, and in spite of a few difficult periods, especially when there was a temporary lack of funds to redeem the notes presented, a moment in 1842 when one of the officers had misappropriated several thousand dollars, and another in 1885 when the cashier overdrew his account by $8,000 and resigned, the bank has survived until the present day.

*The Pacific Bank, circa 1880. Located on the west side of Market Square, it was built in the solid and imposing style meant to convey the security and permanence that the public expected in its leading town bank.*

The Phoenix Bank, however, established in 1812, and false to its name, failed in 1825 and was never resurrected. On the other hand, the Manufacturers and Mechanics Bank, where Burnell was employed, flourished from its foundation in 1825 but succumbed to insolvency and to the Great Fire of 1846, in which the building and some of the records were burned up. Likewise, the Citizen's Bank, in which Matthew had accumulated thirty-five shares, was also destroyed in the fire with a loss to him of $5,000. A second Nantucket Bank, this time with Matthew among the directors, was chartered in 1831 as well, but apparently never did any business. Too many banks, perhaps, for the resources of the island, although a well-known exception is the Nantucket Institution for Savings, set up in 1834 for the benefit of citizens with modest incomes, which is still going strong.

The period from 1790 to about 1850 was, in fact, the time which saw the highest rate of bank failures in the country at large. The main problems of an internal nature appear to have been a lack of experience on the part of the officers in charge, who often did not understand the degree of risk involved; loose accounting methods; reserves that were kept too low; and a lack of oversight by the directors and the stockholders. The Nantucket banks, unfortunately, shared all these weaknesses to some extent and suffered, as well, from a declining economy that could not support so many competing institutions.

The mystery of the Burnell affair began in April 1843, when the books of his bank were audited and the accounts were found to be correct, except that the original capital of $100,000 had been reduced to about $83,000 as a result of bad loans. A year later, another audit showed a recovery of about $12,000. But, as it was discovered later, the real deficit was about $80,000. The figures had been inflated by incorrect entries showing money due from the mainland banks in New Bedford and Boston. In March 1845, another audit revealed a surplus of $5,721, but, in fact, the whole capital stock was missing plus another $17,000.

Although they had not yet realized it, the stockholders had lost their investments, and there were insufficient funds to pay the depositors. Nevertheless, in December of that year, Burnell resigned his position to take up political office and submitted a report showing that the bank was in good condition. His place as cashier was taken by Andrew Morton who, by February of 1846, had discovered, to his alarm, the true state of affairs.

On February 27, the directors met, and it was resolved that the accounts should be balanced each month, that associated banks on the mainland should submit statements on a regular basis, and that an internal audit should be done once a quarter, all sound and proven practices that should have been established at the outset. But the current problem was a delicate one, and it was not until the following June that Burnell was accused of mismanagement, arrested, and imprisoned. The sensational news filled a half-page of the local newspaper.

In time, a bond was posted and he was let out on bail. In October, he was indicted on a charge of defalcation, or embezzlement, in the Court of Common Pleas, and the case was continued until the June term. A civil suit by the Bank vs. Burnell was settled by payment of about $40,000 worth of property. This was done with the intention of avoiding further accusations and a criminal charge. But to no avail. The trial by jury began in June 1847 on the single count "that on 19 February 1844 he [Burnell] had feloniously and unlawfully embezzled and converted to his own use a check for $6,000." The prosecution for the State of Massachusetts, led by J. H. Clifford, the District Attorney of New Bedford, was determined to show fraud and maintained that Burnell's tenure exposed a history of misconduct in violation of the trust he held as an officer of the bank.

An early witness called to testify was David Thain, a friend of Burnell and a director of the bank, who had met the accused in Boston, advised him of the difficulties, and urged his return to Nantucket. He then produced a letter dated February 13, 1846, written by Burnell from the Senate Chamber, which while admitting guilt, appeared to be more a confession of incompetence brought about by inexperience rather than by criminal intent:

> My dear Sir,
>
> Since you left this morning, my mind has been, I assure you, in a pretty bad state. My first course was to go immediately to Nantucket; but connected with that I can see nothing but ruin to myself, or at least disgrace and censure from those with whom I have been intimately associated. And what other course is there for me to pursue? I cannot reflect upon the subject without feeling that my very existence is a burden that I cannot bear; and what course I pursue I know not. Every member of the Legislature treats me with all the respect that I could ask or expect.
>
> Every citizen of Boston, of any eminence, extends to me the hand of friendship; and added to all this, the many friends I have in Nantucket, all conspire to make any stain upon my character the less endurable. I cannot, I cannot come to Nantucket. The Bank will not suffer a loss from funds that I have made use of. When this reaches you, I shall be either in eternity (God forgive me for the reflection), or far beyond the sympathy of those who are dear to me at Nantucket. Death, death. Yes, any thing rather than disgrace.
>
> Your friend,
> B. Burnell[31]

Under the circumstances, suicide, as a solution to his problems, was no more than a passing thought. But it was only natural that he should have found some relief from his overwhelming feelings of guilt and shame and isolation by putting the idea in writing and sharing it with a friend.

The defense was first taken up by Timothy Coffin of New Bedford, who pointed out that it had been shown that Burnell was not the only one at fault. The important firm of

Charles G. and Henry Coffin, the sons of Zenas Coffin, had overdrawn their account at the bank by $50,000. The account of Timothy Hussey, another director, was also overdrawn. Even the personal account of the president was overdrawn. Furthermore, if Burnell was charged with taking $6,000 and the bank was missing $90,000, what happened to the rest of the money? Why were the directors who were careless in their oversight not charged? It was known that Burnell had sufficient funds at hand. Why would he steal?

Abraham Wing, Burnell's business partner, testified that their firm brought in $100,000 a year. In a pertinent aside, Asa Bunker described Wing as "very prudent and extremely cautious, and a very good check on his colleague." This comment suggests that Burnell was considered a bit headstrong, or inattentive to business, or downright careless, and may help to explain how he got himself in this predicament.

Matthew Crosby, called as a witness, confirmed that his son-in-law had capital and income by his wife's inheritance and from his investments in whaling. He also revealed the interesting fact that when he bought from him a one-eighth share in the ship *Navigator*, Burnell had wanted him to keep the money because, he said, he did not need it. But Matthew, in line with his own meticulous accounting practices, had paid him anyway. Here was a mystery to be solved, and it became a theme in the more elaborate argument for the defense by Rufus Choate.

*News of the arrest of Barker Burnell Jr. The article published in the* Nantucket Mirror *included some early and inaccurate facts of the case.*

The Burnells engaged the best legal talent that they could find by bringing Choate in on their side. He had served in both houses of Congress from 1831 to 1845 and was well known as a successful attorney in a number of lawsuits and as an orator much in public demand. What he charged the family cannot be determined, but he was known to have been more interested in the legal niceties of a case than in the fee for taking it on. The reported range was from $50 to more than $200, and it seems reasonable to suppose that Matthew Crosby helped out with the Burnell legal bills. Choate's view, presented to the jury in his florid style as the one that they should adopt, was that Burnell was young and inexperienced, but from a worthy family, and a man with a stainless reputation:

> One of the jewels of the island, married to a wife worthy of his love, a wife who does not desert him today, and who would go with him, if such were the ordinance of the law, to the gallows tree.[32]

His summary was brief and to the point. At one time, young Burnell needed some funds. He took some money intending to repay it. He was careless and too much occupied with his other financial affairs. In May 1847, he had to deal with the death of his son, not quite two years old. He was distracted and the books were not kept up to date. If Burnell were guilty, it was of neglect, not of fraud and embezzlement.

This plea for acquittal was countered by a forceful presentation of the evidence against him by Clifford, who asked for a vote to convict for stealing the $6,000 from the bank. The men of the jury, however, thought otherwise and declared him not guilty. It was a decision probably forced upon them by the troubled web of irregularities, the inconclusive evidence, the number of unanswered questions, and the involvement of too many influential names. It was also the case that some of the records of the bank had been burned up in the fire of July 1846, which doubtless contributed to the disarray of the remaining accounts.

But such was the damage done to the reputation of the family that Barker Burnell and his wife, with his daughter, Mary, and probably his son, Barker, still small children, soon left the island. His house at 48 Orange Street was put up for sale, as the advertisement said, "to close up the affairs of the Manufacturers and Mechanics Bank." It was bought very quickly by Love Parker and her husband, Robert, proprietors of several boarding houses in the town.[33] The store at 16 Main Street, which had been occupied by Barker Burnell for his oil and candle business, was another casualty of the fire of 1846. When the Manufacturers and Mechanics Bank went into receivership, the land was sold to George W. Macy, and a new building was put up which later became well-known as the H. Marshall Gardner art store, and in more recent times, as the celebrated and successful Nantucket Looms.

Matthew did not escape a loss and was obviously greatly affected by the shock to the family. In June 1846, before the trial took place, he had written to his nephew, William Wyer, in Ravenna, Ohio, to explain his view of the affair and to ease the pain he felt by putting the disaster in the larger context of a lesson learned:

> The difficulty with the M & M Bank arising from Barker getting the books in confusion has given us and his family great trouble. The Bank has lost its capital

and there is no accounting for it. I am satisfied Barker never had it. Still, he has been grossly negligent in not keeping the books in order. He has had too much other business on hand. It has over run him. I expect he will lose all his property, which I care but little about, if he can clear himself from the difficulty. It is quite a damp upon all of us and a great loss to the stockholders. The depositors and bill holders will probably get their pay. Aunt Huldah had $100 in deposit and two shares in the stock. I am fortunate in not owning any stock and have but few of their bills. I shall be indirectly interested as our office owns $22,500 in the stock which is lost. I have been fearful for some time, there is great danger in young men going too fast, but better for them to have a lesson when young. It will sometimes be for their advantage. It has troubled me exceedingly, altho I mean not to involve myself with the difficulties that my children run into. I give them my advice; after that I can do but little more.[34]

The trial came to an end. Some of the money was repaid. A reputation was ruined. The family had to leave the island. Those were the facts. But there never was a satisfactory explanation as to what actually happened, or as to why it happened. Two quotations may serve to bring this unhappy episode to a conclusion. An editorial in the *Inquirer* in June 1847 summed up the core of the public uncertainty:

The circumstances of the loss of the money were just as mysterious after the trial as before. Between April 1843 and December 1845 more than $100,000 was lost to the stockholders of the bank. How it went and where it went is unknown. The overdrafts by Burnell do not account for so much as this.[35]

But a writer for *The Bankers' Magazine and State Financial Register* expressed his opinion of the affair in the matter-of-fact logic of a disinterested off-island observer:

This is one of the most extraordinary and unaccountable instances of bad management that we have ever heard of; a commentary upon the practice of placing nominal directors in office, either too ignorant of the routine of business, or too busy with their own affairs, to attend to public duties for which they receive no compensation.[36]

And what became of Barker and Lydia Burnell? Ever since the marriage of Jonathan Burnell of Nantucket and Deborah Barker of Sandwich in 1738, there have been at least six Barker Burnells in the related family lines. The genealogical references are not always accurate, and it is often difficult to be sure which Barker Burnell is being cited. It seems, however, that Barker and Lydia did have three children: Mary (1844–1904), Barker Jr. (1845–1847), and a second Barker (1849–1927) born two years after the bank scandal. According to the Barney list of families, this last Barker followed in the footsteps of some other members of the family and married a woman named Emma M. Newman in Lima, Peru, in 1878.

Barker, his father, who misappropriated the bank funds, is said to have left Nantucket for Chile, and, by a note in the 1850 Nantucket census, to have died in Santiago in 1861, which would fit with the reported exodus to the west coast of South America where there was already a small Nantucket colony. His departure is confirmed by the name "Barker Burnell" listed as a passenger on the steamship *Falcon* which sailed from New York on March 8, 1849, and arrived in San Francisco on August 29. We know that "Barker Burnell and Lydia, his wife," sold land in the Cato lots for $100 to Matthew Crosby in March 1857, and that in January 1863 Matthew and his wife, Elizabeth, sold to "Lydia Burnell, widow," the house and land on the corner of Pine and Pleasant Streets, which had been part of the homestead lot of Zenas Coffin, for $1,000.[37] In February, facing adverse circumstances, Lydia borrowed $1,800 from her father, but Matthew, ever generous to his children, in spite of the "hands-off" posture advised in his letter to William Wyer, gave her the note four years later.[38]

Young Barker evidently returned to California, since there is a gravestone marked "Barker Burnell" with the dates 1849–1927 in the Mt. Hope Cemetery in San Diego. He kept up some connection with the island by annual membership in the Nantucket Historical Association from at least 1905 to 1920, when his address is listed as 1045 Sixth Street, San Diego. After her husband's death in 1861, Lydia must have come back to Nantucket, probably with her daughter, Mary, since she accompanied her father, Matthew, and her half-sister, Emma, on a trip to Detroit in 1866.[39] Lydia and Mary were both buried in Prospect Hill Cemetery.

The children of Matthew and Lydia who grew up and married during the prosperous years of the whaling industry between 1815 and 1845 chose to remain on the island. But it was a sign of the times, and a portent of the general shift in living standards that overtook the island in the mid-nineteenth century, that in the period after 1850, when the economic picture had become much bleaker, most of the children of Matthew and Elizabeth moved away.

If fortunes were rising, why leave? But if fortunes were falling, why stay? The daughters found husbands who were established in trade and the sons, in turn, eschewed the risks of seafaring in favor of the uncertainties of landed business ventures. In this sense, Matthew, who began his career in a packet sloop and ended it in the counting house, may be said to represent this gradual, but significant, change in the economic and social structure of the island. Whaling was still a source of important returns, but not on Nantucket. New Bedford, for example, was fast outstripping the island in the race for wealth. A comparison of three sets of estimated figures for the years 1845 to 1860 will show at a glance the rapid change of affairs:[40]

Table 1.

**Whaleships in service, Nantucket & New Bedford, 1845–1860**

| Year | Nantucket | New Bedford |
|---|---|---|
| 1. The number of whaleships leaving Nantucket and New Bedford. | | |
| 1845 | 32 | 87 |
| 1850 | 15 | 85 |
| 1855 | 16 | 91 |
| 1860 | 6 | 68 |
| 2. The number of vessels employed in the whale fishery. | | |
| 1844 | 78 | 239 |
| 1860 | 21 | 291 |
| 3. The number of barrels of sperm oil imported in 1859. | | |
| | 5,316 | 43,716 |

If you wanted to remain in whaling, although it was obvious to all that it was an increasingly risky business, there was much greater opportunity to make a living in a growing, bustling port where the population in 1850 had swelled to 16,443 inhabitants, than to remain on the island where the number of people had declined to 8,452. Moreover, if the sea no longer held the attraction it once did, New Bedford, with easy inland connections, offered many other kinds of work. It is no wonder that under these circumstances, three of Matthew's daughters, namely Martha, Susan, and Judith, would move there and that two of them would marry businessmen from that town.

But to turn first to the sons and to Matthew Jr., who was born in 1827 and, like his stepbrother William, went into the oil and candle business with his father at an early age. By the summer of 1848, he was set up on Commercial Wharf as a commission agent and dealer in "cordage, duck, sheathing copper, bar iron and steel, naval stores, white lead, linseed oil and paints, potash, flour, sugar, and tobacco." He appears to have continued in this line until the summer of 1853, although along the way, in 1850, he also became an agent for the New Bedford Cordage Company and for the manufacturer of Patent Seam Cotton Canvas for sails. His business sense was evidently appreciated because he was named a director of the Commercial Insurance Company of Nantucket in 1853.

By this time, he had been married for almost four years to Sarah Whitney, the daughter of Daniel Whitney, listed in the 1850 census as "mariner." This being Nantucket, there is, of course, a further connection among the families: Elizabeth, the sister of Matthew Jr., married William C. Gardner, who was a partner with Andrew Whitney, the brother of young Matthew's wife, Sarah, in the newly organized Nantucket Cordage Company.

But Matthew did not linger on the island. Although he still had a hand in the manufacturing business with his father and, in fact, rented the old Zenas Coffin store from Henry Coffin, he left in 1853 with his younger brother, Sylvanus, on an exploratory expedition to Callao, the port for the town of Lima, in Peru. The first American ship, the *Washington*, under Captain George Bunker from Nantucket, had put into Callao in 1792. Since then, it had grown to be an important place where whaleships, which might be at sea for two, or three, or even four years, could be provisioned and repaired, the excess barrels of oil sent home, and the mail picked up and delivered. It was this business that evidently first attracted the Crosby brothers, who established themselves as ship chandlers and commission agents and opened a store.

Among their manuscripts is a form letter written in September 1853 from Boston and signed by Matthew Crosby Jr. announcing his departure for Callao in order "to keep a large and general assortment of ship chandlery and stores, naval stores, …and to furnish to American shipmasters every facility for the despatch of their business."[41] It was addressed to William R. Easton, the father-in-law of Matthew Jr.'s brother, Charles. Easton was highly regarded as a merchant and public figure on the island and, therefore, well positioned to advertise the family undertaking. It is obvious that Matthew Jr. had been careful to lay the groundwork, since the letterhead lists an impressive number of trade references, including Lewis & Tappan in Boston, Josiah Macy & Son in New York, Hadwen & Barney in Nantucket, William Rotch in New Bedford, Palmer, Cook, & Co. in San Francisco, Caldwell, Train & Co. in Melbourne, Russell & Sturgis in Manila, and Nye, Parkin & Co. in Canton. Whaling, with its related commerce, was a worldwide industry.

It's not surprising that Matthew very soon became entangled in Peruvian politics as it is clear that the success of such an enterprise as his depended on knowing the right people. A striking example is his deal with John Ripley Tracy, a tradesman in Hartford, to ship Colt revolvers to Callao using Crosby & Co. as the local agent. In 1854, however, Peru was in the throes of a populist insurrection, and when fifteen cases arrived containing 814 guns valued at $18,198, officials of the government confiscated the weapons. The ensuing correspondence shows Crosby making every effort to recover them, including the usual bribes to customs officers and enlistment of the help of the American Consul, or failing that, to have the government buy the shipment so that he would be able to reimburse Tracy. But early in January of 1855, the populists won a major battle at La Palma, the revolvers were returned, and Crosby was able to conclude the deal and emerge more or less unscathed.[42]

By this time the inhabitants of the town were also making money by shipping guano, the dried droppings of sea birds, which was rich in nitrogen, phosphates, and potash, and widely used as fertilizer. Until the supply became exhausted through mismanagement, it was the chief and an exceedingly lucrative export industry. Whaleship captains often made a little extra profit by acting as carriers for the dusty and noisome product. Even as whaling began to decline and the number of ships stopping in Peru fell off in the 1850s and 1860s, this trade was organized well enough to continue to offer satisfactory returns to investors.

Sylvanus, as we shall see, stayed on, but Matthew returned to Nantucket briefly in 1857 to collect his wife. They made the trip back to Peru via Washington, Petersburg, and Charleston; then traveled by boat to Havana and Colón, the terminus for the recently built railroad that brought them to Panama. There they booked passage on a vessel for Paita, another major port for commercial shipping, provisioning, and recruiting seamen, and finally arrived in Callao. Eventually, Matthew's brother, Francis Lewis, then just seventeen, agreed to join them. He took a job in the store and, like Sylvanus, ended by spending most of the rest of his days there.[43]

Matthew Jr., however, finally decided against a life in the south and by 1865 he was back in Boston acting as the agent for the enterprise in South America, as well as for Bunker, Callott & Co., suppliers of provisions to whaleships in San Francisco. We have a reference to him in some interesting comments on life in the United States and Peru in the letters of his friend, Oliver Chase, a restless young man who had left Nantucket to find work in Providence but was attracted by the promise of a good income in Callao. He first found Matthew living in Boston in "a tip-top boarding place…with some other friends nearby." These included his brother-in-law, Andrew Whitney; Cromwell Barnard (a descendant of Jonathan Barnard and a cousin of Elizabeth, Matthew Crosby's second wife); Benjamin Clisby (a grandson of John Clisby who had married Matthew Crosby's sister, Betsey); and Alexander Pinkham (a distant cousin of Elizabeth Pinkham, the wife of William H. Crosby). With Matthew Jr.'s help, Oliver signed up for a three-year stint with Sylvanus Crosby & Co. as an office clerk with a beginning salary of $1,000 a year, or about $13,000 in present money. But unlike Sylvanus and Francis, Oliver never came to terms with the foreign culture, the language, or the people, and evidently spent a good deal of his time trying to find a way to leave. Unfortunately, the end came suddenly, late in March of 1868, when he died of yellow fever at the age of twenty-five.[44]

Meanwhile, Matthew Jr. remained in Boston, residing in West Roxbury, but continued to make trips to Nantucket with his wife and remained active in his father's business affairs for many years to come. Their commercial interests in Peru also involved Matthew Jr.'s son, Matthew Lewis Crosby, who was graduated from Harvard College in 1877. He journeyed twice to Callao, in 1878 and again in 1881, "to close a business," but whether it was their business or some other one is not clear.[45]

Sylvanus and Francis, on the other hand, soon settled down in their new surroundings and established a lucrative commercial enterprise. Peru had only recently achieved independence from Spain, and the country was still suffering from a depressed economy aggravated by the loss of land after a war with Chile. Foreign trade and administrative expertise, therefore, were welcomed and encouraged.

The Crosby firm in Callao, and in Pisco and the Chincha Islands, prospered as ship chandlers, provision merchants, and forwarding agents. In those days owners, captains, and crews kept in touch by personal encounters at sea and by mail. Letters could be sent addressed to

*An advertisement soliciting new business for the firm of Matthew Crosby Jr. in Callao, Peru, 1853.*

## CROSBY & CO.,
### SHIP CHANDLERS AND SHIP AGENTS,
#### CALLAO, PERU.

**REFERENCES.**

| | |
|---|---|
| MESSRS. SAMPSON & TAPPAN, R. B. FORBES, ESQ., GEO. B. UPTON, ESQ., VERNON BROWN, ESQ. } BOSTON. | WM. J. ROTCH, ESQ., NEW BEDFORD. MESS. PALMER, COOK & CO., MESS. HUSSEY, BOND & HALE. } SAN FRANCISCO. |
| MESS. JOSIAH MACY & SON, JOHN OGDEN, ESQ. } NEW YORK. | MESS. CALDWELL, TRAIN & CO., MELBOURNE. MESS. RUSSELL & STURGIS, MANILA. |
| MESS. HADWEN & BARNEY, NANTUCKET. | MESS. NYE, PARKIN & CO., CANTON. |

Boston, September 10th, 1853.

Dear Sir:

The undersigned, under the name and firm of Crosby & Co., is about to establish himself at Callao, as Ship Chandler and Ship Agent.

It is his intention to keep a large and general assortment of Ship Chandlery and Stores, Naval Stores, &c. He will give devoted attention to the best interest of every ship addressed to his care, and furnish to American ship-masters every facility for the despatch of their business.

He will leave for Callao, via the Isthmus, by the steamer to sail October 5th, and take charge of letters and instructions to captains expected to arrive at that port. Letters addressed to his care may be left at the Office of Mr. Vernon Brown, Boston, or Mr. John Ogden, New York.

Ship owners desiring to write their captains, may at all times enclose letters to his care, which shall be handed them immediately after their arrival.

Matthew Crosby, Jr.

S. Crosby & Co. in confidence that they would be immediately delivered to the designated ship upon its arrival in port. The partners were even enterprising enough to have had water piped into Pisco and then brought down to the beach for the convenience of the seamen on the ships.[46]

In 1862 Sylvanus married Castora Tizón from Callao and began to acquire a prominent position in local society. He held a senior rank in the town fire brigade which, in fact, was an honor of great social prestige and importance, and then served for a time as the United States Consul. His younger brother, Francis Lewis, advanced from clerk to manager, and in 1867 married Mercedes Tizón, a niece of Castora. Good times attracted other outsiders, including a large conglomerate called the American Trading Company, for which Francis became the agent, and the Grace brothers, William and Michael, who descended on the town in 1854. In spite of serious financial problems at the outset, they eventually built up an impressive international company by profits from the guano trade and founded a shipping line from Peru to New York.

When his contract with the company expired, Francis joined the W.R. Grace Co. as head of the sales staff. The firm of Crosby Brothers, however, fell on hard times by the end of the century. Sylvanus died in 1894 and Frank, who still had a stake in the business, sold it. After paying off the outstanding debts, raising fourteen children, and assuming charges incurred by his wife's relatives, he was left with no great fortune to show for his efforts over the years. But like his brother, Sylvanus, he nevertheless made a name for himself in his adopted town and was much praised, both for the organization and leadership of the fire brigade and for his association in the foundation of the Masonic Lodge of Peru.[47]

Although the career of Charles Carroll Crosby, the last of Matthew's sons to be considered here, did not take him away to spend his life on another continent, it is, nevertheless, another striking example of the way in which traditional occupations associated with whaling were overtaken by new and more attractive opportunities from abroad. But in his case, at least, it also reveals the strong ties which still bound him to his island upbringing.

Born on Nantucket in 1836 and educated for a time at the Friends School, Charles left for Manchester, New Hampshire when he was sixteen to learn the trade of a machinist. It was the same shop where John Rogers, who was to become known as the "Norman Rockwell of American sculpture" for his attractive figures and scenes of popular life, was also serving his apprenticeship. Four years later, Charles moved to take a job with the Boston Belting Company, a manufacturer of rubber goods. In 1859, he returned to Nantucket to work as a ship's chandler and to marry Ellen M. Easton, whose father, William R. Easton, as we have noted, enjoyed a position of importance among the citizenry. "Charly Crosby was married to Ellen Easton, daughter of William R., last Monday at day-break, the fashionable hour now for marriages," remarked Elizabeth Pinkham Crosby in one of her chatty letters about island affairs.

By 1863, Charles was employed by Robert Lowden, the saddle and harness maker, in New York City. But this job lasted no longer than the others, and he again came back to the island to work in various capacities in the Nantucket Fishing Company and the Nantucket and Cape Cod Steamboat Company until, in 1879, he established his own firm on Whale Street between Old South and Commercial Wharves, on a dock then known as "Crosby's wharf," as a dealer in "Coal, Wood, and Flour, Buckwheat, Bolted Meal, Grass Seed, Neat's Foot and Sperm Oils."

But having had so many different jobs may have slowed down his success in the business world; a little before this time, his father had made several loans to him, adding up to more than $5,000. Nevertheless, back on Nantucket, trade picked up and improved

*Charles C. Crosby, 1886, at age 50.*

to the extent that Charles found it convenient to open a branch office in Siasconset. From time to time, the advertisements were changed to add other products such as "Lime, Cement, and Hair, Oak and Pine Wood," and, in 1890, "Kerosene Oil," an important sign of surrender to the new age![48]

Within a few years, he also was appointed the agent for the Marine Board of Underwriters, the Old Colony Railroad Company, the Associated Press, and the Western Union Telegraph Company. With regard to the latter position, there was as yet no working cable laid between Nantucket and the mainland, so Charles had the job of writing down messages and sending them by steamboat to Oak Bluffs on the Vineyard, where they could then be sent on by an established cable connection. These were all new undertakings to meet the requirements of the modern age which helped to supplement his income. He also served as the local commissioner of wrecks and shipwrecked goods, and a little later as a founding member and treasurer of the Nantucket Historical Association.

The disastrous fires in Nantucket had heightened awareness of the risks of living and working in wooden structures, and consequently, more importance was attached to a well-organized fire department. Like his brothers in Peru, Charles became a distinguished member of the force, and in 1875, he was presented with a silver and gold-lined trumpet by the members of Engine Company John B. Chace No. 4 for his valuable services.

When he died in 1905, at sixty-nine years of age, he was celebrated by his colleagues as a successful, trusted, and respected citizen of the community.[49] His wife had predeceased him and he had lost three of his four children in the first few months of their lives. Only his daughter, Mary, born in 1868, survived, and it was she who took over the trade on Whale Street, advertising it simply as "Mary E. Crosby, Coal and Wood." She seemed destined to fill her father's shoes, since already in 1889 there was a schooner named the *Mary E. Crosby*, owned by a consortium, which was used to deliver goods to the firm.[50]

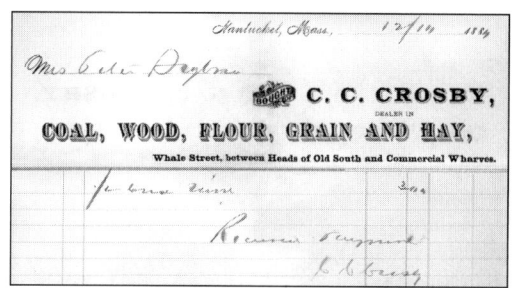

*Receipt for goods sold to Mrs. Peter Sylvia by Charles C. Crosby in 1884.*

The history of the daughters of Matthew and Elizabeth, in keeping with the times, is largely a reflection of the lives of the men they married. In a proportion that might be expected, three of the five chose husbands from off-island, one chose a man from Nantucket, and the youngest remained single. Martha, the eldest child of Elizabeth, moved to New Bedford, and in 1861 married Dennis Wood, a widower with a well-established business. Early in his career, he had been a partner with Willard Nye in the firm of David R. Greene & Co., ship and commission merchants. By 1850, they were reincorporated as Wood and Nye with successful investments

*Old South Wharf, 1880. Schooner* Mary E. Crosby *is at left; the tower of the Unitarian church can be seen in the distance.*

*1870 portraits of Elizabeth Crosby Gardner, Judith Crosby Ford, and Susan Crosby Lowden.*

in a dozen or so whaling vessels. Wood prospered and was elected a director of several banks and an insurance company as a sign of his achievements. He was equally well known for his *Abstracts of Whaling Voyages,* which listed the captains and owners, departures and arrivals, itineraries, and cargoes in oil and bone from 1831 to 1873. To this day, it constitutes a valuable collection of data for research on the whaling industry.[51]

Martha's sister, Susan, in turn, was married to Andrew Lowden, a member of another important merchant family in New Bedford. He died young, at 44 years of age, but not before they had brought eight children into the world, seven of whom survived their father, including Matthew Crosby Lowden, who was living in New York City in 1911. Susan chose to be buried with her husband in the family plot of Rural Cemetery in New Bedford, but her ties to the island were not lost. She remained a member of the Nantucket Historical Association and contributed a poetic trifle to the twelfth annual meeting in July 1906 on the theme of "To thee, our native isle…We bring our humble lay, Fond memories of thy annals past, Are clustered round this day," which was doubtless well received by an appreciative audience.[52]

Judith Crosby, the third sister, also went to live in New Bedford, where she remained for a time before she met James Ford (or Foord), the registrar of deeds in Dedham, Massachusetts. They lived in New Bedford from April 1864, but afterward moved to Dedham, where Judith died in childbirth a little more than a year later.[53]

Elizabeth, the next of the girls, was named for her mother. Although she later lived abroad and died in Brooklyn, N.Y., she had a Nantucket connection in her husband, William C. Gardner, whose father, Edward, had been a whale-oil importer and had married into the Hussey family.

The fifth and last sister, Emma, born in 1839, never married; she evidently stayed on the island for some time, as she is mentioned by her father near the time of his death as the one child who knew most about his business affairs and was the person to be consulted should questions arise. Afterward, she moved to Bedford, New York, where she died in 1892, aged fifty-three.

Although Matthew had thirteen grown children, with almost thirty years separating the first-born from the last, as well as at least twenty-eight grandchildren and numerous great-grandchildren, we know very little about their relations with each other. It is apparent, however, that Matthew was solicitous of their welfare and concerned that, as far as possible, they should benefit from his good fortune. In a much-quoted letter to his children, written on April 12, 1878, a month before he died, he made it clear that over the years he had supported a large family and that he had spent "many thousands of dollars" for their benefit.

In recording his payments, Matthew is not always clear to distinguish gifts from loans or to note loans which became delinquent and were cancelled. Assistance to William, Charles, Susan, Sylvanus, and Emma, for example, amounted to over $32,000, but the breakdown is not specified. Certainly, his intent was to do good. One of his last wishes was that "all of the

*Six friends and four Crosby relatives in 1855. The daguerreotype portrait was made as a farewell gift to Emily T. Barnard (sitting, center) on the occasion of her wedding. Sitting to Emily's right is Sarah Howland, and to her left is Susan B. Crosby (Mrs. Andrew Lowden). Standing left to right are: Elizabeth B. Crosby (Mrs. William C. Gardner), Elizabeth Whitney (sister of Sarah Whitney who married Matthew Crosby Jr.), and Helen Pinkham (sister of Elizabeth Pinkham who married William H. Crosby).*

children in need of assistance should be helped by those who were able to do so in a reasonable way."[54] In order to forestall any complaints of favoritism, he made it a point to cite heavy financial losses from investments late in life, which reduced the total amount he could leave to them. He also mentioned that providing for his daughter, Susan, and her family had taken a large cut. Evidently, they had endured a good deal of hardship after the early death of husband, Andrew Lowden, who had left her with seven children to raise.

The distributions made in Matthew's will also reveal not only his generosity, but also his desire to balance earlier gifts with later bequests without sacrificing the principle of more or less equal benefits. There were forty-nine named beneficiaries divided into four groups, beginning with the three daughters from his first marriage, Mary, Ann, and Lydia, each of whom was to have the income from $3,000 invested in stocks, "free of control by their husbands." By including this precaution, which was not unusual in deeds and wills of the time, Matthew may well have been thinking of the losses incurred by the Burnell disaster.

In the second group was a list of individual grants: $1,600 to Phoebe, Elizabeth's daughter, the wife of Oliver Macy; $200 to Dennis Wood on the death of his wife, Martha, Matthew's daughter (but, as it turned out, he died long before she did); $200 to Susan Coffin, the sister of Matthew's wife; and $100 to his nephew and faithful correspondent, Captain William C. Wyer, the son of Matthew's sister, Mary, who lived in Ravenna, Ohio.

In the third group were thirty-three grandchildren and great-grandchildren, each of whom was to receive $100 to be invested until he or she was "of age or was married."

Finally, the remaining assets were to be divided among Lydia's son, William H. Crosby, and the children of Elizabeth, Matthew's second wife, namely, Martha Wood; Matthew Crosby Jr.; Francis L. Crosby; Sylvanus Crosby; Charles C. Crosby; Elizabeth B. Gardner; the impoverished Susan B. Lowden; and the unmarried Emma L. Crosby. Likewise, these daughters were to have their portions "free from and clean of control of their husbands."[55]

The value of the probated estate in September 1878 was about $57,000. Accounts submitted by the executors in July 1879, August 1883, and May 1885 showed an increase to almost $60,000 through income and the sale of assets until the final distributions were made. An estate of that size in 1878 would be worth about $1,350,000 today, and proportionately, $3,000 would be worth about $68,000 and $100 about $2,200. All in all, the allocations seem to have been made with care to provide a welcome subsidy to those with established careers and an encouraging gift to those just starting out.

Nevertheless, as we have seen in the case of Zenas Coffin, money given away is always open to question. Heirs and onlookers want to know who got what, how much did he get, and who failed to get enough, or got nothing at all. In this case, Benjamin F. Coffin, the husband of Matthew's daughter Mary, raised a mildly dissenting voice. Mary died just three months after her father, and Benjamin had waived all rights to her inheritance. But at the same time, he wrote a letter to his elder children, Jared and Marianna, which he marked "private," giving them a summary of Matthew's will and complaining that eight grandchildren and great-grandchildren had been excluded and received no inheritance.[56] These were three children of Francis Lewis Crosby, two of Sylvanus Crosby, one of Susan Crosby Lowden, and two of his own family. Since Benjamin did not name those excluded, it is not possible to determine which ones he thought were left out. Thirteen offspring of these same children were, in fact, beneficiaries, so that the picture is perhaps not as bleak as he

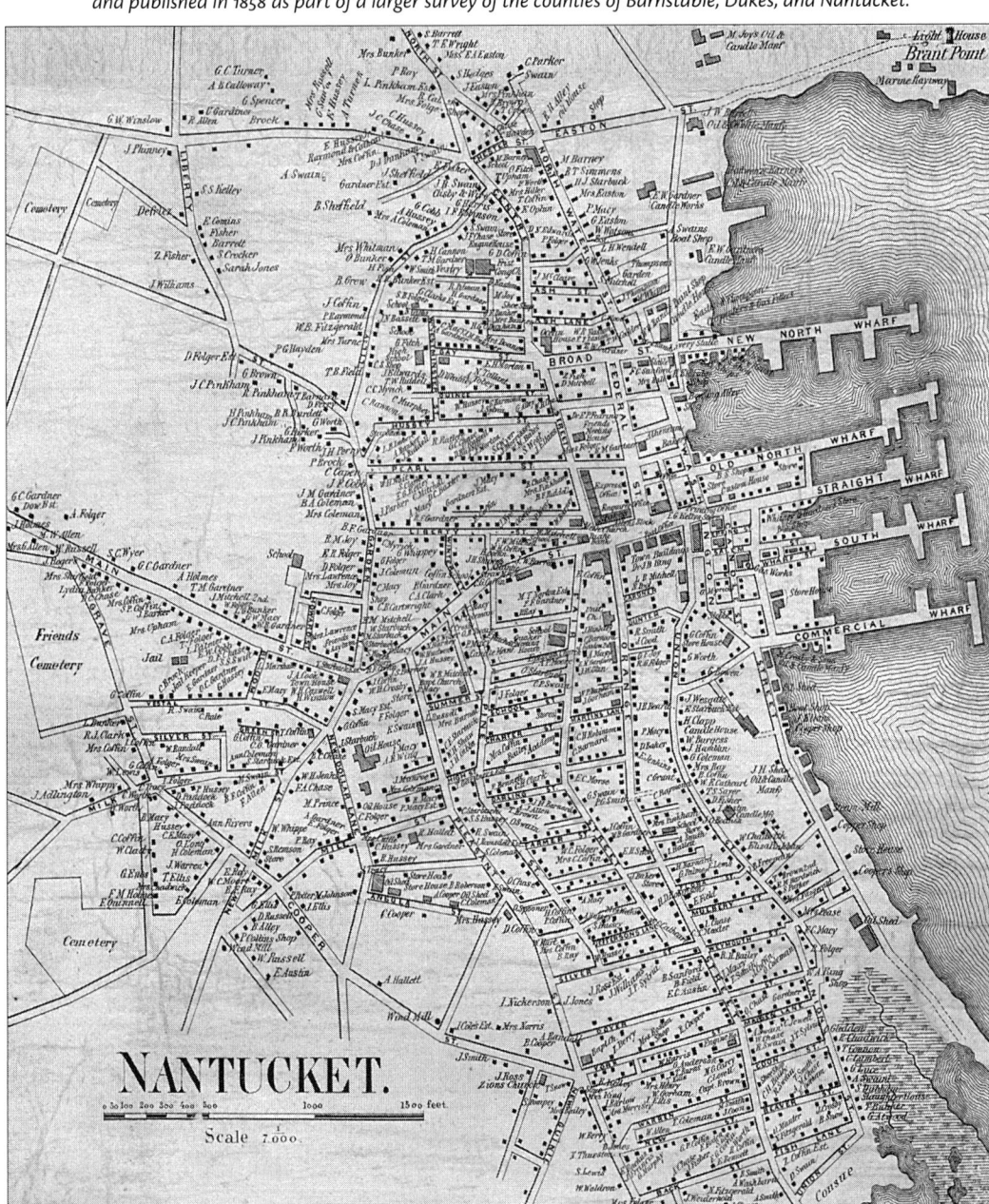

Map of Nantucket town drawn up under the direction of Henry F. Walling (1825-1888), and published in 1858 as part of a larger survey of the counties of Barnstable, Dukes, and Nantucket.

described it. Later in the letter, after listing the assets inherited by Matthew's son, Charles, which amounted to the 'Sconset house and land, as well as some property in town, his comment was, "a poor bargain for Charlie." But it would be hard to say that Charles was discriminated against, since he also received an equal share of the assets left to the descendants in the fourth group.

No other documents have been found which might shed some light on the reason for Benjamin's letter. Recriminations by the heirs to such an important estate were hardly unexpected. Among a large group of descendants there may well have been a few who were passed over inadvertently, or, indeed, on purpose. Matthew certainly must have had his likes and dislikes among all the children in his two families. But if this were, in fact, the case, who would be so well informed as to question his judgment with regard to the final distribution of his wealth?

By his own account, Matthew attributed his decision to give up seafaring to the onset of problems with his health. But the early death of his wife, Lydia, the responsibility for a son and three daughters, a second marriage with a new family and the need to manage the Coffin legacy must have also convinced him that a change was necessary.

As we have seen, it was a propitious move. His active mid-life years from 1820 to 1850 were to coincide with an exceptional period of prosperity on the island. With the capital he had accumulated in the coastal trade, increased by inherited real estate and other assets, Matthew was well positioned to see his investments grow and to have his importance in the community recognized. The new American republic may have disavowed old-world nobility and title in favor of a new aristocracy based on wealth and talent, but social standing and political power were still grounded, as it were, in landed property. Without it, a man had little to say and no vote to cast. Those familiar fundamental rights of the citizen, recited in a variety of revolutionary documents, were not only life and liberty but also property. It was more important than personal liberty which was based upon it. Life was given, liberty was won, and property was acquired; while happiness, so elusive a condition, was constantly pursued. "Property," declared John Adams in 1787, "was as sacred as the laws of God."[57] Of all the outward signs of a man's wealth in the nineteenth century, the most visible, distinct, and permanent were his land and house.

On Nantucket, much of the new money from the whaling industry not given to ships, wharves, and warehouses came to be invested in private homes worthy of successful merchants. This decision to build in the Grand style was certainly encouraged by the decline in Quaker influence and the growth of religious groups which were important enough in numbers to put up an impressive display of new structures for themselves. The Methodist and Congregational churches on Centre Street, the Congregational Unitarian Church on Orange Street, the Universalist Church on Federal Street, the Baptist Church on Summer Street, and an early Episcopal Church, first on Broad Street and then on Fair

Street, were all built, with later additions, between 1822 and 1850. Designed in that period according to the classical values of "stability, function, and beauty," using quality materials and constructed with care, several of the churches and a great many of the houses have survived to the present day.

One astonishing result of this rush to build is the cluster of elegant residences on a short stretch of upper Main Street, and in the surrounding neighborhood, which belonged to Zenas Coffin and his children and in-laws, including Crosbys, Macys, and Swifts, and to Joseph Starbuck and his family. Altogether, there are about a dozen significant properties between Fair Street and Pleasant Street that constitute a kind of little Coffin-Crosby enclave within the larger community and another half dozen which belonged to the Starbuck dynasty.

This is the familiar scene today, when every visitor who has time to spare is told "to see the houses on Main Street." But to frame the picture correctly, we should keep in mind that this not the way it looked in, say, 1840. Since many of the well-to-do lived in their mansions and worked nearby, next to many of them were the factories, sheds, and storehouses which were required to process the oil and candles. Zenas Coffin had a candle factory adjoining his residence, and Matthew had another between Traders Lane and Pine Street, as well as several barns and sheds with stables for horses and cattle next to 90 Main Street. When Hadwen and Barney purchased 100 Main Street in 1829, it included a candle factory with various out-buildings; Joseph Starbuck had a brick storage shed and tryworks, as well as a candle works, constructed in New Dollar Lane as early as 1807; and another was owned by Isaiah Coffin on a lot south of Mill Street. To have the utilitarian instruments of trade, and

*The indecorous backyard of 82 Main Street seen from Ray's Court, circa 1890.*

the accompanying noise and smell, so near the elegant living quarters would now be zoned out of existence, but at the time it seemed hardly incongruous or objectionable.

Worse, certainly, were the noisome effluent and the spread of disease from inadequate drains. As late as 1884, a State Board of Health report cited:

> …the foul odors noticeable in the streets of the town and the contamination of wells by fecal matter percolating through sandy soil…The present sewers are evidently inefficient, improperly constructed, and devoid of any general plan, their outlets being a public nuisance.[58]

It was thought that the configuration of the town, with a concentrated population, narrow streets, and with "close cesspools, privy-vaults, and wells," was a principal reason for the abnormally high rate of disease on the island which, at the time, exceeded the average for

*Pleasant Street looking south from Main Street, circa 1870, with 1 Pleasant Street on the right and the corner of 96 Main Street on the left.*

the state. Moreover, an unforeseen complication was that with the introduction of a public water supply, "it became common practice to convert the abandoned wells into cesspools with the certainty of the pollution of the surrounding soil and the difficulty of the removal of their contents." Indeed, the extension of upper Main Street, beyond a thin line of houses that stretched northwest to the Burying Grounds, was still rural. It was where the country began and where the Lowells, the Folgers, and the Coffins had their farms and vegetable gardens. Main Street was unpaved until 1837 when the first cobblestones were laid from the wharves to the Pacific Bank, while the further stretch, from the bank to Pleasant Street, where the great houses were built, remained dirt, sand, and mud until 1861.

Among the boons and benefits that Lydia Coffin had brought to her marriage with Matthew were the plans for a "mansion house" on Main Street. Apart from a discussion of the project, evidently nothing was decided until just before her untimely death in July 1823. A few weeks afterward, Matthew bought a lot at auction on the corner of Traders Lane, owned by the estate of Sally Jones and sold for $1,500 to pay off her debts. But it was not until 1828, or thereabouts, that he contracted for a two-and-a-half-story Federal-style clapboard building at what would be number 90.[59] In finished form with a five-bay façade, double ridge-chimneys, a balustrade on the edge of the lower roof, and a raised doorway with sidelights and a fan, it was a striking addition to the new architecture. We may assume that a portion of the cost was a gift from Zenas to his daughter. Certainly, it seems true that in

*Matthew Crosby's "Mansion House" at 90 Main Street, circa 1870.*

his well-known generous spirit, he was determined that the new house should be as much for Matthew and his new wife, Elizabeth, as it would have been for Matthew and Lydia. He may even have lived long enough to see the foundations laid and the framing erected. Zenas himself, however, like his own father, Micajah, and in spite of his great wealth, lived in a large but far more modest shingle house built in the late eighteenth century, just around the corner on Pine Street. Joseph Starbuck at 4 New Dollar Lane and Walter Folger at 8 Pleasant Street, both leading citizens, were also content to spend their lives in spacious yet relatively simple houses devoid of external architectural embellishments.

But the new generation desired not only a new look, but to be looked at, and that meant Main Street. Charles G. Coffin, the prosperous elder son of Zenas, put up an expensive, but rather somber, brick dwelling at number 78 in 1832. A year or so later, his brother and business partner, Henry, did the same across the street at number 75, but in a more engaging style with a cupola on top. Asa Bunker thought that the funds to build the houses were borrowed from their mother, Abial, "who was worth at least $70,000, but not more than will come to them from her estate."[60]

Gilbert Coffin, the brother of Zenas, lived at number 83, but the building burned down in 1876 and was not rebuilt. The Coffin daughters, as we have seen, brought houses to their husbands with their father's money. Matthew's new home may have so impressed Thomas Macy, the husband of Eunice, that about 1830, when Thomas transformed a smaller building of the late eighteenth century at number 99 (inherited from Zenas Coffin) into a larger

*Ninety Main Street in modern dress, circa 1960, with the architectural harmony impaired by the added west wing.*

mansion, its design and structure closely resembled the one at number 90. The Sylvanus Macy house at number 89 was also rebuilt in the same style, but whether it served as an early model for the other two or was restored at a later date to copy them, has not been determined.

Another older and smaller building across the street, at number 91, was remodeled around 1820 by Mary Coffin and her husband, Henry Swift, with a simple four-bay façade, a single ridge chimney, and, in typical Nantucket fashion, an entrance doorway at the corner, which gave it an asymmetrical look. Thus, in a relatively small space we can count six houses for Zenas Coffin, his father, his brother, and his three married daughters.

For the daughters of Matthew Crosby and Lydia, we can add another two. The house that Mary and Benjamin Coffin built in 1836 at number 98, for example, retained the five-bay architectural style of the one his father-in-law had put up six years earlier and of the more recent one of Thomas Macy. Corner pilasters were set in place, an elegant recessed doorway added, and end chimneys built to give it a look of refined solidarity.

Mary's sister, Ann G. Crosby, in an unusual move, bought the Joseph Allen house and lots at 86 Main Street, on the corner of Pine, for $4,240 in December 1838, when she was still a single young woman just twenty years old. It was adjacent to land on the south side owned by her father, and because she was very soon married to George C. Macy, it seems that it was intended as part of her wedding gift, with partial funding from the Zenas Coffin bequest. It is uncertain to what extent she altered the building to the present configuration of a three-bay, gable-end structure facing the street. Built over a high brick basement with a raised off-center entrance and stoop and an odd Gothic-style window in the third-floor

*The Benjamin F. Coffin house at 98 Main Street, circa 1870.*

*William H. Crosby's house at 1 Pleasant Street, circa 1890, showing the elaborate gable end.*

*The same view of 1 Pleasant Street, 1970, largely unchanged since the whaling days.*

wall, it is not as striking as some of its neighbors, but it nevertheless fits the style of the street with solid simplicity.

As already noted, Lydia, the youngest daughter and the wife of Barker Burnell Jr., abandoned Main Street for Orange Street. Oddly enough for them, this section of town was growing in favor as the place of residence for the captains of whaleships, as opposed to wealthier owners. She and her husband settled in there until his financial embarrassments forced them to leave the island.

Finally, there is the mansion of William H. Crosby, the only surviving son of Matthew and Lydia. Around 1837, he decided to build on the lot at 1 Pleasant Street, which he had bought from Alice Barnard two years before. With the further purchase of a small strip of land adjoining the property of his brother-in-law, Benjamin Coffin, who lived on the corner, there was no difficulty in considering William to be part of the Main Street family. He and his wife, Elizabeth, had at first occupied a house owned by Zenas Coffin, ever-present in death, it seems, as in life, while plans were drawn up for the new one. Just as Zenas had provided funds for Matthew's new home, so the latter contributed to the cost of William's. In design, materials, and ornate details it was an expensive undertaking, and soon recognized as one of the more elegant structures in the upper town. The gable-end turned toward the street which gave it a narrow appearance and the impressive exterior that included three bays, a raised stoop with an elaborate portico supported by two columns, and a cupola on top, is still there for all to see. Inside, the kitchen and dining room were in the basement, double parlors led off the first floor, and the bedrooms were on the floor above.

We can catch a glimpse of the interior furnishings of the period from a brief description by Elizabeth Crosby Plaskett. She was the daughter of Henry Plaskett, who served as mate on the whaleship *Joseph Starbuck* from 1839 to 1842, and Mary B. Pinkham, the sister of William's wife. Named after her favorite aunt, the young Elizabeth Plaskett was a frequent visitor to the new residence. While impressed by the marble mantelpieces, the mahogany

*An interior view of two of the parlors at 1 Pleasant Street, circa 1870, furnished in the heavy style of the period.*

doors with silver knobs, the French windows which opened onto an unusual wrought-iron balcony, the hand-blocked wallpaper, and many other luxurious appointments, including a Chickering piano, she struggled, somewhat, to reconcile this display of extravagance with the traditional island simplicity with which she had grown up:

> But the Quaker leaven in our New England loaf kept us plain, although we prided ourselves on city modes and manners.[61]

It was, perhaps, a lingering feeling of guilt, quickened by the surrounding luxury, that first attracted her to the Ladies Howard Society, a union of three earlier charitable groups concerned with the temperance movement and aid to poor women and children. Her continued devotion to the destitute, and to the important part women should play in world affairs, later carried her to the presidency of the local chapter of the better known and more influential Sorosis Society, founded in New York City in 1869. The members endeavored to promote a freemasonry among women to gain the vote, to care for the unfortunate, and to enhance their own status for the general improvement of society.

In 1874, Elizabeth gave a stirring speech at the Atheneum, resounding with echoes of the Declaration of Independence, which culminated in an invitation to the public to join her in the noble enterprise:

> Resolved: that the rights and powers of government are simply aids or instrumentalities to promote the great ends of human rights and liberties; that whenever any form

of government becomes destructive to those ends, it is the right of the people to alter or abolish it; that we unite in forming a Nantucket Women's Suffrage Association, believing that a government of the people must be composed equally of men and women; and that we pledge ourselves to labor for the ballot, which is the very essence of equality, until we are recognized as citizens of this great republic.[62]

In sounding the trumpet for social equality, Elizabeth Plaskett was as refreshingly out of the ordinary in her way on conservative Nantucket as was her aunt, Elizabeth Crosby, who cultivated the grand style of housekeeping on Pleasant Street.

Sadly for William and his wife, however, this came to an end when the oil and candle factories and the warehouses on which his business depended, and which were only partially covered by insurance, burned down in the great fires. In spite of help from his father and his continued employment in the family firm, William apparently was unable to regain a strong financial position. In January 1866, they sold their landmark house and land to Orrin F. Adams and moved to a more modest establishment on Fair Street. William died in 1896 and his wife a year later, both respected members of the island community.

Unlike most of the Crosby wives, however, about whom we know very little, Elizabeth is of more than passing interest for her thoughts about life on the island, recorded around mid-century in her journal and in letters to her sisters. There are the usual notices about the latest fashions in clothes and hats and furnishings for the house, but literate, sophisticated, and perceptive (she attended readings of Shakespeare and her mother insisted on French lessons) Elizabeth spent a good deal of time airing her views on the conceits of different family members, on conflicts of favoritism and jealousy, on loves and lovers among her friends, and on those accepted and those rejected, along with the reasons why. Moreover, as a Pinkham of her generation, she was eager to report on the success of meetings and discussions by advocates for women's rights.

Yet from time to time, there appear hints of uneasiness and apprehension in her own mind which are given expression in lengthy musings on the meaning of happiness, unhappiness, loneliness, and fear, and in complaints about her own sufferings. Perhaps as a result of personal disappointment, she comes down hard on churchmen as the most ignorant of all people of human nature and the least able to provide good advice. She fretted over sudden headaches, spinal pain, and erysipelas (an unsightly bacterial skin infection), compounded by distress over the failure of her husband's business. William and Elizabeth had no family of their own, and the paradox of her own feelings of isolation on an island then in decline, in spite of signs of growth and an ever-widening contact with the world outside, is also part of her confession:

> I had, perhaps, but an hour before, called every body insane who could live in a place fast going to decay if they could afford to go anywhere else. I have often heard my friends

say, when they have returned from a journey or a visit, that they were glad to get home, that they enjoyed every moment of their journey or visit, but were delighted to return. I never yet could say so.[63]

There is a discipline of mind necessary to live in a place hemmed in by the sea amid a small community of neighbors with a limited world of experience, and Elizabeth was sensitive to its demands. But hers may have been a special case exacerbated by her sudden change of fortune.

As for the Starbuck family, the three identical brick houses built by Joseph Starbuck on Main Street for his three sons, George ("West Brick," no. 97), Matthew ("Middle Brick," no. 95), and William ("East Brick," no. 93), along with the two magnificent Greek-revival mansions opposite, at no. 94 and no. 96, built for William Hadwen, undoubtedly compose the most striking group of all the town buildings. The men of the families had their houses on the north side of Main Street, and the women had theirs on the south side.

*The "Three Bricks," at 93, 95, and 97 Main Street, built by Joseph Starbuck and his three sons, 1836–1838.*

The Starbuck-Hadwen connection centers on Joseph's daughter, Eunice, who married William Hadwen, and lived at number 100 until the great house at number 96 was finished in 1844. Within a year or so, Hadwen built the similar mansion at number 94 for Mary G. Swain, the daughter of Eunice's sister, Mary. A third Starbuck daughter, Elisa, married Nathaniel Barney, the business partner of Hadwen. They were dealers in whale oil and manufacturers of whale-oil candles. Eliza and Nathaniel also lived at number 100 for several years until they moved off-island and sold their house to their son, Joseph.

This collection of family-related dwellings, of course, was a small part of the hundreds of houses, old and new, that lent a distinctive appearance to the other parts of town. Farther down Main Street, at number 69, stood an early brick mansion similar in proportion and materials to three houses of Joseph Starbuck, built in the 1820s for Frederick W. Mitchell. Another outstanding example in the Grand style, but constructed of clapboard rather than brick, was the John W. Barrett house at number 72, near the corner of Fair Street.

But, in fact, it is not solely the succession of fine buildings of this kind that makes the neighborhood so attractive and first draws the eye of the visitor. Rather, what he comes to appreciate is the far more interesting random intermingling of simple with elaborate structures, of old with new, of shingle here, clapboard there, and brick mixed in, which make up an integrated, harmonious, and ultimately successful, architectural assembly. Examples of this unintended artistry can be seen in the course of a few-minutes' walk down the west side of Pleasant Street. There, the William Crosby house is the first and immediately impressive structure. Next door is the simpler shingle Dow house built about 1800, which, in turn, stands in contrast to the impressive mansion of oil merchant Isaac Macy at number 7. The latter dwelling has more in common with the late eighteenth-century home of Walter Folger at number 8; and then, in sudden contrast, looms the large brick pile of Jared Coffin's *Moors End* on the corner of Mill Street. Built at some distance from Main Street, it was located on what was then considered the very edge of town.

Dozens of other convincing examples in this living museum may be found in almost any of the other nearby streets. The "typical Nantucket house," we are told in many a treatise on the subject, was one that stood close to the street and was built two stories high with an attic, a three- or four-bay façade with exterior weathered shingles or painted clapboards, a single ridge chimney, a simple offset front doorway. A group of them together seen from a distance lent a distinctive somber appearance to the town, quite in line with the unadorned respectability of the Quaker faith.

But even among these houses, a close-up view will reveal an imaginative variation in the treatment of windows, doors, chimneys, front stoops, and placement on the site. They are not uniform and boring like modern row houses, and it is the small stylistic differences that make them attractive. In this sense, of course, the great houses on upper Main Street are not typical, since they represent the endeavors of a small group of wealthy merchants in a relatively short period of fifty years or so to build with a different motive to a different plan. But in just the same way, and due in large part to the quality of design and materials, the unexpected contrasts they present cannot fail to sharpen an interest in the history of the island and quicken the pleasure of those who visit them.

The pleasant irony, of course, and a stark indictment of modern taste, is that none of these grand houses so admired today, nor even some of the lesser ones, would be permitted under current laws and regulations meant "to preserve the historic architecture." Faced with an unprecedented growth in new construction and fearful of the impact that unregulated architectural styles and materials would have on the appearance and prosperity of the island, the citizens voted to establish the Nantucket Historic District Commission at a meeting in February 1956. Rules were drawn up to preserve what was considered to be the historical character of the town, and the village of Siasconset, and a committee was appointed to enforce them. In view of the success of this endeavor, coverage was extended to the whole island by an act of the Massachusetts legislature in 1970.

*Main Street looking east from no. 73 to the Pacific Bank, circa 1870.*

# 3. In the Counting House

*"Sperm whaling off Hawaii," a painting by Thomas Birch from a sketch by C. B. Hulsart, 1838.*

**S**HIPS AND MORE ships! Big ships, strong ships, sturdy ships. Ships designed and built to sail the seas in every kind of weather for months and years until the casks on board were filled with oil. They were the keys to the whaling treasure-house. No ships, no whales; no whales, no oil; no oil, no profits. Beneath the lofty rhetoric of Melville's description of the fictional *Pequod*, lies the real-life image of the old and battered, yet tough, staunch, and still seaworthy whaler familiar to sailors up and down the coast:

> She was a ship of the old school, rather small if anything; with an old-fashioned claw-footed look about her. Long-seasoned and weather-stained in the typhoons and calms of all four oceans, her hull's complexion was darkened like a French grenadier's who has alike fought in Egypt and Siberia. Her venerable bows looked bearded. Her masts, cut somewhere on the coast of Japan—where her original ones were lost overboard in a gale—her masts stood stiffly up like the spines of the three old kings of Cologne. Her ancient decks were worn and wrinkled, like the pilgrim-worshipped flagstone in Canterbury Cathedral where Becket bled… A noble craft, but somehow a most melancholy.[1]

But whether old, or new like the *Acushnet* built in 1840 and not yet "weather-stained" with "ancient decks," when Melville began his apprenticeship on her a year later, whaling vessels had a recognized slightly chubby look, with the galley placed aft to leave the forward deck clear for cutting-in the carcass and trying-out the blubber, and with the whaleboats hung over the side ready to be lowered as soon as the call was heard. In his journal of a whaling cruise in the *Chelsea*, about the same time as Melville was at sea, the practical-minded William Davis sketched the essentials without the poetry:

> She was sharp in the bow, broad in her beam, and clean in her run; small in her hold, with broad and roomy decks…Our ship, bark-rigged, and registered 400 tons, could stow 300, equivalent to 2400 barrels of oil. We carried four boats on the cranes, and three spare boats on the spars above the quarter-deck. To each of the four boats was assigned a crew of six men, viz., a boat-header, a harpooner, and four oarsmen. Besides the twenty-four men assigned to the boats, we had a carpenter, a cooper, a cook, a

*A photograph taken in 1862, and later retouched by Henry S. Wyer,*
*of ships docked at Straight Wharf with the Unitarian church tower in the background.*

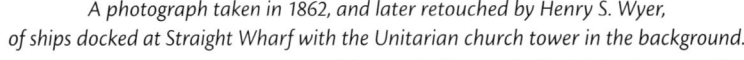

steward, a cabin-boy, and three spare men, or thirty-two all told. The captain, cook, steward, and cabin-boy did not stand regular watches; they aided as ship-keepers when the boats were off. This gave the starboard and larboard watches each fourteen men, sufficient to handle sails in nearly every emergency.[2]

These were the vessels that made the fortunes on Nantucket when, for a brief moment in her history, the growing demand for oil could be readily supplied from the sea. Indeed, the course of the rise and fall of the whaling industry in the nineteenth century can be seen by reference to the table below, which shows the estimated number of whaling vessels that left the port in different years from 1815 to 1870 and the estimated number of barrels of oil imported.

Table 2.

**Whaleships leaving Nantucket and oil imported: 1815–1870**

| Year | Whaling ships sailed | Sperm oil (imported bbls.) | Whale oil (imported bbls.) |
|---|---|---|---|
| 1815 | 43 | 1,025 | 20 |
| 1820 | 33 | 20,749 | 11,726 |
| 1825 | 26 | 31,780 | 7,194 |
| 1830 | 21 | 36,013 | 7,758 |
| 1835 | 19 | 38,824 | 4,497 |
| 1840 | 28 | 43,330 | 2,275 |
| 1845 | 31 | 45,864 | 6,280 |
| 1850 | 15 | 17,989 | 1,328 |
| 1855 | 16 | 9,852 | 5,067 |
| 1860 | 6 | 5,316 | 2,335 |
| 1865 | 2 | 6,242 | 1,366 |
| 1870 | 0 | 2,500 | 70 |

In 1800, the prosperity of the country, then composed of sixteen states, depended heavily on the maritime trade with foreign partners which, in turn, relied upon the fisheries. Since Matthew Crosby was, to a large extent, an investor in whaling vessels, it is worth keeping in mind how the industry was organized in the nineteenth century in order to understand the issues he would have faced in making a living.

In the early days, most of the vessels in use were sloops or schooners of moderate size with a capacity of 75–120 tons. But once the Nantucket men sailed into the Pacific Ocean at the end of the eighteenth century to make a business of hunting sperm whales, voyages were prolonged to several years and much larger ships, barks, and brigs of 250–350 tons were required.[4] Needless to say, even in a period of relatively stable prices, they became increasingly expensive to build, to outfit, and to operate. In 1791, at the very beginning of the expansion, the cost of the ship *Beaver*, ready for a voyage to the Pacific, was about $10,000. By 1830, it might have risen to as much as $20,000 or $25,000 to buy a ship and another $15,000 or $18,000 to outfit her. Ten years later, it would have been no surprise if the total cost of a 350-ton ship were $50,000 or $60,000.[5] Whaleships were made to withstand rough use and, consequently, the largest outlays were for the best yellow pine and white oak timber, quality canvas for sails, prime cordage for rigging, copper for sheathing, and the skilled labor needed to put the materials together.

Once the work was finished and the vessel ready for sea, she had to be outfitted with an impressive quantity and variety of goods. Spare boards, extra sheathing, canvas and cordage, lengths of chain, and supplies of tar and nails had to be put aboard, as well as several whaleboats, each with a requisite set of oars, lines, and whaling hardware. For the crew, there were casks of beef, pork, codfish, flour, corn, beans, peas, rice, potatoes, salt, dried apples, sugar, molasses, butter, raisins, coffee, tea, rum, vinegar, tobacco, pipes, rolls of cloth, hats, gloves, shoes, blankets, candles, as well as firearms and, perhaps, a medicine chest, all of which had to be purchased, delivered, and loaded.[6] A whaleship, therefore, viewed as a source of income for the owners and the crew after a successful voyage, nevertheless required substantial expenses to be met even before she set sail. At the same time, her preparation furnished jobs, wages, and other payments for a small army of builders, riggers, manufacturers, suppliers, recruiters, shipping agents, owners of boarding houses, shopkeepers of various kinds, insurance companies, and banks. From an estimate of some of the more expensive provisions needed for a fully-equipped ship in the successful years of the 1840s, it is clear that a good many people could make a good deal of money:

| | |
|---|---:|
| enough wooden casks to hold 2,800 barrels of oil | $ 3,500 |
| 240 barrels of beef and pork | $ 2,040 |
| 220 barrels of flour | $ 1,15 |
| 1,600 gallons of molasses | $ 432 |
| 900 pounds of butter | $ 117 |
| ready-made clothing | $ 2,500 |

Considering the cost of all the equipment, foodstuffs, and the labor in port consumed annually by the more than 600 American whaling vessels at sea in January 1844, the value of which has been estimated at about $3,845,498 (or about $116,500,000 in current dollars), the business opportunities are apparent.

When the bills were added up, it was obvious that the cost of a vessel was beyond the means of most single investors. Few men went out and bought a whaleship. Instead, they

*The bark* Charles W. Morgan *under full sail, circa 1910. This sturdy and dependable whaler was built in 1841 and named for a successful New Bedford merchant who married the granddaughter of William Rotch Sr. of Nantucket. The last surviving American whaleship, she is now berthed at the Mystic Seaport Museum in Connecticut.*

*"Opening bid." The scene in a trading office on the waterfront by the English artist, Walter Dendy Sadler (1854-1923). Published by Frost & Reed, London, 1894.*

bought shares, so that by pooling their resources, they could together finance a ship that none of them could have afforded individually.

This kind of fractional ownership was a modern version of a very old commercial arrangement. It shows up, for example, in medieval Italy as the so-called *commenda*, whereby one partner furnished the capital and stayed at home, while the other traveled abroad to invest it. On the return of the latter, the earnings, if any, were divided according to whatever agreement had been made.

In the case of the whaling fisheries, the owners furnished the ships and the outfits, and the captains and the crews supplied the labor while at sea. This way of doing business had the advantage of attracting new money by offering a variety of investment opportunities and by spreading out the very real risks involved among several different vessels. It also kept the larger share of the profits in the hands of a small group of men, usually fewer than a dozen for each voyage, for whom ownership of the ship and/or outfit might be divided into parts of one-half, one-quarter, one-eighth, one-sixteenth, or even smaller amounts.

In practical terms, if the outlay for vessel and outfit was $40,000, the part-owner-agent with, say, a one-fifth share, had an investment of $8,000; he with one-eighth share, $5,000; and the one with one sixty-fourth share, $625. If the ship were the *Charles Carroll*, which sailed from Nantucket on the August 30, 1836, and returned on February 14, 1840, with

2,678 barrels (or about 85,000 gallons) of sperm oil, when the average price was a high $1.02 per gallon, the gross value of the cargo amounted to $86,700. This figure would be modified depending on the quality of the oil, and from it were deducted various costs, such as depreciation, insurance premiums, wharfage and dockage charges, pilot fees, and general maintenance and repair, which might amount to $2,000 or more. Even then, most of the oil had to be graded before it was sold, a process which added to the overhead and increased the price.

It seems to have been often the case that the owners took as much as 50%–75% of the proceeds, leaving 25%–50% to be divided among the captain, the mates, and the rest of the crew in shares called "lays." These might range from $\frac{1}{12}$ to $\frac{1}{15}$ for the captain, $\frac{1}{28}$ to $\frac{1}{60}$ for the mates, $\frac{1}{80}$ to $\frac{1}{120}$ for the boatsteerers, and $\frac{1}{120}$ to $\frac{1}{180}$ for the other hands, according to their duties and experience. That is to say, in theory, each seaman, depending on his fractional worth, received one barrel of oil (in fact, the dollar equivalent) out of every 15, or out of every 28, or out of every 80, or out of every 180, In the example above, if the allocation to the owners on the return of the ship was, say, 70% of the value of oil, they would have made something like $60,690, which would be divided among them according to their shares and diminished by the various amounts mentioned. Similarly, the allocations to captain and crew at 30% would have amounted to $26,010, divided according to their lays, but subject to charges for advances, clothing, fines, and other miscellaneous costs.

But all these figures are estimates and they varied with each voyage. When all was said and done, a principal owner might only have come close to breaking even on a single vessel, or he might have made a profit of several thousand dollars, whereas a minor investor might have made no profit at all, or perhaps just a few hundred dollars. The crew, on the other hand, put up relatively little money in advance, but had free board and lodging, such as it was, for the length of the voyage. Their earnings in round figures, minus deductions, might have been $2,100–$1,700 for the captain, $900–$400 for the mates, and $200–$150, or less, for the seaman who had never been on a whaleship before. Unless some of the oil had been shipped home previously aboard another vessel, there were no earnings for either owner or crew until the ship had put into port and the cargo gauged, valued, and sold at the current market price.

For an investor like Matthew Crosby, the risk centered on the ship. If no whales were found, or too few, or if the vessel were wrecked, he took a loss. But he paid nothing to the crew. On the other hand, he had the luxury of sending out half-a-dozen ships at the same time to ensure that at least some of them would return after a successful voyage.

The crew, who were paid no daily wages, risked not only their time and labor, but also their health and, perhaps, their lives. They had no choice but to take whatever came to them when the final, and seemingly mysterious, calculations were made at the end of the voyage after two or three years of hard work.

"Whaling on Japan Grounds," August 1843, from a watercolor by George A. Gould aboard the Columbia *from Nantucket. As boats from different ships attack the school, their waifed whales are marked with flags. The black whaleboat (left of center) belonged to the ship* Charles and Henry *of Nantucket, which was owned by the sons of Zenas Coffin.*

No matter how much success in whaling could be laid to good planning and management, and to experienced captains and disciplined seamen, it was always recognized by those who played it as a game of chance. The point was seized upon by Walter Tower in his book on the history of the American whale fishery:

> One of the most potent causes working toward the downfall of whaling is found in the nature of the industry itself: the uncertainty of the business. It would be hard to find any other business, employing so much capital, where the uncertainty of profitable returns is so great as has always been the case with the whale fishery. One year may bring successful voyages and good profits, only to be offset the next year by heavy losses of life, money, and property.[8]

Samuel Millet, who shipped aboard the bark *Willis* out of Mattapoisett in 1849 for a short voyage of a year in the eastern Atlantic, shared the same sentiment, based on first-hand experience:

> July 6. Spoke the bark **Persia** and brig **Rodman** both of New Bedford. The **Persia**, six months out, with 145 barrels of sperm, and **Rodman**, fourteen months out with 165 barrels sperm and bound home. The crew were rather discouraged, for some of them would go home in debt without anything to pay for their outfits with, and this is one great evil in going a-whaling, for it is too much like lottery business.[9]

In addition to the calamities which might overtake the vessel and the crew in the course of the voyage, Millet alludes to the constant difficulty for those on land in knowing where the vessel was at any given time. News to reassure the owners about the number of whales taken and the amount of oil extracted, and to comfort the families of the men aboard about their safety, came only haphazardly and at irregular intervals. The fate of an investment of $40,000 or $50,000 and the well-being of twenty or thirty men were often unknown for months at a time. Leaving aside the critical value of human life, it was as if the present-day stock-holder, who spent several thousands of dollars on a venture in September, had to wait until Christmas, or even longer, before he knew if he had lost or gained and how much the sum might be.

Still, there were far more successful voyages than poor ones in the best years to keep men betting on a good return. A reasonably fair idea of what might have been expected of Nantucket ships may be had by a comparison of the known average prices for sperm oil in the years from 1813 to 1870 with the quantity imported, the time at sea, and the estimated gross value. A summary is given in the following table with the name of the vessel, the date of sailing and returning, the number of months at sea (in brackets), the number of barrels of oil, the approximate equivalent number of gallons, the average market price in the year the vessel returned, and an estimate of the gross value of the sperm oil.[10]

Table 3.

Comparative returns of selected Nantucket whaleships, 1822–1851

| Ship | Sailed-returned (months at sea) | Barrels | Gallons | Price/Gallon | Value |
|---|---|---|---|---|---|
| Lydia | 1822–1825 (35) | 2,388 | 71,640 | $.72 | $53,730 |
| Maro | 1825–1828 (31) | 2,437 | 73,110 | .63 | 46,059 |
| Sarah | 1827–1830 (35) | 3,497 | 104,910 | .66 | 73,437 |
| Loper | 1829–1830 (14) | 2,280 | 68,400 | .66 | 45,144 |
| Montano | 1833–1836 (35) | 3,097 | 92,910 | .88 | 78,974 |
| Fabius | 1833–1837 (47) | 863 | 25,890 | .83 | 22,265 |
| Catharine | 1835–1838 (39) | 3,016 | 90,480 | .86 | 79,622 |
| Peru | 1835–1839 (42) | 676 | 20,280 | 1.05 | 21,294 |
| Three Brothers | 1837–1841 (46) | 2,719 | 81,570 | .94 | 76,676 |
| Joseph Starbuck | 1838–1842 (40) | 3,321 | 99,630 | .73 | 72,730 |
| Maria | 1840–1842 (21) | 2,413 | 72,390 | .73 | 52,845 |
| Zenas Coffin | 1840–1843 (33) | 3,049 | 91,470 | .63 | 57,626 |
| Charles and Henry | 1840–1845 (51) | 689 | 20,670 | .88 | 18,190 |
| Scotland | 1845–1851 (52) | 2,660 | 79,800 | 1.27 | 99,750 |

To take the case of the ship *Loper*, for example, she had a remarkable voyage of only fourteen months, but returned with a cargo of 2,280 barrels of oil, whereas it took the *Scotland* almost four times as long to bring in 2,660 barrels. Thanks to an increase in the price of oil, the latter made a greater profit, but it took her longer to get it. Outstanding was the success of the *Sarah*, out for thirty-five months and then home with 3,497 barrels of sperm oil.

121

Further down the list were the more disappointing efforts of the *Fabius*, out for forty-seven months with only 863 barrels worth $22,265; or the *Peru*, out forty-two months with 676 barrels of sperm oil, but at a higher market price of $21,294; or the *Charles and Henry*, out fifty-one months with 689 barrels of sperm for a lower total price of $18,190.

Obviously, a good deal of success depended on the prevailing market price, which was a business risk beyond the control of the investor. What the buyer would pay per gallon for sperm oil in all American markets ranged from about $.63 a gallon in the decade 1821–1830, to $.86 in 1831–1840, $.93 in 1841–1850, $1.39 in 1851–1860, $1.85—$2.55 for a short period after the Civil War, and then back to an average of $1.62 in the years from 1861 to 1870. But Nantucket, as we know, was largely out of the picture by the late 1850s and, therefore, did not benefit greatly from the temporary spike in demand which was fed, in part, by an increase in returns from more intensive fishing in the Atlantic and Arctic.

Nevertheless, with so many ships constantly at sea, whaling was big business. If you came in with the tide, so to speak, as Matthew Crosby did, and managed carefully, there was a sizeable fortune to be made for yourself and your family. From the time of his days in the packet trade, Matthew had invested in a variety of sailing vessels. As his capital grew, he bought and sold more and more shares, so that over the course of his business life, until he was well into his eighties, he acquired interests in some twenty-three ships, barks, and brigs, as well as twenty-four schooners, twelve sloops, and six steamboats.

How he managed these risky ventures, which could end in handsome profit or in discouraging loss, is a useful measure of the way in which he built his financial success. The ship *Washington*, 308 tons, provides a good example because we can trace her fortunes over a thirty-year life at sea. Built on the North River in Hanover, Massachusetts, in 1819 by the well-known firm of John and Elijah Barstow, she was first owned by Zenas Coffin, Matthew's father-in-law and benefactor, and Reuben Swain, her captain. As noted previously, the ship had come to Matthew in 1828 as part of the Coffin bequest to be used for the support of Zenas's grandchildren. Matthew's business-like obligation was signed and dated on November 6:

> This day by an agreement of the heirs of the estate of Zenas Coffin I have taken, as guardian to my children, the hull and apparel of ship Washington at $8,000, said ship is now at their risk to take her when she arrives back from this present voyage with all her materials, excepting the cargo, of which they draw one-fifth of two-thirds.[11]

The *Washington* had already made three round-trips to the Pacific and returned with a little over 6,000 barrels of sperm oil. Calculated at the average price for the oil in each of those years, the gross value of the cargo amounted to about $120,000. This was a promising record, and the ship, in which Matthew seems to have had a variable interest of one-half to two-thirds over the long term, turned out to be a sound investment. The full sailing schedule can be seen below. Note that time at sea was money in whales so that the turn-around period in port was always made as short as possible.

All told, the *Washington* completed eight voyages under six different captains in twenty-eight years and brought back almost 14,000 barrels of oil before she finally gave out on the ninth voyage and was left to die in Hawaii with a small residual cargo. Adding in the amount already gained by 1828, the value of the total return must have been something over $300,000.

Table 4.

**Sailing schedule of the whaleship *Washington*, 1819–1849**

| Sailed | Returned | Barrels of Sperm Oil |
|---|---|---|
| December 26, 1819 | February 14, 1822 | 1,920 |
| June 23, 1822 | February 26, 1825 | 2,054 |
| July 17, 1825 | April 5, 1828 | 2,027 |
| July 24, 1828 | May 24, 1832 | 1,774 |
| November 5, 1832 | December 30, 1835 | 1,538 |
| July 14, 1836 | December 1839 | 1,780 |
| May 14, 1840 | September 24, 1843 | 1,095 |
| December 2, 1843 | June 12, 1847 | 1,613 |
| October 30, 1847 | Condemned at Oahu, 1849 | |

These figures naturally raise the question of how many whales had to be killed to produce that much oil and earn that much money. Estimates have been made based on the assumption that one sperm whale of average size might have produced about twenty-five or thirty barrels of oil. Therefore, 14,000 barrels would have required 400–600 whales. Keeping in mind that some whales were harpooned, but never caught, and afterward died of their injuries; that some part of the animal, and the oil, was often lost to sharks and to rough cutting-in practices; that a portion of the oil was wasted in filling the casks and by leakage on the way home; and that we are dealing with imprecise numbers all around; a realistic cost in whales might well be even higher. Overall, it has been calculated that in the 1830s perhaps some 5,000 sperm whales were killed each year.[12]

Whether or not the nineteenth-century industry caused a serious depletion in the world whale population, a question modern conservationists like to ask, is one that has not been satisfactorily answered. Too many variables and unknown quantities are involved to allow a straightforward answer. From what statistics are available, it would appear that it did not, or at least not on the scale that some critics would allege. If certain kinds of whales are now thought to be in danger, the cause is the massive onslaught of modern mechanized and heavily-subsidized industrial fishing practiced since 1945, rather than the relatively less destructive invasion of the whaling grounds by the old sailing ships.

Killing whales, of course, inevitably brought up moral issues that were often argued by those least involved with the work. Henry T. Cheever, for one, a Protestant minister who shipped aboard a whaler to the south Pacific about mid-century, was much concerned with "the lawfulness and expediency of the whale fishery." He reported what he had once been told by an old seaman:

> Whales has feelings as well as any body. They don't like to be stuck in the gizzards, and hauled alongside, and cut in, and tried out in them'ere boilers no more than I do.

This, he acknowledged, was true, but wrote it off as a foolish saying. Far more serious, to his way of thinking, was the fact that men were pursuing whales:

> in flagrant violation of the Sabbath…[with] the consequent disastrous effect upon the moral and religious characters of those engaged in it…The all inclusive cause which perpetuates and lies at the bottom of Sabbath-whaling is…the lust of lucre. Whaling captains and owners are seldom willing, for the honour of God, or regard to his law, to forego the profits which they think accrue from Sabbath-whaling.[13]

But this style of censure was commonplace among zealots of the American evangelical movements at the time, and it was, in turn, ignored by the men who were risking ships and lives to put as many casks of oil aboard in as short a time as possible. Cheever undoubtedly had some satisfaction in making his views known to the public, but certainly aware of the wealth generated by the whaling industry, he must have had little hope that they would be fulfilled.

A summary of the figures, as they are laid out above to underline the economic importance of the industry, makes it clear why men were drawn to put their money into whaleships. But the numbers fail to convey the level of constant anxiety the owners must have felt with so many ships scattered across the globe. Nor can they paint an adequate picture of the unceasing labor, fraught with uncertainty and danger, that was demanded of the crew.

We have already been witness to the hardships and boredom recounted by Matthew's father, Sylvanus, on the *Asia*. Judging from many of the other terse accounts in log books and sailors' memoirs, it would seem that several years at sea, while now and again enlivened by exotic landscapes, unusual visitors, and time off in ports of call, often came down to killing whales, killing time, and thoughts of killing each other.

In the case of the *Washington*, we can cite a few examples to illustrate the difficulties encountered. When not quite two years into her first voyage, in October of 1821, she was surprised near the Juan Fernández Islands off the coast of Chile, and boarded by escaped

*"Taking a Whale," a woodcut by Robert Weir Jr. (1836-1905) based on a drawing from his journal kept aboard the Mattapoisett bark* Clara Bell *in 1866.*

convicts from a nearby penal colony. A desperate counterattack led by the Nantucket captain, Reuben Swain, with harpoons, spades, and knives, and any other make-shift weapon at hand, succeeded in killing some of the intruders, capturing the rest, and saving the ship.[14] On another occasion, a chance meeting of the *Washington* and the New London whaleship *Chelsea*, in Lee Bay off Isabela Island in the Galapagos, probably in August 1837, afforded an opportunity for an exchange of recent news. In one of the classic records of a whaling voyage, William M. Davis, who had shipped aboard the *Chelsea*, reported the following incident:

> When cruising a while in Lee Bay, we spoke the Washington, of Nantucket, thirteen months out with four hundred barrels of oil. She had two men killed by whales, and her third mate was very severely injured, having been caught across the thighs in a whale's mouth and nearly drowned by the whale's repeated dipping beneath the surface…We also spoke the Ocean, of Nantucket, eleven months out with six hundred barrels of oil. Her mate had been killed by a whale; just how, we did not learn.[15]

We know that the *Washington* sailed from Nantucket with Stephen Bailey, master, for what was to be the last time on October 30, 1847. In the spring, she was at Callao, where the captain evidently ran into difficulties with the port authorities because there is the report of a claim made by Matthew Crosby, who we assume was the father since he was referred to as the owner, and ultimately lodged with the Peruvian Claims Commission for the seizure of part of the cargo in 1848. The brief notice in the Congressional Record reads that:

The articles were subsequently returned, but it did not appear whether this was done in accordance with a judicial or an executive order. A week after this seizure, the Washington obtained permission to leave the port, and they [the articles] were returned by another vessel. The umpire found that the seizure was made in accordance with the laws of Peru, on account of Crosby's failure to comply with the customs regulations, and that the claimant consequently was not entitled to an indemnity.[16]

*A watercolor of the whaleship* Washington, *circa 1825, by William W. Morris (1780–1847).*

A partial explanation of the matter can be found in two letters written in September and October of 1856 by William L. Marcy, then Secretary of State, to Matthew Crosby in Nantucket. As he explained it, a part of the cargo was sequestered by the customs officials in 1848 for a technical violation of the revenue laws. Matthew complained that the act was illegal and the goods damaged and filed a claim for $2,500 in the following year. Captain Bailey, concerned that time wasted in port meant a loss in profits and eager to put to sea, empowered Mr. Johnson, the United States Vice-Consul in Lima, to act for him. An appeal was carried to the Tribunal of the Consulado, where the original decision was confirmed.

Johnson then appealed to the Superior Court, which in due course ordered the restitution of the goods in what was termed "a compromise," meaning that the penalty was rescinded, but that the fees and costs, amounting to $700, were to be paid. The goods were then loaded on to the ship *Persia* to be delivered to Matthew Crosby, the lawful owner. Marcy suggested that the reason for the seizure of the cargo was that the agent contracted by Bailey, a Mr. Coombs, "bore the reputation of having been engaged in smuggling transactions." Besides, he added, "the quantity and description of the goods may be considered to have afforded some ground of suspicion that the articles were intended to be smuggled." There is no mention in these documents of what the goods were, but a letter of James Buchanan, Secretary of State in 1845–1849, written to Joseph Grinnell and dated June 26, 1848, referred to "a quantity of clothing" which had recently been seized by the customs officers from the *Washington* in Callao. This may have been the cargo that was the cause of the problem. We can also cite the case in 1854, referred to previously, when Matthew Crosby Jr., then in business in Callao, acted as the agent for a shipment of Colt revolvers which were seized by customs officers, but later returned. There is no obvious connection between the two incidents, which occurred several years apart, except that it was not unusual for whaleships, which routinely put into foreign ports, to act as carriers of unauthorized and undeclared goods, whether known to the captain or not. It is clear from Marcy's letters that the younger Matthew had entered a second claim for the cargo of the *Washington* in the extraordinary amount of $57,820, which cannot be explained and is impossible to reconcile with the penalties imposed. Marcy's comment was that:

> the utmost demand, as the Department views the question, which can be made upon Peru is one arising out of the equity of a claim for a reimbursement of the judicial expenses incurred… It is apprehended, however, that the exaggerated and exorbitant sum made up by your agent, instead of the original amount claimed [i.e. $2,500], will operate very much to your prejudice in procuring an adjustment of the claim.[17]

A list of claims against Peru submitted to the Commission in Lima in November 1863 includes another one made by Matthew Crosby for $20,000.[18] It's possible that Matthew Jr. had reduced the $57,820 to $20,000 in the hope of obtaining a favorable decision, but to no avail.

Once he left Callao, Bailey began to sail back and forth in the "off-shore grounds" of the southern Pacific, just south of the equator, trying to find enough whales for oil to fill the casks. The ship was reported at Nuku Hiva in the Marquesas Islands in October, at Pitcairn Island in November, and in the beginning of 1849 she had returned nearer the coast, but with only eighty barrels of sperm oil. By the beginning of summer, she was at Paita, a port town on the north-west coast of Peru, having managed to stow away 130 barrels.[19] But more worrisome than the lack of whales was the discovery that the old vessel was leaking badly. So much so that we next hear of her arrival in Oahu in Hawaii on August 13, 1849, where, according to letters received from Captain Bailey, she was afterward condemned, sold at auction, bought by the Hawaiian government for $1,375, and broken up for firewood.[20] Bailey is said to have gone home as master of the ship *Mary*, and the mates as officers on other vessels, while the rest of the crew apparently set off for California and the gold mines!

The fate of the oil remains uncertain. The notice printed in the Whalemen's *Shipping List* confirms that it was saved and later transferred to the *Romulus*, a ship out of Sag Harbor, to be brought back. The *Romulus*, however, had her own troubles. She was reported condemned in Honolulu in the spring of 1849 and abandoned. Nevertheless, the necessary repairs must have been made, since she sailed again from Honolulu late in 1849 under a different captain, but like the *Washington,* sprang a leak and put back into port, where she was also condemned and sold at auction for $2,900.[21] Matthew seems likely to have lost not only his ship but perhaps also the cargo.

Of further interest with regard to the *Washington* is a copy of the certificate of registration issued on October 30, 1847, on the eve of her final departure, which makes clear that ownership was a family affair. Matthew, as the major investor, is listed with his son, William H. Crosby; his son-in-law, Benjamin F. Coffin, husband of his daughter Mary;

and another son-in-law, George C. Coffin, husband of his daughter, Ann. As we know, Benjamin Coffin, who held a one-eighth share including outfit and cargo, sold it back to Matthew for $3,000 in September 1849, when he decided to leave the island to make a living in California.[22] If Benjamin held an eighth worth $3,000, we might then assume that the whole ship in good sailing condition must have been valued at about $24,000 at the time. On the face of it, this seems a reasonable amount, but we do not know if the sale was made at a premium by Matthew to favor a member of his family. In his journal for 1845, Asa Bunker, the credit-rating agent, thought Matthew had a one-half share worth $15,000 which is not too far out. But without more reliable figures, it is impossible to be sure. Nor can we determine the monetary extent of the loss. The sale price might have been discounted, we are unsure about the disposal of the cargo, the insurance coverage is uncertain, and the ship was sold as a hulk for a pittance. In his ledger under "losses," Matthew noted the value of the ship at $9,700 and his interest as $2,830, which may be what he finally salvaged from the wreck. But it was not unusual for him to enter different figures for the same account as his memory served him, nor always to differentiate between total cost and his own share. But however these amounts are to be interpreted, even setting the highest loss against the estimated returns for the twenty years or so he owned the vessel, he undoubtedly came out ahead.[23]

*Whalemen's Shipping List, August 21, 1849.*

Every ship had a history, but for the purposes of illustrating particular aspects of the whaling industry that directly affected Matthew's investments, some are more interesting than others. Without trying to reconstruct so many voyages for so long a time, it is worth considering a few pertinent examples.

Like the *Washington*, the *American* was an old vessel. Built in 1822 as a merchantman, but later converted for whaling, she crossed and re-crossed the Pacific Ocean for more than forty years. Over that long period, the total return amounted to over 12,000 barrels of sperm and whale oil brought into port. It was the kind of success that encouraged investors to buy fractions of the vessel. Matthew initially had a one-fifth share, and his sons, Matthew Jr., William, and Sylvanus, bought smaller amounts. In the golden years of the 1840s, Asa Bunker estimated that the one-tenth share held by William Crosby was worth about $3,000, so that Matthew, himself, must have had about $6,000 tied up and floating about somewhere west of Peru.

He was lucky with the *American*. In the summary letter he wrote to his children just before his death, he put the total profit the ship brought him at over $9,000. She ran the course without a major mishap until 1853, when, in a deal that presaged the fundamental shift in commercial activity on Nantucket, she was sold to a firm in Edgartown on Martha's Vineyard. It has already been shown that easy access to the harbor there, at a time when the home port was blocked by the sandbar, meant that more and more whaling masters chose to unload cargo and to refit their vessels on that neighboring island. By the time of her last voyage in 1857–1861, it was late in the day for American whaling.

After such long and worthy service, it is sad to relate that, along with twenty-five or thirty other venerable whaleships, the *American* was purchased by the Union government in November 1861, loaded with stones and cement, and sailed down to Charleston, South Carolina, where the hulks were sunk in an attempt to block the passage of Confederate vessels in and out of the harbor. The "Stone Fleet," as the convoy was called, proved to be another wasteful and expensive bureaucratic undertaking which failed to accomplish any practical purpose. It did, however, provide the incentive for patriotic self-congratulations in the northern press, and it did inspire a dissenting poetic lament by the ex-whaleman, Herman Melville.[24] Overall, the Civil War resulted in the destruction of more than 200 whaleships. This was a blow which could not be absorbed, and it encouraged a partial migration of the industry to the west coast, with the development of San Francisco as the chief port.

*Wreckers pick apart the ships of the ill-fated Stone Fleet in Charleston Harbor. From an illustration in* Harper's Weekly, *December 1863.*

By way of contrast, the ship *Mariner*, built in 1832 and worth $32,000, although ridden with worms after fourteen years of whaling, was spared such an ignominious end. For some time she had also proved to be a good investment for Matthew (a three-sixteenths share) and his son, William (a one-sixteenth share), but later suffered a string of misfortunes. After an ill-omened departure from Nantucket in May 1849, she returned in late July with the captain sick and the first-mate injured in a fall from the masthead. She departed once again in August with a different captain, but over the next four years the crew managed to bring in only about 800 barrels of sperm oil. This was too little cargo for such a long time. In the spring of 1853, she put into Paita, where

*A marble memorial tablet inside the Seaman's Bethel in New Bedford. William Swain had previously been in command of several British whalers, but later in life he shipped aboard the* Christopher Mitchell *as a mate. "The chaplain had not yet arrived; and there these silent islands of men and women sat steadfastly eyeing several marble tablets, with black borders, masoned into the wall on either side of the pulpit." – Herman Melville,* Moby-Dick

the vessel was condemned. But someone evidently saw a future for her, for she was refitted and rechristened to sail again as the *Sophia Somontes* under a new owner. This was likely the firm of José Somontes & Son, commission merchants, in Tumbes, Peru, northwest of Lima on the coast. But Matthew gained nothing from her rebirth. After the insurance was paid, he incurred a net loss of about $1,000.[25]

Two other examples of ships closely held by family interests were the *Nantucket*, one of the few whaleships built on the island and launched in 1837, and the *Navigator*, built four years later. Matthew Crosby Jr. joined his father with shares in the former vessel, which made five voyages in twenty-two years and returned over 9,000 barrels of oil. She ended her days close to where she had begun them, wrecked on Nashawena Island off Martha's Vineyard in 1859.[26]

As for the *Navigator*, which was worth about $40,000 in 1856, Matthew Jr. and William, as well as Henry Swift, the son-in-law of Zenas Coffin, and the captain, George Palmer, had shuffled various sixteenths, eighths, and quarters of value among themselves over the years the vessel was in service. By the mid-1850s, she was removed from Nantucket to Edgartown, and Matthew appears to have sold his interest in her about 1863.

But even in her after-life, she still commanded attention, for a half-hull model taken from the Jared Coffin House was sold at Northeast Auctions in Portsmouth, New Hampshire, in August 2014 for $780. An engraved plaque bore the inscription: "Navigator. Built for Matthew Crosby in Medford, Mass. by J. O. Curtis in 1841. 333 tons." She was also noted as one of the few whaleships whose captain took his wife with him. Eliza Palmer, unfortunately, fell ill on the third voyage out, died, and was buried on Pitcairn Island in September 1850. Ever after, when he found himself on a sailing course nearby, her husband made a point of stopping there to visit her grave.[27]

Matthew and a group of close relations that included his son William also owned the *Lima*, built in 1804. Sporting the Crosby house flag, the whaleship spent thirty-eight years at sea, ten more than the whaleship *Washington*, yet returned with about the same number of barrels of sperm oil before being condemned at Rio de Janeiro in 1842. An inefficient producer, the *Lima* represented a net loss to Matthew of about $1,700.

The ship has more of a claim on our interest, however, than just its disappointing accounts. When Herman Melville was serving as a deck-hand aboard the *Acushnet* out of Fairhaven, he recorded a meeting with the whaleship *Charles Carroll* from Nantucket, probably late in 1841. He mentioned speaking with the captain, a man he thought was Owen Chase, one of the survivors of the *Essex*, and the supposed author of the famous narrative that described how the ship was stove by a whale in 1820.

But it was not Owen Chase, because the captain at that time was Thomas S. Andrews, and Owen Chase had long since returned to Nantucket to deal with a painful problem all too familiar in a community where husbands were absent at sea for months and years at a time. His wife, Eunice, had given birth to a son early in 1838, sixteen months or so after he had left on the *Charles Carroll*. This unhappy fact led to charges of adultery, and a trial was

*Whaleship* Navigator *of Nantucket, 1845. Watercolor by Nantucket whaleman George S. Clark (1825–?).*

held before the visiting chief justice of the Massachusetts Supreme Court, Lemuel Shaw, whose daughter Melville would later marry. In the climate of increasingly liberal views on domestic relations, and Shaw's own equitable outlook, a divorce was granted.

Yet shortly before the encounter with the *Charles Carroll*, the *Acushnet* spoke the *Lima* and hove-to long enough to exchange news and visits of the crews. It was then that Melville appears to have met not Owen Chase, the author of the famous narrative, but his young son, who gave him a copy of the *Essex* tragedy. Thus, the *Lima* was the unlikely agency for the "surprising effect" of the story, admitted by Melville in his confused notes about the narrative, which served as the inspiration for *Moby-Dick*.[28]

When the *Lima* was broken up, her tiller was somehow preserved and came into the possession of Matthew's son, Charles Carroll Crosby, the local merchant and the treasurer of the Nantucket Historical Association, who used it to decorate a signboard over the door to his office on Whale Street.[29]

Whereas the government thought that it would benefit at the beginning of the Civil War by sinking the *American*, and other ships, in Charleston harbor, a group of businessmen on Nantucket were confident that once the war was over, they could improve the economy by purchasing the Union warship *Bohio* in order to outfit her as a whaler. This revival of interest in a failing industry was encouraged by an editorial in the *Inquirer and*

*A painting of the Nantucket whaleship* Spermo, *296 tons, attributed to John Fisher. She made only one voyage to the Pacific (1820-1823) before being sold and subsequently lost at sea. The crew is shown "cutting in" the whale by hoisting a massive piece of blubber to a point where it can be reached by those onboard.*

*Mirror* in May 1868, written with enthusiasm in the much-will-be-done-if-we-do-but-try style of Samuel Smiles:

> Take courage all, and favor this local enterprise. Thus will we reflect credit upon the brave deeds of our fathers, instead of presenting to the world that abortion of requital which is the offspring of timorous, feeble natures, ever wailing over the past, never up-and-doing for the future. Rather let us aid any local enterprise, which is honorable, by our hearts and hands.[30]

The *Bohio*, a brig built in 1856, had been used on blockade duty in the Gulf of Mexico during the war. Decommissioned in 1865, she was sold to a party of investors led by Joseph Macy, a prominent resident and insurance agent on Nantucket, who owned a good deal of real estate and was, appropriately, a member of the town finance committee.[31] His wife was the daughter of Barzillai Coffin, a successful ship's captain in the early part of the century, so he had sufficient credit in wealth and background to propose staking the future on a refurbished whaler. As the day of launching drew near in July, another editorial provided the needed flourishes:

> For many weeks past familiar sounds have engaged our ears. The ring of coopers' hammers, the rattling of blocks, and that strange noise of new rigging strained into place, have awakened in many a bosom the days of past thrift and livelihood on Nantucket, while all these present omens have given us fresh glimpses of a possible future of success in our island's early business—whaling. And we are now on the road to prosperity, if we will

*A selection of the signal and house flags for the Nantucket whaling vessels. Matthew Crosby's is at bottom right.*

have it so…We look upon the sailing of the Bohio as a good example. Let others be brought here on a like errand.[32]

On July 12, 1868, she left the dock, under the command of Captain Henry W. Davis. In response to the general optimism, Matthew had bought a one-sixteenth share, apparently in the outfit, in April 1868, and a little later a one-sixty-fourth, for a total outlay of about $650. It was a sufficiently generous subscription to show his support for the venture, but not so much as to cause a major upset should it fail. It was typical of his style of conservative investing. Moreover, he may have had misgivings about the idea of recapturing the golden days, especially with an old warship. Besides, he was seventy-seven years old, with other interests to consider, so it may have seemed altogether too late. Alas, he was right.

The *Bohio* failed to make good on her first voyage, and there is no record of later substantial returns in either oil or bone. The captain put into Paita in November 1871, and then into Callao in December, where, through the brokerage office of Matthew Crosby Jr., the ship was sold for $6,000. It was an unintended irony on the part of Captain Davis, who had taken the *Bohio* out in an effort to revitalize the commerce based on sailing vessels, that he left the ship, traveled to Panama, and embarked for New York in February 1872 as a passenger on the steamer *Rising Star*.[33]

Nor was the *Bohio* the only sign of a falling market. The bark *Islander*, built in Fairhaven for Matthew in 1856, sailed for the Pacific in August in a partnership with Zenas Adams and other friends, and returned in June 1861. After five years at sea, she had only 800 barrels

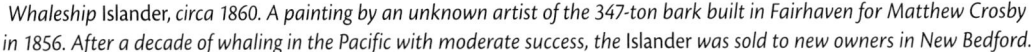

Whaleship Islander, *circa 1860. A painting by an unknown artist of the 347-ton bark built in Fairhaven for Matthew Crosby in 1856. After a decade of whaling in the Pacific with moderate success, the* Islander *was sold to new owners in New Bedford.*

of sperm oil. A shorter voyage from June 1862 to July 1865 proved to be more successful with 2,400 barrels of sperm oil, as well as whale oil and bone. Evidently, this was not enough to calm fears for the future, and soon thereafter, she was sold to a firm in New Bedford.[34]

In a case similar to the *Bohio*, the *R.L. Barstow*, a bark built in Mattapoisett in 1851, had also been purchased by the Joseph B. Macy consortium to recapture the profits in whaling. Once again the news was greeted with enthusiasm by the local newspaper.[35] She was worth a sixteenth to Matthew in 1862 and up to an eighth in 1867. Her cruising grounds were mainly confined to the Atlantic, but after six voyages, although the crew had filled about 4,000 barrels with oil, she was sold at a loss in Callao in February 1873. This time, Matthew's other son, Sylvanus, acted as the commission agent. It was fitting that an epitaph appeared as the headline in a New Zealand newspaper in June 1873, in a part of the world that had once been the source of great profits:

> Nantucket no longer owns a whale ship. Thirty years ago the port of Nantucket, Massachusetts, sent nearly 100 whalers on fishing voyages, and recently the last whale ship hailing from Nantucket, the *R.L. Barstow*, was sold at Callao. How a great business can decay is thus sadly exemplified.[36]

With the high cost of equipment and cargo and so much money invested, financial and legal problems were a constant worry to men involved in the whaling industry and a hidden threat to every voyage. For the owners, there were careful estimates of expenses to be made,

"South Sea Whale Fishery." An aquatint after an 1835 painting by Ambroise L. Garneray (1783–1857).

precise bookkeeping records to be kept, necessary calculations as to what range of debt was affordable, and what reserves were deemed sufficient. The entries in Matthew's account books show that he was forever reviewing his assets, adding up profits, subtracting losses, stating and restating current balances to bring them up to date, and, since a good deal of business was done on credit, noting how much he had borrowed as well as how much he had lent to others. The general impression is that there was as much activity in the counting house as there was on the high seas.

One illustration of the issues involved was the fate of the ship, *Clarkson*, owned by James Athearn. Newly built in 1826 and a successful whaler for sixteen years, she was caught in a hurricane in October 1842, which damaged the hull. Temporary repairs were made, but ultimately they proved insufficient. She put into Talcahuano, a port on the coast of Chile, in 1845. There the vessel was inspected and estimates were given for the necessary work. Total costs amounted to more than $14,000. As a result, she was condemned

*"Sperm Whaling With Its Varieties," a lithograph by J. H. Bufford, Boston, 1870, after a drawing by Benjamin Russell.*

and sold at auction for $4,842 minus commissions. The last of the oil, amounting to 1,200 barrels, was shipped home care of the Pacific Bank. There was $4,000 insurance coverage on the ship and its cargo, written by the Commercial Insurance Company of Nantucket and by other firms.

At that point, Matthew, a director of the Commercial, stepped in and agreed to rent his warehouse for several months to store the oil. Then, with Hadwen and Barney, partners in the importing firm, and Edward W. Gardner, he was engaged by the Pacific Bank to go down to New York to deal with claims. Questions had been raised over the amount of oil lost before the casks were unloaded, and the Mutual Insurance Company of New York refused to accept the decision to abandon the ship and, therefore to acknowledge its own liability. In the end, the cargo was divided up among the three merchants, with each one purchasing a portion.[37]

Other difficulties in buying and selling can be found in a letter written by Matthew addressed to Henry Phelon in March 1842. Phelon had been the captain of several well-known whaleships, including the *Neptune*, the *Ploughboy*, and the *Three Brothers*, but he was then living in Springfield, Massachusetts. He had evidently complained to Matthew about a note due him for the purchase of sperm oil. Matthew, representing his firm of Matthew Crosby & Son, replied that he understood that Phelon had agreed to wait on payment until the oil was sold and was surprised to have been asked for the money so soon. Nevertheless, he wrote, if Phelon could wait no longer, the note would be paid at once. In a nice parting touch, he also took the opportunity to correct an error in his own favor that Phelon had made in the calculation of the interest.[38]

The correspondence also reveals some of the risks in dealing in the oil market. Because Matthew not only bought oil but also refined it, he kept large stocks on the wharves and in a shed behind his house on Traders Lane. In February 1841, the value of the oil in storage was $37,245. In addition, he had about $12,000-worth at market, but as yet unsold. Such a large quantity stored for weeks or months in hundreds of wooden casks piled up in wooden sheds was a constant liability, not only because of the ups and downs of market prices, but especially because of the ever-present danger of fire, as many merchants had found out in 1836 and 1838 and would find out again in 1846.

The accumulation of debt, of course, was an everyday reality which reflected the structure of most businesses, particularly of the whaling industry. In the busy decade of gains and losses from 1850 to 1860, Matthew himself ran up large amounts: as much as $11,677 in 1850, $29,384 in 1854, and $16,800 in 1857. But these high figures were offset by the proceeds from the sale of oil and candles, so that in 1861 his debt had decreased to $2,558. Considering the balance of income and expenditure, Matthew was constantly concerned about the amount of money other merchants owed him, when they might pay it, and if they did not, what he could do about it. A few examples will illustrate the problem.

In January 1848, he listed $19,915.07 in "bad debts" from more than sixteen different firms. Among them was Henry A. Kelley, a prominent oil and candle manufacturer on Nantucket and an agent for oil sales in New York, who also acted for the Charles G. and Henry Coffin firm; Albert S. Ashmead, an oil and bone wholesaler in Philadelphia with connections to the brokers A.A. Lane in New York City and to Edward M. Robinson and Isaac Howland in New Bedford; and Thomas Potter, a supplier of provisions on the island.[39]

Kelley had sold oil to Lane for Matthew, but his IOU notes were not honored. The debt evidently lingered on with no resolution in sight. In 1867, Matthew declared it "worthless," and gave the case to Alfred Macy for collection, "at no expense to me, but Macy to have a third of what he can collect." The problem of who owed what to whom apparently was compounded by the passage of funds through different hands over several years. In the end, Matthew obtained a judgment against the Ashmead firm and settled for $500. The outcome of the controversy with Potter, who owed almost $3,000, is unclear, but it was apparently settled before 1867.

A list of commercial firms in Nantucket published as an inset to the Henry F. Walling map of 1858. "M. Crosby & Son" appears under "Oil and Candle Manufacturers."

In a similar case, Matthew held notes from Sampson & Tappan amounting to the large sum of $13,653 by 1861. In particular, he had accepted twenty-two shares in the Boston Belting Company as collateral for a debt of $4,250 incurred by Sampson & Tappan. The latter was an important Boston merchant firm with a fleet of clipper ships, but prone to controversy and legal action over money matters and labor practices. (Boston Belting was closely associated with Sampson & Tappan and Matthew knew about it because his son, Charles, was employed there for several years). The shares, as it turned out, did not carry the intended value, payment was not forthcoming, and Matthew filed a suit, allowing George B. Upton, who held his stock certificate, to see what could be salvaged. This time, however, nothing could be done. Matthew noted the disappointing outcome in his ledger, "We have lost the case. Fraud in S. & T."[40]

Still, in spite of numerous reverses and little formal training, he turned out to be a successful manager of his finances. In a period when, as we know, quite a few merchants went under financially, Matthew took pride in the fact that, as he said, he had never put off a payment large or small during his lifetime.

# 4. New Markets for New Wealth

*An engraving by S. E. Brown of the inner harbor and the town from the Creeks, published in John Warner Barber,* Historical Collections, *1841.*

**I**F WHALING WAS an undoubted source of profit for many years, investment in island and mainland real estate and business corporations grew to be another important alternative. Matthew, as we have seen, had bought and sold property and shares in various enterprises ever since his packet days. Eventually, as fewer ships were sent out and oil production was reduced, merchants were driven to look to other options for income.

Well before mid-century, the entries in Matthew's account books reveal a perceptible shift from a concern focused on how well his ships were doing to a broader interest in other opportunities at home and abroad. Among the interests he added to his portfolio were banks, insurance companies, and various startup ventures, as well as railroads, gas and mining concerns, and state and municipal bonds. Although he spent most of his life on Nantucket, his outlook was engagingly, but prudently, cosmopolitan. Ever since his days as packet captain, he had traveled regularly to New York and to towns along the shore of the Sound, and even to Boston, and many of his children and his friends had left the island for lengthy periods. By the time he was intent on exploring new ways to broaden his commercial contacts, he had already developed a familiar way of doing business beyond the small community at home. Since these activities became a fundamental part of his professional life, and of the lives of his merchant colleagues, it is important to look not only at the changes on the local scene, which were extensive, but also to consider how well he managed in the world beyond.

As if to underline the notion that in any consideration of the prosperity of the island the land and sea were joined as one, Main Street descends in two marked curves through the town and straight out over the water on the pilings of the wharf planned and erected in the early eighteenth century. Straight Wharf, as it was called appropriately, was the first of five major structures built adjacent to one another during the next hundred years to serve the growing needs of the town merchants. There followed in succession Old South Wharf and Commercial Wharf, and, for a time, "Crosby's Wharf," which was fitted between them and named for its owner, Charles C. Crosby, Matthew's son, who had business there. Then came Old North Wharf, and finally New North Wharf, which as a sign of the change necessary to accommodate more passengers coming to the island, soon became known as Steamboat Wharf.

As part of the legacy of Zenas Coffin to his sons and sons-in-law, Matthew had inherited one-fifth of a share in Old South Wharf. He had also come into possession of a portion of the brick warehouse located there, with an oil and candle factory and the surrounding land. On the basis of this investment, he continued to buy property on and near the waterfront for many years. Of particular interest to him were the connected parcels in the so-called South Beach lots along Washington Street facing the harbor where the wetlands had been filled in to extend the use and the value of the real estate. The Coffin map of 1834 shows the

*Commercial Wharf seen from Washington Street, circa 1880, with the cluster of factories, sheds, and warehouses.*

lots between Straight Wharf and Commercial Wharf along Whale Street and to the east of Candle Street heavily built up and crowded with small factories, storehouses, oil refineries, shops, and sheds. It was, therefore, natural that Matthew's sons, Matthew Jr., William, and Charles, and his son-in-law, William C. Gardner, as well as Charles G. and Henry Coffin, the sons of Zenas, all became important property owners in that part of the town with its easy access to the shipping.

This concentration of money and activity led to the organization of a group of investors in January 1831, dominated once again by related members of the leading families, to undertake the design and reconstruction of Commercial Wharf to the south. Joseph Starbuck, the builder of the "Three Bricks" on Main Street, and his brothers, Levi and Simeon, headed the list, which included old Abial Coffin, the wife of Zenas; and Gilbert, Zenas's brother; Gilbert's son, William B. Coffin; Gilbert's nephew, Jared Coffin; Zenas's sons Charles G. and Henry Coffin; Henry Swift, the husband of Zenas's daughter Mary; Philip H. Folger, a prominent public official, shipowner, and merchant who had married the daughter of Levi Starbuck; and Matthew Crosby, who, in accordance with the rotation of offices, became president of the association in 1838 and treasurer in 1847.[1]

*The waterfront between Commercial Wharf and South Wharf with a view across the harbor to Pimnys Point, circa 1890.*

143

That it was an expensive proposition is suggested by the number of high-level participants who were also property owners. Matthew operated a candle factory on the south side of the wharf with his son Matthew Jr., and nearby was the warehouse of Charles G. and Henry Coffin. Matthew's calculations put the initial cost of construction at about $38,000, equal to the price of a new whaling vessel of 350 tons. By 1835, the estimate had risen to more than $46,000, with fifteen shares outstanding. Matthew paid for his by installments over two years, for which he received a dividend of 7%. He remained a proprietor through another building phase in 1850, when a new stone foundation was laid at a cost of $60,000.

Debt continued to be a pressing problem in this undertaking, which led to frequent meetings to discuss the best way to reduce it. As one way of assuring a flow of income, a schedule of wharfage and dockage fees was drawn up and put in place by mid-century. Whaling and fishing vessels, for instance, were charged three mills per ton per day (a mill was one-tenth of a cent); bags of coffee, two cents each; coal, ten cents per ton; posts and rails per hundred, twenty-five cents; salt per bushel, one-half cent; ship timber per ton, twenty cents; bedsteads, three cents each; carboys of vitriol, two cents each (carboys were large glass containers protected by wickerwork), stoves, two cents each. Many other items were included in the schedule, and we are reminded once again of the extent to which Nantucketers were dependent on outside suppliers.[2]

In February 1857, Matthew moved, and it was voted that all the interest due and as much of the outstanding principal as possible be paid whenever sufficient funds from receipts on the wharf account that were not required for maintenance became available. Yet in March 1861, in a special meeting, his motion that the proprietors be assessed an amount sufficient to pay off all the debt on the wharf was deemed too drastic and was voted down. Instead, Henry Coffin asked the board to assess the proprietors the amount of the note due to the estate of Joseph Starbuck and, when it was collected, to pay that portion. This proposal evidently appeared to be more reasonable and was approved. The rich grew wealthy by good fortune and by careful management resulting in wise allocation of the funds they had.

But very soon disaster was to strike this growing, prosperous, and congested waterfront. Serious fires and the loss of lives and property were the plagues of towns and cities across the country. In a list of outbreaks on the island from 1760 to 1870, published in the *Inquirer and Mirror* in 1876, there appears to have been one almost every year.[3] A terrifying few hours occurred on the night of October 22, 1799, when, as Obed Macy tells it:

> [The fire] started in Isaac Folger's boat-builder's shop, then to Silvanus Coffin's dwelling house which very soon was all on fire, but fortunately there was about fifty pounds of powder in the garret, that when the fire took, blew the roof completely off, and with it about half the fire, so that it enabled the people to put out the remainder of the fire on the house, but about one third was destroyed.[4]

In August 1800, a group of about thirty concerned citizens, called The United Fire Society, was formed for the purpose of assisting one another in case of an emergency. This was a sensible and well-intentioned step forward, but still inadequate to deal with the threat. Heavy damage to Straight Wharf and Old South Wharf and to the warehouses and shops, estimated at $11,000, occurred in a spreading blaze in November 1812. That the townsmen were well aware of the danger is shown in a section of the bylaws printed for the public in 1823, and renewed thereafter, which "forbade anyone to carry open fire in the town, including smoking cigars or any kind of tobacco on penalty of a fine of $2.00 for each offence."[5] Officers known as firewards were appointed by the Town Meeting, and Matthew did his duty in 1830 and in 1832. There was an effort made to keep a supply of water in cisterns built at strategic places in the town, and the volunteer department had several horse-drawn engines housed in sheds at its disposal, but there was no way to rule out human carelessness. Moreover, strict building codes and approved construction practices—measures absolutely necessary to ensure adequate protection—were far in the future. If the losses on Nantucket did not constitute enough warning for all the citizens, there were examples nearby that touched some island interests. New York City suffered during a very cold December in 1835 when the water froze in the hose lines and seventeen

*A lithograph by Thomas Moore of Boston based on E. F. Starbuck's painting of the fire on Main Street, May 10, 1836. The view is westward from the bottom of the Square on Main Street.*

blocks worth several million dollars were destroyed in lower Manhattan. Ten years later another blaze started in July in a whale-oil factory in the same district, spreading from Wall Street to Pearl Street and laid waste another expensive section of the city. It is easy to say that Nantucketers might have been wiser, or more careful, or better prepared, or more fortunate than they were, but they were unable to avoid a similar run of disasters at almost exactly the same time.

The fire that broke out on May 10, 1836, in the back of the Washington House hotel on lower Main Street, burned down several stores and, spread by a strong southwest wind, threatened considerable damage. But the immediate response by men, women, and children was organized and effective. The pumps were in operation, sparks that lighted on neighboring buildings were quickly extinguished, and the damage was confined to a narrow strip of the docks. The excitement of the moment was captured in a well-known painting by E. F. Starbuck, later sold as a lithograph print.

Far worse for Matthew, and for many of his friends and relatives, was the conflagration two years later on the night of June 2, 1838. The blaze began in a ropewalk between Union and Washington Streets and quickly swept across the greater part of the lower town. Feeding on the half-dozen oil and candle factories which lay in its path, the fire consumed the buildings owned and leased by Matthew, as well as by Daniel Jones, Philip H. Folger, James Athearn, Valentine Hussey, and several others. Shops of boat-builders, blacksmiths, riggers, coopers, sail makers, storehouses sheds, and dwelling houses all went up in flames and smoke. "Everything," reported the *Nantucket Inquirer*, "between Union Street and the harbor…was burnt as bare as the shore beach." It was a major catastrophe, and the horror of it was reflected in the dramatic description given in the editorial:

> The nature of the materials on fire was such as to fill the firmament with thick clouds of the blackest smoke, from out of which, at a vast height, the angry flames were occasionally seen to burst, throwing a lurid light upon the shuddering multitude below, already partially illumined by the lava-like fires which flickered on the subjacent waters. Large quantities of oil floated through drains beneath the ropewalk into the low and marshy ground to the west, much of which was afterward dipped up into casks, while still greater quantities saturated the earth whereupon it had flowed, filling also a ditch which extended along the whole length of the ropewalk and presenting a living sheet of flame for hours after the whole area had been swept of its buildings.[6]

From the author of an unsigned letter to the newspaper, we learn that winter sperm oil was stored in a candle factory occupied by James Athearn, so that:

> As the tide was coming in, the burning oil communicated with Mr. Crosby's premises and from thence to others, until the lower part of the town was in imminent danger. The

women…were employed in carrying around hot and refreshing drinks to enable the men to sustain, so far as they were able, the fatigue and labor to which they were called.[7]

Estimated losses for the leading firms published in the *Inquirer* amounted to the enormous sum of over $150,000, broken down as follows:

Table 5.
**Estimated losses in the Nantucket fire of 1838**

| Firm | Loss Estimate |
|---|---|
| James Athearn | $ 46,000 |
| W.S. French and Benjamin Coffin | 32,000 |
| Matthew Crosby and William Crosby | 24,000 |
| Daniel Jones | 23,000 |
| Joseph James | 13,300 |
| Valentine Hussey | 10,000 |
| Philip H. Folger | 8,000 |

In his account book, Matthew put his own loss at about $17,000, which suggests that his son's interest was another $7,000, but the apportionment of the amounts is not entirely clear. In any case, although Matthew was lucky enough to have some of his stores preserved, the consequences were serious, particularly for several other proprietors whose stocks could not be saved. On June 6, a card of thanks, among many others like it, appeared in the newspaper:

> The undersigned offer their sincere and grateful acknowledgments to their friends and the public who, at the peril of life, succeeded in saving their store and most of their oil on Commercial Wharf and likewise used their utmost exertions in attempts to rescue their other buildings and their sheds of oil, oil house, etc. which were entirely destroyed in the conflagration of 2d inst. Matthew Crosby & Son.[8]

Already on the night of the fire, a town meeting was hastily called and the following resolution was adopted:

> As the sense of this meeting that the losses sustained by individuals of our community are, in their practical operation, a loss and a detriment suffered by the whole public; and linked together, as we are, not only by ties of affinity, but by the intercourse of society and of business, we feel that in the late visitation a common calamity has befallen our people.[9]

On the theme of perseverance in adversity and strength in unity as an inspiration for the future, the confirmation was *de rigueur* for a public announcement in the wake of a major tragedy. A call went out for assistance from the mainland, people of goodwill responded, and the task of rebuilding was begun.

But not everyone was sympathetic. In one instance, at least, the devastation to the town brought to the surface latent ill-feelings toward the inhabitants by an anonymous correspondent. Undoubtedly the consequence of some personal injustice, real or imagined, in the years gone by, the letter was picked up by the editor of the *Nantucket Inquirer* as a piece to enliven his columns. In itself it is of no great historical significance, but it is worth quoting, if only as a reminder that commercial pursuits on Nantucket were not always shaped by communal feelings of fellowship and charity but, as anywhere else, often directed by opposing views stirred by self-interest or benevolence, greed or generosity, honesty or deceit, as the case may have been, whereby some gained and prospered while others lost and suffered:

> The Nantucket fire is making stir and people are called on to assist the sufferers. No doubt they will be willing to receive all the assistance that can be sent to them, but who ever heard of their being guilty of a benevolent act? All that is done for Nantucket men will be like the showers which fall upon the barren sands—they are swallowed up and produce no vegetation. Let the rascals live on their own whale scraps until they learn to have a fellow-feeling to others in distress.[10]

As would be expected, the attack elicited a vigorous rebuttal from the newspaper. The writer was accused of being generally depraved, uncivilized, and of criminal intent, but in which the general charges were not refuted.

The last fire of those middle years, on July 13, 1846, coming as it did on the heels of the other two, and at a time of increased emigration from the island and a noticeable economic decline, was a disaster from which the town was never able fully to recover. It is known as the "Great Fire," great in extent, great in the destruction of houses and factories, and great in the long-term deleterious effect it had on the life and work of the people. It is ironic that the author of a compendium of the histories of all the towns in Massachusetts published in 1840 thought it worthwhile to describe Nantucket as:

> very compactly built, most of the streets narrow, and the homes mostly constructed of wood. The inhabitants seem sensible of their exposure to sweeping fires, to prevent which they have an efficient fire department and eighteen public cisterns and wells.[11]

But being aware of the danger could not prevent its occurrence. The Map of the Burnt District, published in the *Nantucket Inquirer* on July 24, and the more detailed drawing printed by Samuel H. Jenks Jr., showed that the loss of property extended in a broad crescent from the wharves (Commercial Wharf excepted), up Main Street to the Pacific Bank, along

*The extent of the disastrous fire of 1846 is shown in the shaded portion of the map by Samuel H. Jenks Jr. Lithograph by Bufford & Co., Boston.*

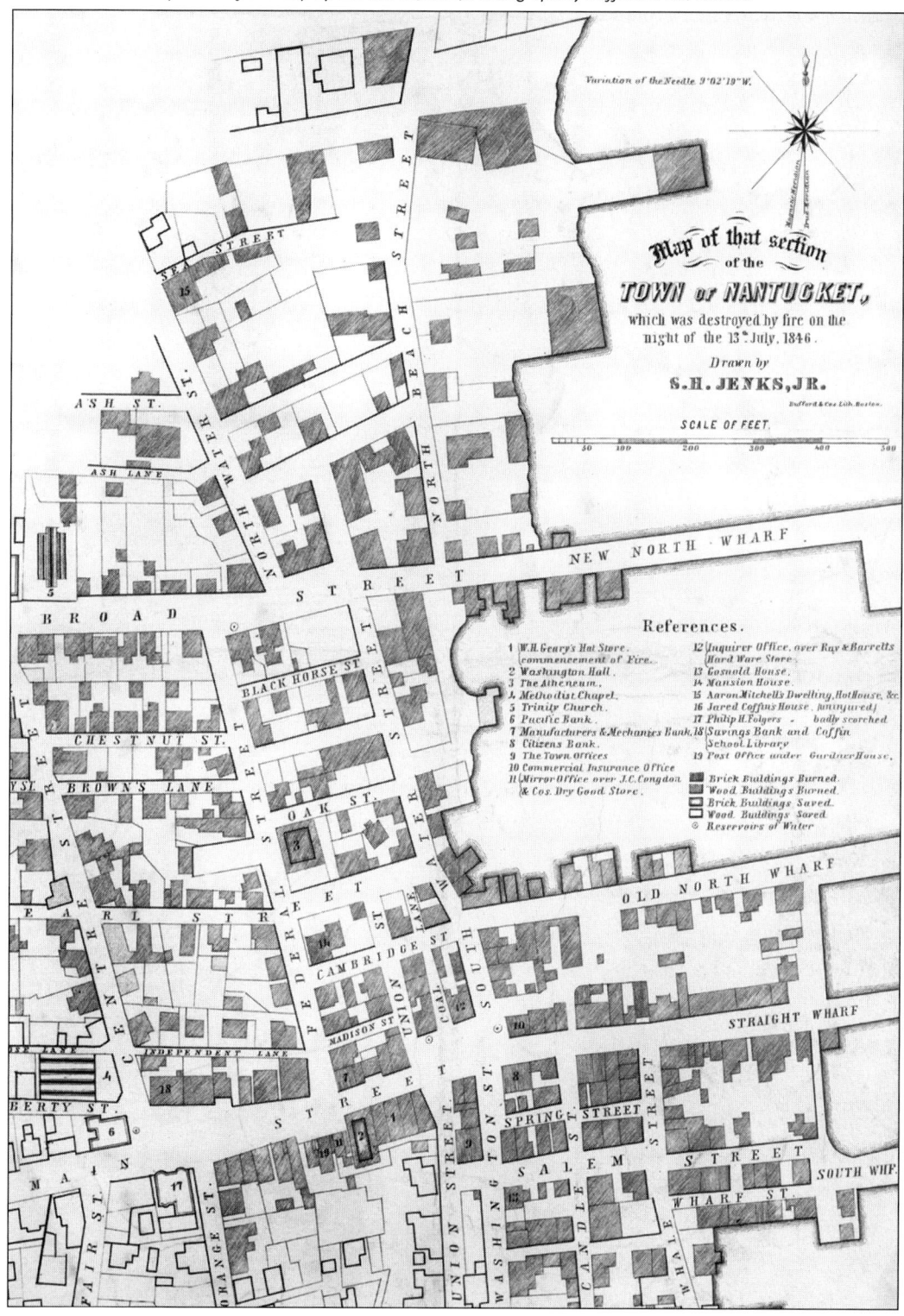

Centre Street, and then north to Sea Street, taking in all the waterfront and inland buildings. This time, most of Matthew's property was spared, but other merchants were forced to move temporarily to other premises. Gorham Macy, whose son George had married Ann Crosby, announced that he "offers his services in the auction and commission business at the store of Matthew Crosby, head of Commercial Wharf;" and T.W. Calder gave notice that "My customers and others can be supplied with the best family groceries at Benjamin M. Hussey's store in Pleasant Street next south of William H. Crosby's house."[12]

Nevertheless, the Crosby family did not go unscathed. William, as noted above, had lost much of his oil stock in the fire of 1836, and in 1846 he lost the rest. Even for Matthew, although the material loss was less than in 1838, the cost was still high. Casks and tools and oil that he had stored on Straight Wharf were destroyed and several adjacent shops had to be rebuilt. He put the value of the damaged buildings and equipment between $18,000 and $25,000. The consequences, of course, were felt in ever-widening circles. Suddenly reduced oil stocks, for example, meant an insufficient supply on the island and on the mainland for use in street lamps, lighthouses, and industrial machinery. Christopher C. Hussey, who was twenty-six years old at the time and who was conspicuous in working to rescue goods, as well as people, from the flames, recalled the melancholy aspect:

> After the fire had burned itself out, the scene of desolation was utterly indescribable. I remember one thing in particular. In the ravaged districts great heaps of coal and oil rubbish remained smoldering all summer. When the wind fanned the flames, they would shoot up and throw a weird, ghastly light through the streets. If the wind was east, the odor of burning substance would pervade the town with a gloomy, depressing effect.[13]

To help with reconstruction, gifts of money, food, furniture, and manpower were once again solicited, and donations flowed in from nearby communities. This time, no indictment of the townsmen for being mean-spirited has so far come to light. Slowly the ruins were cleared. Advantage was taken of the vacant spaces to widen some of the principal streets, new buildings were constructed, businessmen opened their doors again, and the islanders had reason to believe that they might yet recapture some of the faded wealth of recent years. Although the returns from whaling had declined from the mid–1830s (when twenty-five or thirty vessels might have brought in over 30,000 barrels of sperm oil a year) to the mid–1840s (when there were fifteen or twenty vessels returning a yearly average of about 22,000 barrels), Nantucket continued to produce a respectable profit in the industry into the early 1850s.

There is no doubt, however, that the fires had a depressive effect on the island economy. Once an assessment had been made, it was found that nearly a million dollars' worth of property had been destroyed. Even if the portion covered by insurance and the aid contributed by sympathetic donors are taken into account, the net loss was probably close to $500,000, or in Nantucket terms, the value of a dozen or so whaleships. To absorb as large a figure as that required a heavy dose of optimism followed by stern resolve and hard work. In practical terms, what was needed, as a frank, but well-meant, writer to the paper suggested in July 1847, was diversity in the economy:

> If the people of Nantucket ever needed a thorough stirring up, they need it now... The truth is, we are on the downhill road. A few good voyages will not save us and we shall not be able to rally again, as we have heretofore, after a year of bad voyages and low prices. If our capitalists desire to remain here and if our real estate owners want their property to continue [to be] worth anything, they must put shoulder to and start some new branches of business...[14]

But "new branches of business" had never been a proposal to which the islanders had reacted with much enthusiasm. Although it was a very small community, Nantucket had always supported a limited variety of industries, but most of these, such as rope-making, boat-building, the manufacture of barrels and casks, candle manufacturing, and oil processing, were ancillary to the whale fishery. Closely associated with them was a woolen factory put into operation by Obed Mitchell in 1812, and a brass foundry on South Beach, established in 1821.

But other untried local ventures of this kind met with only moderate success. With a commendably larger vision, but hindered by insufficient capital and output, and a restricted customer base, it was difficult to make a living. As mentioned previously, Aaron Mitchell opened the Atlantic Silk Company on Gay Street in 1836, but whether the mulberry trees failed to thrive in the New England climate, or the worms did not cooperate, expenses overrode income, and it was shut down eight years later. The Atlantic Straw Works, established

*Rear view of the Hadwen and Barney warehouse, previously the Hadwen candle factory, and later the Nantucket Whaling Museum, 1880s.*

in 1852, in which Matthew bought two shares by way of encouragement, was also closed soon afterward. A boot and shoe industry was in existence in 1846, but burned in 1873 and was never rebuilt. On the other hand, real estate and well-founded corporations offered opportunities for regular returns that seemed more attractive to many of the wealthy merchants and their families. They thereby diversified their assets in the years of declining income from oil and bone and, in the process, provided some benefits to other members of the community.

It is clear from Matthew's notebooks that he had been actively pursuing real estate in all parts of the island for many years. His investments ranged from land in Madaket and Head of Plains in the west to Coskata, Squam, and Siasconset in the east, and from Trot's Hills in the north to Smooth Hummocks and Southeast Pasture in the south. Some of the properties he kept, others he sold or exchanged soon after purchase, and a few he rented out. In January 1866, for example, he bought the Daniel Macy house next to his own on Traders Lane, thereby consolidating his home estate, but then leased it out to provide a monthly income.[15] In a few cases, these transactions were denominated in the so-called sheep commons. Over time, these amounted to land values worth hundreds of dollars. It is of some historical interest that in Matthew's day a sheep common was a usual and acceptable measure of value. The practice dated from the earliest settlements when most of the island was given over to grazing sheep and cattle on land held in common and only a small portion was set aside for individual, privately owned homesteads.

A sheep common, therefore, was proof of the right to keep one sheep on the undivided land. How much land did one sheep need? In the eighteenth century, it was thought to be about one acre or 160 square rods. This, in fact, was the amount that had been deemed sufficient in 1678 for one household when the Wesco house lots were laid out to the west of the present-day town. They were bounded by Liberty Street on the south and west, by Broad Street and Quince Street on the north, and by Federal Street on the east. But then, homeowners were not roaming about in search of forage and water. They liked to live close together, and so the developed land became more expensive.

Since originally there were twenty-seven proprietors, and the common was estimated to consist of 19,440 acres, each man had the right to keep 720 sheep (or the equivalent of eight cows or sixteen horses). With a sheep common representing one acre of land, it quickly acquired a certain value, and several of them could be traded back and forth for interests in real estate.

Over the next century and a half, the sheep commons were passed down to the descendants of the first owners, but they became divided into smaller and smaller parts. If one of the first men had $1/27$ of the common and left it in equal parts to his five children, then each child theoretically would inherit $1/135$, or 144 sheep commons and equivalent acres. If the man with the $1/135$ died and left his share to his five children, then each one would have had $1/675$, or 29 sheep commons and acres. Finally, if the man with $1/675$ had two children to inherit, each one would have received ⅟₃₅₀, or 14 sheep commons and acres. The system grew unwieldy and became less useful, but the real challenge came from groups of landholders in the early nineteenth-century who sued in court to have their portions of the common set off as private property, thereby improving individual lots but diminishing the extent and the value of the whole. It was the inevitable outcome of the hardship brought about by a growing population living on fixed acreage, something landlords in England had been dealing with since the fifteenth century.

The nominal right to graze a sheep gradually grew less valuable as there were fewer sheep to graze, and the common became less important for trading purposes. But in Matthew's time, it still retained some worth, and he and his friends who were knowledgeable in the old ways had no hesitation in using it to buy and sell in the land market. In April 1833, for example, he paid $445.50 for 396 commons in the South Beach shares, which put the average price for each at $1.12. A year later, he bought 148 commons in another share in the same division for $.81 each, and in 1839, in still another share, where the cost had risen to $1.45. Toward the end of his life, in March 1870, he sold off a mass of almost a hundred commons in divisions across the island for an average price of $.80–1.00.[16] It is doubtful if Matthew ever spent much time in the sheep business, but he did buy a sheep tag from one Daniel Barney, with his own mark of a *fleur de lys* for the left ear, whereby owners could be identified and charged for washing and shearing the animals.[17]

*The last of the Nantucket sheep gathered at Quaise, circa 1890.*

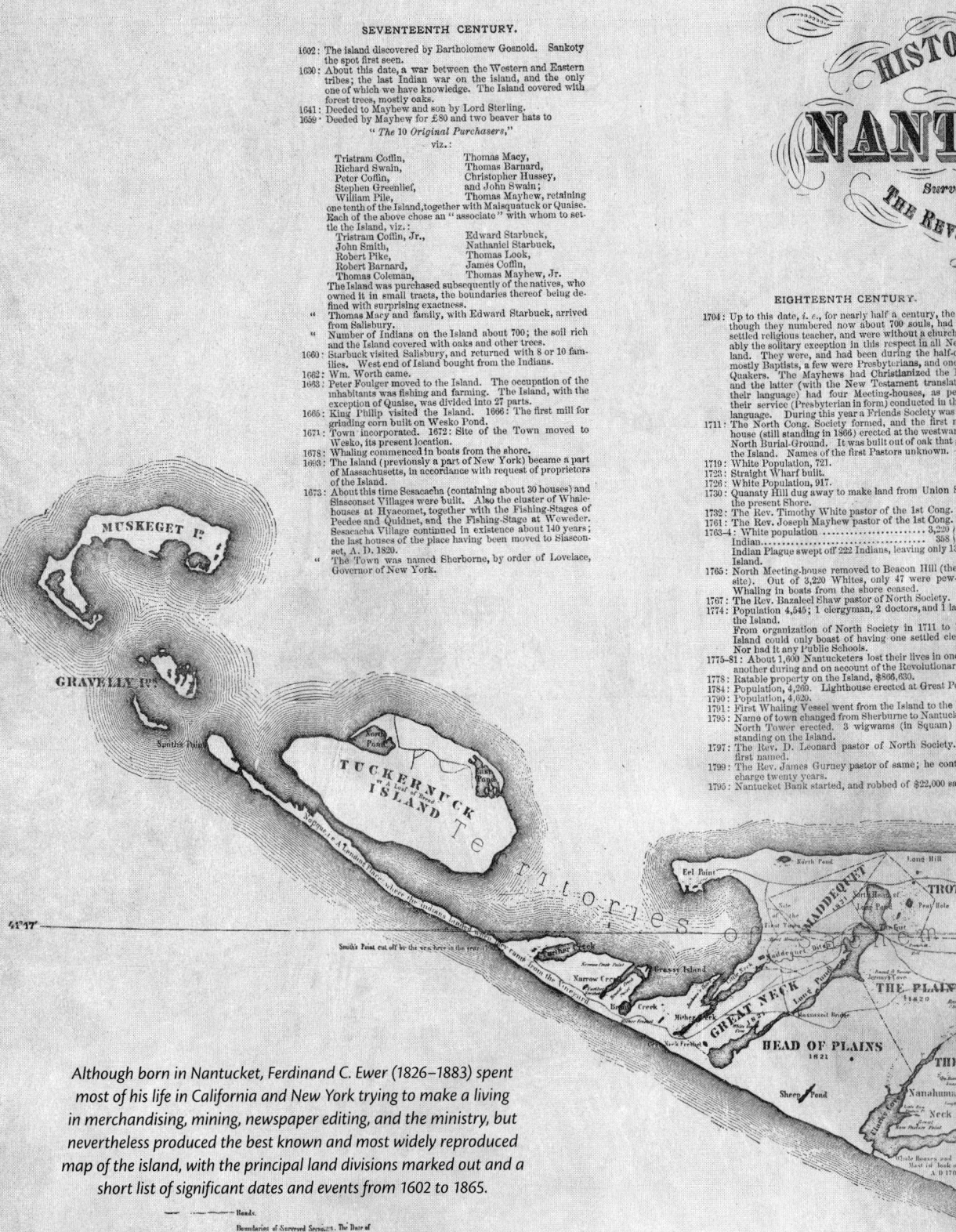

Although born in Nantucket, Ferdinand C. Ewer (1826–1883) spent most of his life in California and New York trying to make a living in merchandising, mining, newspaper editing, and the ministry, but nevertheless produced the best known and most widely reproduced map of the island, with the principal land divisions marked out and a short list of significant dates and events from 1602 to 1865.

### NINETEENTH CENTURY.

1800: The Academy incorporated, and the building erected. It was not a public School.
" Bell (weighing 1,000 lbs.) placed in North Tower.
" The Methodist Society organized.
" Population, 5,617.
1804: Pacific Bank and two Insurance Offices established.
1809: The Unitarian Society formed, the Rev. Seth P. Swift, Pastor. The North Society languishing on account of losing members to the Methodist and the Unitarian.
1810: Population, 6,807.
1815: Social Library instituted: Josiah Hussey, Esq., President.
1816: The Nantucket Gazette issued. It had but a brief existence.
1820: The Rev. Abner Morse pastor at the North. The Mechanics' Association, a literary society, was formed.
" Population, 7,266. 72 ships (21,600 tons) engaged in Whale Fishery.
1823: Columbian Library Association formed.
1827: Two Public Schools established and the Coffin School opened.
1830: Population, 7,202.
1834: The new North Meeting-house erected. Athenæum incorporated. 1836: Great Fire.
1838: High School opened. Great Fire in the town; loss $300,000.
1839: Trinity Church (Episcopal) erected; the Parish having been organized a short time before by the Rev. Moses Marcus, B. D.
1840: Population, 9,712.
1846: Great Fire, July 13 and 14. Whaling declines.
1847: Pine trees planted by Josiah Sturgis.
1850: Population, 8,779.
1852–3: Other Pine groves planted.
1854: Gas lighted for first time on the Island. 185–: Abram Quary (last man with Indian blood in him) died.
1860: Population 6,094.
1865: Population, 4,830. Alumni Association (of High School) organized.

Although the town bought most of the remaining sheep commons in the mid-twentieth century, there are still a few in private hands. But who can say how much they are worth or what parcels of land they represent? Because the common land was not titled, and because of the confusion in rights, exacerbated by the private setoffs, too much of the real estate on the island in later years was plagued with flawed descriptions and false claims. This unfortunate state of affairs, as many older citizens know, has enabled some unscrupulous individual and corporate owners, local lawyers, town officials, and off-island developers to exploit the tracts of "land of owners unknown" to their own advantage and profit.

Matthew also invested in mortgages and made a modest income from that business. He would make a loan to a homeowner and take a lien on the property as collateral. Interest hovered around 6%. An example can be taken from the flowery description of a February 16, 1839, where "a certain lot of land and dwelling house in that healthy and pleasant part of Nantucket called Newtown, south by Dover Street," was conveyed to Matthew by Rowland M. Coffin, cooper, for $160.23, with the right to repurchase within twelve months. He settled on May 28, 1844.[18]

But of particular importance for Matthew, for many of his friends, and, indeed, for the growth of Nantucket as a whole, was the continued development of the land on the east coast of the island. By the middle of the nineteenth century, in the northeastern states, it had become fashionable for wealthy upper-class families to forsake the hot and noisy cities

*Broadway in Siasconset, circa 1860.*

in the summer months for the cooler air and leisured pace of the mountains or the seaside. New Yorkers packed up for Newport or the Adirondacks, Philadelphians went to the Jersey shore or to the lakes and islands of Maine, and, wonderful to relate, merchant families on Nantucket, surrounded by the ocean and enjoying an ideal climate, bought or built cottages in Siasconset, less than eight miles away, to escape the bustle of town, to breathe what was thought to be purer air, to gaze across the ocean three thousand miles to Portugal, and to enhance their social standing. Although the growth of this custom may seem surprising in such a small locality, on consideration it is perfectly understandable. The census figures for Nantucket in 1840 reported a population of about 9,200 people, up from about 7,200 in 1830. The town by this time, as mentioned before, was congested, noisy, and dirty, and the air was heavy with the smell of smoke and oil even in the residential quarters. A healthy change of scene and pace was easily achieved at minimum time and expense. In 'Sconset quite a few of the old fishing shacks were converted to serve as small, but proper, residences and, in the course of time, as more people gathered there, new streets were laid out and new houses were built. "The Nantucketer…made 'Sconset his watering place," announced

*The old fishing shacks in Siasconset, circa 1880.*

A. Judd Northrup in a book of memoirs published in 1881.[19] But the exodus from town had, in fact, begun long before. The pleasant, simple life in the village was praised by Obed Macy in his *History of Nantucket*, which had appeared in 1835. He found that even such a small town could become too formal, too mannered, and forgetful of honest country ways:

> At Siasconset, all are on a level, or rather on an equal elevation. Useless forms and ceremonies are laid aside, and the little community, for the time being, indulges in a reciprocity of good feelings and interchange of civilities, which can be found in no place but one situated precisely like Siasconset, and no other such place exists in the known world.[20]

Society moved east. Barretts, Bunkers, Burnells, Crosbys, Folgers, and a clutch of Gardners, Husseys, and Starbucks, to name a few of the leading families, all set up summer housekeeping near the 'Sconset Bluff.

*A posed photograph of several different family members amid the shacks on Front Street, Siasconset, 1860.*

Matthew, himself, having heard the siren song, had begun to buy land there as early as 1830 and continued to do so for many years. In the fall of 1836, he purchased a lot from Philip H. Folger, 91 feet across the front and back and 231 feet from front to back, for $175 and contracted with Charles Pendexter, a local carpenter, to build a family house with a barn behind it.[21] This appears to have been on Main Street at the corner of the present Morey Lane in the village, nearly opposite the site of the Atlantic House Hotel. Next door was the residence of John W. Barrett, a close friend and a successful merchant banker in the firm of Barrett & Upton, who owned the grand mansion at 72 Main Street in town. Within the year, Matthew enlarged his holdings with a two-acre lot from Barrett; another nine acres in 1847 from Fredrick W. Mitchell, a co-director of the Pacific Bank; three acres in 1864 from William C. Gardner, his son-in-law; and numerous other parcels here and there in the expanding village from other owners. Besides these luminaries, his other close neighbors were Charles G. Coffin, Henry Coffin, William Hadwen, and Barker Burnell, altogether a group of well-established friends and relations who could have been picked up bodily from Main Street in Nantucket by some miraculous power and set down comfortably on Main Street in Siasconset. Only the scenery and the architecture would have changed.

*An inset of Siasconset from Henry F. Walling's Map of Nantucket, 1858. Matthew Crosby's house is marked on Main Street next to his neighbor, J. W. Barrett, across from the Atlantic Hotel.*

The rough plans for Matthew's house make it clear that it was to be a modest structure. They called for a 11' x 11' bedroom, a 16' x 15' front room, a front and a back entry, closets in all the rooms (a modern touch), walls of lathe and plaster, shutters on all the windows (another novelty), three chimneys, a cellar, a cistern with a capacity of seventy barrels with a pump, a porch, and a terrace with a balustrade and a fence in front. The original price by Pendexter was $1,812, but once the design had been laid out it may have seemed overly restrained for a wealthy merchant. Matthew enlarged the porch, added a floor with two more windows and doors, and bought some additional acreage. His own figures show that he spent almost $4,000 when all was done. We know from details specified in the contract that the finished work inside was to match the quality carried out in the house of Frederick W. Mitchell at 20 Main Street in 'Sconset, especially the glass, which was to be "of the best kind," and was to be of the same size. Thus it was, and to some extent still is, the custom to have the owner lay out the plan, to have the carpenter build it after his fashion, and to duplicate and incorporate the best ideas and designs of other buildings as needed. According to Matthew's son, Frank Lewis Crosby, it was:

> a very small pretty home with a coach-house, horse stalls, workshop, and land given to pasture and vegetables. [We] lived in town October to June and the rest of the year at the farm.[22]

Not long after Matthew settled in, he began to buy into several ventures with an eye to improving the living standards in the community. He joined Frederick Mitchell as a trustee

*Matthew Crosby's house at 28 Main Street in Siasconset with the barn behind it, circa 1880.*

of the Franklin Schoolhouse Association, which owned land (known as Plainfield) between 'Sconset and Sankaty Head donated by George B. Elkins, a Nantucket businessman. Elkins ran a rooming house near Sankaty for a few years, where he entertained John Quincy Adams in September 1835 and several other prominent men from town. Matthew retained an interest in the Association until February 1878, a few months before his death, when, as the sole surviving trustee, he sold out to the Town of Nantucket for $200.[23]

In 1841, with some of his neighbors, he paid for a subscription to the Atlantic Pump Company, and a little later he also thought it worthwhile to join a group of fourteen other investors to support the new Atlantic House Hotel. The latter, an impressive sign of the popularity of the little village in which Matthew bought four shares, opened its doors in 1838 with the promise of "pure fresh air, magnificent ocean scenery, and fine fishing."[24]

North of Plainfield and the bluff at Sankaty lay the large pond and the very old fishing hamlet called Sachacha. By Matthew's time, several of the huts had been taken down and moved to Siasconset, but the choice location itself gained a new life by attracting a group of wealthy merchants, including the old friends, Frederick Mitchell, Philip H. Folger, and John W. Barrett, who liked to gather there. Matthew had a small house built in a shared ownership arrangement and kept a boat for fishing and picnics. It is pleasing to imagine members of these families and their guests trundling out to Siasconset by horse and cart, glad to escape

*Atlantic House circa 1870. The grand hotel in Siasconset was built about 1848 by a consortium of businessmen in which Matthew Crosby was one of the partners.*

the routine at home by a few days in the country and to spend some time entertaining themselves on the eastern shore. Certainly, the feeling of "getting away from it all" was enhanced by the fact that it took almost two hours by horse and wagon to complete the journey from Nantucket to the village. Moreover, there was as yet no good road, certainly not a paved one, which probably added some excitement to the outing. An anonymous letter to the *Inquirer* in July 1855 described the poor state of affairs:

> I took a ride across the island to Siasconset last evening. The road across the plain is nothing more than a series of wheel tracks side by side. As fast as one track is worn through the surface to the loose sand, another one is made beside it, and so in some places there are as many as a dozen parallel carriage paths.[25]

By mid-century, with more and more residents and the increase of traffic to and from the village, murmurs of complaint began to be heard more loudly and a petition to the selectmen was published in the newspaper over several weeks in the summer of 1855. It was signed by a group of prominent citizens, including Matthew's son, William H. Crosby, and resulted in the calling of a town meeting to resolve the issue.[26] Strong contrary views on the matter provoked a surprisingly acrimonious discussion and argument giving rise to majority and minority reports relating primarily to the location and width of a new road.

*Measuring ruts on the improved Milestone Road from the town to Siasconset, circa 1890.*

Even on Nantucket, where so few people lived so close together, whatever was proposed in the public interest was sure to be opposed by another portion of the public will. In the event, after several more meetings, the majority view for a hardened road was upheld. The location and dimensions were slightly altered to appease the minority, the plan was finally voted on and accepted, and construction began in September. But for some old-timers, ever resistant to sudden change, it seemed that "faraway 'Sconset" would now be too easy of access, and that another bit of the charm of the little village perched on the rim of the island would fade away.[27]

Matthew, the businessman and dealer in 'Sconset property, appears in an interesting contract that he wrote toward the end of his life when he was in the process of selling off a portion of his real estate holdings. It concerns a small part of the so-called "Fisher Lot" he owned. It was adjacent to his other land, next to the property of his daughter, Lydia Burnell, on one side and that of R.B. Pitman on the other:

> This is to certify that I have sold to William H. Bowen a part of my Fisher Lot at Siasconset…and he is to pay me for the same in labour or money from time to time when ever I want him at the rate of one dollar per day, he to put up and enclose the same with a good fence at his own expense, and after he has paid for the same with interest, he can have the rear west part at fifty dollars on the dotted line on the plot within. After he has paid for the same, I or my administrators are to give him a clear deed of the same. We both sign and agree to the above & each have & sign a copy.[28]

Although the full price is not stated and the attached plat is not drawn to scale, the intent was to sell almost half the lot to Bowen in two stages; first, one portion including a new fence in return for work or cash, and then, if this had been paid for, a second part to round out the purchase with the rest of the land for $50.

Billy Bowen, it should be said, was not the ordinary purchaser and Matthew could afford to be indulgent. Born on Nantucket in 1830, Bowen shipped out on several whaling voyages in the sunset years of the industry. Only five feet tall and of sunny disposition, but never prosperous, he eventually retired to Quidnet, and then to 'Sconset, where he first spent the summer months in a one-room shack with his wife on the site of the later village post office. Within a short time, however, he moved the building to a lot on Morey Lane, which appears to have been the one purchased from Matthew in 1876. There, the shack was enlarged to four rooms and named "Sea Shell." Bowen was evidently something of a character in the village and a popular tourist attraction who held court in the guise of the "old salt." This notoriety may account for the slightly unusual terms of the sale. As the years went by, he came to spend the winter months at the asylum on Orange Street (renamed Our Island Home in 1905), where, as he always said in his picturesque way, he would like "to drop anchor at the end of the voyage." His ship came home to port in December 1915.[29]

As a successful merchant in a small community, Matthew naturally held investments in other local enterprises in addition to his capital in vessels and real estate, and, in a few cases, he gave of his time and money to help manage them. We have already noted his connections with several banks in the discussion of the Barker Burnell affair, and while several of them continued to produce a significant return, they often came at a high cost of concern and worry. The disaster with Burnell had occurred in the spring of 1843, but just a few months previously, there had been a similar scandal in the Pacific Bank that had the potential to do considerable damage. As we well know, there always had been a close relationship between banking and whaling, and bank officials were often owners of whaleships. As a director and stockholder, Matthew was immediately involved and he thought it important enough to write up a lengthy description of what happened. Because his account brings to light some more of the inner workings and family relations of the institution, it is worth a brief comment.

For Matthew, the drama began late in the day of December 27, 1842, between eight and nine o'clock, when he was called upon by John W. Barrett, his neighbor in 'Sconset, and asked to go down to the bank. Barrett said he felt "very bad" because there was some difficulty involving the president that would be explained when they got there. On arrival, Matthew met William Mitchell, the cashier, and two other directors, and learned that a recent audit of the books had turned up a delinquency in the accounts. This amounted to about $63,000 in the New England Bank of Boston, and about $30,000 in the Phoenix Bank

*The poor house and asylum on lower Orange Street, 1860s, which was removed from its former location at Quaise.*

of New York, which large sums had been drawn down without the knowledge of the directors of the Pacific Bank. The president at the time was James Athearn, who had a long record of faithful service from the time he had been appointed cashier in 1810. By investing heavily, and successfully, in real estate and whaling, he had built up a considerable fortune. His assets included a house on Centre Street, an interest in the Washington House hotel on the corner of Main and Union, a brick warehouse at 2 Union Street, which is still standing, and in partnership with Edward H. Barker, his son-in-law, he owned a small cordage factory and several whaling ships. But Athearn was one of the unfortunates who was hard hit, first by the fire of 1836, which destroyed the Washington House, and then by the fire two years later when he lost most of his oil stocks. He never recovered his fortune. The avalanche of troubles that overwhelmed him was the most obvious reason for his attempt as the chief officer of the bank to raise enough cash to tide him over without the burden of a formal loan. "I was struck with astonishment," wrote Matthew,

> and did not know what course we had better take. I, however, said I was fearful that we had not security enough for the Bank and that our whole aim ought to be to get all the security for the Bank we could both from Athearn and also Barker & Athearn and, if possible, try to sustain the Bank and the public from any loss, which was acceded to by all present.[30]

Matthew also recommended that all the directors should be informed of the whole matter, but it was thought best to get the security first since it was not known if Athearn was also indebted to them or their friends. Such was the delicacy needed in handling the problem when so many were dependent on each other through business and family relations. Matthew added that all the directors had the "greatest confidence in Athearn's integrity and ability to pay all his liabilities and to have a large amount left." He was convinced that "the Bank was as sound as any other in the state." At least he hoped so, because at the time he owned thirty-two shares of stock in the institution and members of his family had an equal proportion. Still, they all probably had reason to be optimistic. While on further investigation it was found that Athearn had withdrawn as much as $169,000, the securities he offered, considered to be "good, bad, and indifferent," were appraised at about $213,000. Nevertheless, the directors deemed it expedient to sign a bond for $75,000, whereby they would be responsible for that amount to redeem the bills, should it be necessary.

Two days later, on the evening of the 29th, all the directors met again, except for Levi Starbuck, then in his seventies, who excused himself "because of family connections." (His daughter, Lydia, had married Athearn's son, James F. Athearn, and there were social conventions in place in the community that had to be observed.) "Athearn came in," Matthew wrote, "looking and feeling sadly. I never witness [sic] a person in more apparent distress.

He stated he alone was to blame in getting the Bank and himself into this difficulty." It was the familiar lament of the wrongdoer caught in the act, but Athearn does seem to have been able to reimburse the bank for most of the funds he had withdrawn, although the directors were still tidying up the books well into 1849. Having done this, he had next to nothing left. Soon afterward he left the island, an insolvent debtor, and moved to Boston, where he died in 1852. But the bank was saved!

Matthew continued in the directorship until the end of 1874. Judging by the minutes preserved in the archives of the bank, he took an active part in the management, although he was by no means assiduous in attendance at the regular meetings. He served on a variety of committees, brought a solid and thoughtful view of current issues to the table, and showed his confidence by acquiring sixty-one shares and by keeping a trunk for his important papers, notes, and deeds in the bank strong-room. By then, he was eighty-three years old and on Christmas Day he sent in a letter of resignation in which he expressed confidence in the institution and, doubtless in the shadow of the sorrowful Athearn and Burnell episodes, a certain satisfaction in his own reputation:

> To the president and directors and officers of the Nantucket Pacific Bank, Gentlemen: Being far advanced in life, my health rather feeble, deficient in hearing, and having been a director for the past forty-two years, I now tender my resignation as a director to take place on the 25 day of the present month. 25 day of 12 mo. 1874. I have the fullest confidence in the present management of all the officers and directors of the bank and as far as my knowledge extends, I believe the bank is in first rate condition. I believe that my account has never been overdrawn, always having a balance in my favour and never having been indebted to the bank in any shape to the amount of my stock in said bank. [Signed] Matthew Crosby.[31]

His resignation was accepted, and in a letter sent to him, the directors resolved that:

> We desire to express our full appreciation of the valuable aid rendered by him during the long period of his service as a director and the great loss the bank will sustain in the resignation of one who has heretofore taken so active a part in the management of the institution and who has been so deeply interested in its welfare.[32]

By all appearances, a form letter issued for the occasion, but, nevertheless, of value to the modern reader in adding support to the view that Matthew was widely honored for his integrity, thoughtful counsel, and consistent service. It was more than the directors would have said of James Athearn.

Like the well-managed banks, equally well-managed insurance companies also prospered in the best days of the whaling industry and continued to thrive on new business long after the years of decline. As Elmo Hohman put it:

> The greatest safeguard against the inevitable hazard of whaling…lay in the system of marine insurance which was readily available to owners throughout the period after 1820.[33]

If not "the greatest safeguard," for the quality of the boat, the captain, and the crew, were of comparable importance, insurance did provide a measure of security in port and at sea and an incentive to expand the industry. A typical carefully written policy insured against:

> the Seas, Fires, Enemies, Pirates, assailing Thieves, Restraints and Detainments of all Kings, Princes, or People, of what nation or quality soever, Barratry of the Master (unless the insured be owner of the vessel) and of Mariners, and all other losses and misfortunes which have or shall come to the damage of the said Ship."[34]

There followed, of course, in fine print, a long list of exceptions and exemptions that would come into effect under certain specified conditions. Like the banks, therefore, the insurance companies were attractive investments.

The Union Insurance Company opened in Nantucket in 1804 and it was followed by several others, including the Phoenix and the Commercial. Matthew bought stock in the latter two, was a trustee of the Phoenix, and served on the board of the Commercial for several years. With Hezekiah Barnard and Timothy Hussey, he even tried his hand at the game. On April 6, 1838, the three partners were granted a corporation known as the Howard Insurance Company in Nantucket with a capital of $75,000 to make maritime loans and write insurance against maritime losses. But for whatever reason, ineffective management, lack of subscribers, or too little capital, there is no evidence that it became a profitable undertaking.[35]

In other ways, too, Matthew was ready to adapt to changing conditions on the island that offered new ideas and new opportunities for investment. As proceeds from whaling diminished, he took up the slack by buying into some of the smaller and less expensive vessels owned by several newly organized fishing companies on the island. With a relatively modest capital outlay, three or four of them operated in the Atlantic with about fifteen schooners and sloops, mainly harvesting cod and mackerel. In spite of his earlier disappointment in the insurance venture, Matthew thought well enough of the project to join Joseph B. Macy and Joseph C. Chase in the foundation of the Nantucket Fishing Company on March 26, 1866 "for the purpose of carrying on a general fishing and freighting business, capital not to exceed $60,000 divided into shares of $50 each."[36] This was a reasonable decision since the state mackerel fishery by itself in 1831 comprised about 400 vessels and was valued at over a million dollars. Obviously, it was a going concern. He subscribed to ten shares, Charles C. Crosby to thirty shares, and William Crosby to two shares. But, alas, Nantucket did not

*Nantucket fishermen at South Wharf prepare small schooners and sloops for summer mackerel fishing, circa 1900. The fishing industry had thoroughly replaced whaling by the 1870s. Using small purse seines and gill nets, Nantucketers fished from May to December, landing mostly mackerel to sell as the fresh catch and salting the remainder.*

always reflect the prosperity that enlivened the mainland. Not enough profits were generated and the company wound up its affairs early in 1871.

In Matthew's younger days, it had been early to bed on Quaker Nantucket. The streets were not lit, and few homeowners left a light by the door. Should you have wished to walk about, or to have read or worked beyond the natural hour, a candle or an oil lamp had to be found. The widespread industry of manufacturing sperm candles, in which Matthew and so many of his friends were occupied, prospered by putting a superior product on the market at a premium price.

Likewise, there were constant improvements being made in the design and manufacture of lamps. The introduction of the Argand burner at the beginning of the nineteenth century, with a newly designed hollow wick, provided a brighter light with minimal smoke and proved to be less noisome than tallow or hog fat. Imported and much extolled by Thomas Jefferson, it was a luxury item costing more money, but of interest to Nantucketers because it was filled with whale oil in order to give the best light. There was plenty of the fuel for use on the island, but some merchants of a conservative turn of mind considered this a poor choice. It made more sense, they argued, to ship the oil abroad and sell it, rather than to squander the money at home. It seems hardly the case, however, that the consumption of a little of their own oil by the small group of merchants who could afford it would decrease their profits in a major way.

But the answer to the problem of more efficient lighting, as we know, was out of their hands. It came first with gas from coal, in use tentatively as street lighting by 1810; then kerosene, initially from coal in 1850, and then more widely from petroleum in the 1860s; and, finally, electricity, available with the Edison bulb in 1882, but too late for Matthew to appreciate its superior quality. Gas for public spaces in the mainland cities was already installed during the 1820s and 1830s, but it took a good deal longer to reach the island. The writing, however, was on the wall. In October 1854, James S. Kelley ran an advertisement in the *Inquirer* offering to convert chandeliers, mantle lamps, and girandoles into gas burners.[37] The Nantucket Gas Light Company was chartered in the same year, a manufacturing plant was built, mains run, posts erected, and in November lower Main Street was suddenly lit up as never before. Matthew may have viewed this innovation with some uncertainty, because he waited eight years, until 1862, before he bought two shares in the company.

Other public business ventures offered further possibilities. The sea link to Cape Cod, New Bedford, and New York was always a concern to men on Nantucket, so that the introduction of a service in 1818 by steamboat, rather than by sail, was a significant development. The *Eagle*, driven by wood-fired boilers, proved to be short-lived, but another attempt was made in January 1833 by friends of Matthew. With his support, they organized The Nantucket Steamboat Company to connect the island with Martha's Vineyard

The steamboats Island Home (1855–1895) and River Queen (1871–1884) at the wharf in Nantucket, circa 1870.

and New Bedford on a regular schedule. The company survived until May 1855, when the route was shifted to Hyannis and the name changed to The Nantucket and Cape Cod Steamboat Company. New Bedford was thus left out of the picture. To remedy this omission, yet another group was backed to promote The New Bedford, Vineyard, and Nantucket Steamboat Company, with Matthew as the island representative who held a seat on the board. A succession of side-wheel steamers came and went: the *Telegraph* in 1832, the *Massachusetts* in 1843, the *Eagle's Wing* in 1854, and the *Monohansett* in 1862. They were expensive vessels (the *Monohansett* cost almost as much as an outfitted whaleship), but Matthew bought shares in all of them. He had returned to investing in ships and the sea, which idea may have appealed to him more strongly than helping to pay for the gas works. Indeed, the steamboats appear to have done well, except for the *Eagle's Wing*, which caught fire and burned to the waterline in July 1861. But, for Matthew, that was a bad year all around, with losses from some of his whaleships, a drop in the price of oil and candles, and debts he was unable to collect on.

As whaling declined, and as the tourist trade picked up, fast, regular, safe, and comfortable transport became essential to the island economy. Here the new and well-appointed steamers played a major role. But an even more significant development that increased the

*Certificate for shares in the New Bedford, Martha's Vineyard, and Nantucket Steamboat Company, 1886-1919.*

importance of the boats was the extension of mainland rail lines to the busy seaports of New Bedford, Woods Hole, and Hyannis. This development allowed the trains to connect with Boston, New Haven, New York, Baltimore, and Washington which, in turn, served as hubs for further travel and transport inland. Railroad construction began in the 1830s and continued at a frantic pace, accompanied by increased settlement along the routes, a rise in property values, and a greater quantity of goods transported. As large firms, the railroad companies prospered by instituting efficient accounting methods and administrative practices that were soon imitated by other companies. Far from being "a distant shore," mainland America, or, "the continent," as Nantucketers liked to call it, imitating the English view of Europe, although never so far away as some people thought, or hoped, was now a far more insistent and integral part of island growth and welfare.

Railroads became an accepted part of life on the mainland and on the island. How else was Matthew to go to Detroit and back again within the space of a few weeks with relative ease, as he did in 1856? How else were the merchants to ship their boxes of candles quickly and safely? A consortium on Nantucket even started up its own little line from the town to Surfside in 1881, and thence to 'Sconset three years later. It is no surprise, therefore, that Matthew began to enlarge his portfolio so that by the 1860s he had stock in eleven different rail companies, of which seven were in New England. At the same time, he expanded his investments and spread the risk among a number of mainland banks, insurance companies, and similar undertakings.

*The Nantucket Railroad beside the Easy Street boat basin, circa 1900. It ran in fits and starts from 1881 to 1918 when the project was given up and the rails and rolling stock were shipped to France for the use in the last stages of the Great War.*

The table below, which gives the name of each company and extent of Matthew's investment in it in 1868, is the easiest way to see the range of his interests:

Table 6.

**Matthew Crosby's investment portfolio, 1868**

| Railways | Amount |
|---|---|
| Boston and Providence | 30 shares |
| Boston and Worcester | 11 shares |
| Boston and Albany | 14 shares |
| Burlington and Missouri River | $1,000 bond |
| Cambridge Horse | 5 shares |
| Cincinnati | $1,000 bond |
| Eastern | 10 shares |
| Kennebec and Androscoggin | $1,000 bond |
| Michigan Central | 21 shares |
| New Bedford and Taunton | 30 shares |
| Philadelphia, Wilmington, and Baltimore | 20 shares |
| **Banks** | **Amount** |
| Bank of Commerce, Boston | 30 shares |
| Commercial Bank, Boston | 20 shares |
| Granite Bank (Second National), Boston | 55 shares |
| Mechanics National Bank, New Bedford | 10 shares |
| Webster National Bank, Boston | 40 shares |
| **Other Investments** | **Amount** |
| Brooklyn Water Loan bond | $1,000 |
| Massachusetts State bond | $2,100 |
| New Bedford City bond | $4,000 |
| New York City bond | $4,000 |
| Pewabic Mining Company | 31 shares |
| Union Coal Company | 23 shares |
| United States bond | $5,500 |
| Vermont State bond | $1,000 |

As was his custom, Matthew invested with a limited number of shares in a few selected companies, and his accounts, for the most part, show satisfactory returns on a regular basis.

Disappointing results occurred with the Pewabic firm, which had operated a copper mine in Michigan on Lake Superior since 1853. It was dependent on a group of investors from Massachusetts and was acquired by Matthew to satisfy a debt. In 1870 it was merged with the Concord Company with a loss in the value of the shares to Matthew of over $1,500.

Likewise, Union Coal in Pennsylvania proved to be an unsatisfactory choice. It fell into financial straits and was ultimately sold to the Delaware and Hudson Canal and Railway Company, as Matthew noted, "…to pay debts, and all came to nothing, a swindle of no value, nothing left for stockholders."[38]

Matthew's success in his business ventures did not escape the notice of Asa Bunker (1802–1869), whose manuscript on credit ratings has been referred to previously in connection with several of Matthew's children and relations, including William H. Crosby, Barker Burnell, and George C. Macy.[39] Already in 1841, Lewis Tappan, the radical abolitionist (not the Lewis Tappan who was the husband of Mary Swift, the granddaughter of Zenas Coffin), had founded the Mercantile Agency in New York City, following the example of the Baring Company in London and Boston. His purpose was to gather and sell information sent in by an army of informants relating to the character, commercial contacts, and financial reliability of hundreds of business customers. The reports were written out longhand in folios in Tappan's office and then made available to merchants who had subscribed to the firm. Tappan's brother-in-law, R.G. Dun, took over in 1858 and much later, in a merger with an older company, the firm became known as Dun and Bradstreet.

The early submissions relied upon the local attorneys, cashiers of banks, and other town and county officials who were supposed to have some personal knowledge of the men in question. At first, there was no uniform system of collecting the data and no standard of reporting, so that what information was turned in was often no more than personal opinion subject to undisclosed prejudices. But gradually the methods were refined, a consistent format was adopted, and the information came to be cast in a useful analytical framework. With more and more firms buying and selling on credit as a matter of convenience and necessity, this was a service that was destined to be a mainstay of the expanding economy.[40]

Such was the growth of the business that in February 1843, The Mercantile Agency opened its first corresponding office in Boston, and very soon, other offices in Baltimore and Philadelphia. In 1844, Warren A. Cleveland (or Cleaveland), who had worked for Tappan, established his own agency in New York and, it would seem, also in Boston. It was to Cleveland that Asa Bunker sent his reports on the Nantucket businessmen, thereby joining a widespread group of informants that included Abraham Lincoln and Ulysses S. Grant among many others of less renown.

For more than thirty years as the Register of Deeds in Nantucket, Bunker had ready access to the tax records and other useful documents related to businesses on the island, as well as an ear for gossip, rumor, and hearsay. The advantage he played was that he knew things that others did not: "My dear friend," he wrote to an anonymous correspondent 1854, "What can I find to write to you from dull, old Nantucket, especially as you have a wife and daughter and numerous friends to favor you with news, yet I may hit on something which all of them may omit."[41] His work, which lasted for several years, consisted of brief, straight-forward assessments of business acquaintances with some details on their ethics, their families, their current assets, and their status in the marketplace.

How great was the risk, the clients of the agency wanted to know, if you lent these merchants money? Could they be counted on to pay their debts? The value of Bunker's information, considering his purpose, his sources, and his method, was generally dependable, but the facts were few and the comments perfunctory.

Naturally, there were the critics who decided that this kind of rating was not convenient, because it involved increased paperwork and expense for the merchant; not necessary, because if the customer did not have the cash, he should not make the purchase; not reliable, considering that business affairs changed too quickly to remain valid in a dated report; and not democratic, in view of the fact that it was the kind of transaction that favored the upper class over the lower. Orison Adams, for one, a tradesman in Nantucket, announced in the *Inquirer* in 1855 that:

> The subscriber having satisfied himself by many years' experience that the credit system is both unequal and disadvantageous has resolved that on and after January 1, 1855, he will offer his present complete stock of goods for cash only at such prices as will suit all who may favor him with their patronage.[42]

A later blast from the opposition, which made it clear that not all the faults in the system had been corrected, was published by William Yates Chinn in 1896:

> In the role of busybodies and tale-bearers, the mercantile agencies make of themselves not only a neighborhood nuisance, but they have made themselves a national menace, oppression and a fear of them a very natural result.[43]

Moreover, secrecy was paramount. Since credit reports could easily be considered spying and ready-made material for a lawsuit, all the parties involved were bound to operate in private. Bunker found that the information he sought had to be collected and transmitted with great care. He sounded a warning in the postscript to one of his letters to his correspondent:

> N.B. My acquaintance with the character of merchants inspires me with the belief that your subscribers on receiving post haste information will be careful not to implicate the informant. Should a subscriber in consequence of the above information immediately give Barrett to understand that he was informed as to the above, how natural would it be for me to be suspected and the more so as they probably do not know of such an agency. Mr. Cleveland must bear with me for a while. I shall soon get over my qualms. I write not to get reassurance. These things naturally suggested themselves on account of my delicate position.[44]

But the undercover transfer of sensitive business information was as common then as it is today. When Francis L. Crosby arrived in Peru in 1862, he worked for a short time in a sugar factory owned by his brother Matthew Jr. and his cousin, the other Lewis Tappan. Asked by the manager to report in secret about what he had heard said among the employees with regard to the operations of the firm, he refused to comply and quit the job. Needless to say, he was probably shortly replaced by someone whose ethics were more pliable and more in line with usual practice.[45]

Bunker's entry for Matthew, "ship owner and manufacturer of oil and candles" reads as follows:

> Has a family, his mansion $2500, Candle house $1000, land and buildings at head of Commercial Wharf $3000, Siasconset house $1400, lot on Washington St. $400, grass lots $500, probably one share Commercial Wharf $700, assessors give him ½ Ship Washington $15,000, 3/16 Ship Mariner $6000, ⅕ Ship American $6000, 5/16 Ship Navigator $12,500, interest in Ship Senator $1000, oil stock, notes, cash, etc. $40,000, his family is large and their expenses no doubt at least $2000 a year, very methodical in business.[46]

The value of the listed assets amounts to about $90,000, but by itself, that figure does not convey enough information to enable us to establish Matthew's real worth. We are dealing with a very general measure of wealth at a specific time and not with a precise statement of income and expenses over the course of several years. Bunker leaves out of his calculation, for instance, several other vessels, houses, and lots, as well as the proceeds from the sales of oil and candles, and the value of other investments, rents, and mortgages, all of which returned a profit. These assets, however, may have been considered too numerous to include separately in a summary report and some, or all, were likely gathered up in the catch-all category valued at $40,000. Given the margin for error, the total of $90,000 does, in fact, come fairly close to Matthew's own recent balance sheet. In 1841 he estimated the gross value of his assets at $141,418. If the losses on ships, oil stocks, and debts owed were deducted, the total net worth might be reduced to about $88,500. In 1843, when there was less debt, but also less income, the net worth was down to about $80,000. Bunker then probes a little deeper based on information obtained from an unnamed informant:

> N.B. it has been said by some one that this person is always full of money, yet he could not see how it could be so unless he hired a considerable money; that his ships could never have made much money; that the firm of Matthew Crosby and Son did not exist; that about two years since a dissolution of co-partnership was announced once or twice in the newspaper and quietly withdrawn. I have good reason to believe that he hires 18,000 dollars.[47]

The reference to the Crosby firm (presumably of Matthew and his son, William) is hard to explain, in that if it did not exist, then why were the announcements of dissolution withdrawn? We know from Matthew's letter to Henry Phelon in 1842 that he and his son were acting together in what might well have been considered a firm. Whether it was registered legally is another question. There appears to be no way to substantiate the allegation, which may be more rumor than fact. As if he, himself, were also inclined to question its value, Bunker admits, "but in point I may be misinformed."[48]

More interesting is the charge against Matthew that his ships were less profitable than they appeared to be and that he had borrowed as much as $18,000. It is true that, often enough, whaleships returned to port with too little to show for several years at sea, but there is no way to know what Bunker's correspondent thought was a good return, nor to be sure what particular year, or years, he had in mind. With so many factors involved, we have seen earlier how difficult it is to calculate precise figures for profit and loss. Nevertheless, since we are already familiar with four of the five ships cited by Bunker, we can take a single voyage for each one during the years concerned as an example to estimate the returns and to gain a better understanding of what Matthew was able to earn from investments in whaling. Assuming that Matthew's share included the vessel and the outfit, a comparison can be set out in the following table of estimated values:

Table 7.

**Matthew Crosby's interest in selected whaleships**

| Ship | Matthew's interest | Years at sea | Sperm oil (barrels) | Value | Matthew's share |
|---|---|---|---|---|---|
| Washington | ½ (50%) | 1843–1847 | 1,613 | $ 52,132 | $ 18,246 |
| American | ⅕ (20%) | 1841–1845 | 1,890 | 53,222 | 7,450 |
| Mariner | 3⁄16 (19%) | 1840–1844 | 1,632 | 47,524 | 6,321 |
| Navigator | 5⁄16 (31%) | 1841–1845 | 1,737 | 55,841 | 12,117 |

As was customary, and as noted above in the case of the *Charles Carroll*, the value of the cargo was divided between the owners-agents of the vessel on the one hand, and the captain, officers, and crew on the other. If the share of the owners was 70%, a not unusual amount, Matthew's gross profit may be calculated on that portion of the total value. In the case of the *Washington*, for example, in which he held a 50% interest, this amounted to about $18,240. But there were further expenses to be deducted, such as those costs listed in Chapter 3, which we might estimate at 5%–10%. The net profit to Matthew, therefore, might have been between $17,000 and $18,000. The table shows only sperm oil, but the *Washington*, the *Mariner*, and the *Navigator*, also brought small quantities of whale oil and whalebone which probably increased the combined proceeds of those vessels by another $1,000 or so.

If Matthew's initial investments in the four ships amounted to almost $40,000, according to Bunker's reports, and the four voyages cited brought him about $44,000–45,000, his net gain was relatively modest. But he was glad to get what he could. Given the risks involved, his outlook was invariably conservative. In a letter written in 1840 to his nephew, William Wyer, who managed a farm in Ohio, Matthew surveyed the returns on several whaleships as, "all doing a fair business, although we cannot as you do get [a good] crop every year; if we get a good one every four years we think ourselves lucky."[49]

On the other hand, the results of these four voyages have to be seen as a part of the productive thirty-five years that the ships were at sea. The *Washington* made nine voyages (three for Zenas Coffin and six for Matthew) over twenty-one years; the *American* made seven over twenty-six years; the *Mariner* made five over seventeen years; and the *Navigator* made three over thirteen years. All together, they brought home nearly 40,000 barrels of sperm oil for a market value of a little over a million dollars. This amount of oil returned by Matthew's ships, moreover, was in line with the average number of barrels returned per whaling cruise by all American vessels as set out in the following table:[50]

Table 8.

**Average return of sperm oil landed by American ships, 1842–1847**

| Year | Barrels | Year | Barrels |
|------|---------|------|---------|
| 1842 | 1,973 | 1845 | 1,291 |
| 1843 | 1,641 | 1846 | 1,350 |
| 1844 | 1,419 | 1847 | 1,505 |

One swallow did not make a summer, and one whaleship, as we have seen, generally did not make a fortune. Matthew, like most owners, had several vessels at sea during the same time, so that the aggregate profit was certainly more than that entered here. Although there are doubtless many lacunae in these calculations, such as the amount of oil sold during the voyage; oil shipped home but not reported; the final market price when the oil was sold; and the added costs of refining and transport, the figures are substantially correct. We know that Matthew was well regarded as a successful businessman in the select group of leading Nantucket investors, and that there seems to be no question that, in spite of later major losses, he was earning more than enough during the period we are concerned with to offset the negative view reported by Bunker's informant

It is also true, as noted previously, that Matthew, like most whaling merchants, carried a good deal of debt. What he borrowed, however, was well managed and what he owed was paid off. The assertion in Bunker's letter that Matthew could not be worth so much unless he hired money and that, in fact, he now had $18,000 outstanding, was included as a standard part of the credit-rating report and, by itself, should have raised no concerns. It probably was not taken to imply that borrowing was, in some way, suspect. Unless debt grew unchecked by inattention or over-confidence to the point where it exceeded assets, it was not to be considered a weakness in his financial arrangements. The new American nation, after all, was born in debt, and more was added by the War of 1812. But it survived, barely, by finally putting in place a unified taxing authority.

In 1851, Abner Forbes and J.W. Greene published a book entitled *The Rich Men of Massachusetts, Containing a Statement of the Reputed Wealth of about Fifteen Hundred Persons*. Their purpose, they said…:

> …was not only to furnish encouragement to the young from contemplation of success resulting from a suitable combination of those sterling qualities: Perseverance, Energy, Carefulness, Economy, Integrity, Honesty, but also to excite in the minds of the wealthy, and of all who shall become such, greater attention to the importance of an enlarged system of Benevolence.[51]

It was an endeavor that sold copies by appealing to the abiding interest of the public in knowing who had the money, how they got it, and what they did with it. Their wealth was made to appear acceptable, first by having been acquired honestly through hard work, and second, by having had a portion of it shared with the poor. It was an expression of the familiar Puritan work-ethic secularized in the nineteenth century to emphasize the importance of labor considered as much a "vocation" as a way to be socially useful.

In the list for Nantucket, the names of twenty-three men were arranged in alphabetical order with a note, where possible, on their occupation, whether their fortune was made or inherited, and to what extent they were charitably-minded. Matthew Crosby is there (rated at $50,000), along with Joseph Starbuck ($200,000) and his three sons, George, Joseph, and William (each at $60,000); Nathaniel Barney ($100,000); William Hadwen ($150,000); the two sons of Zenas Coffin, Charles and Henry (each at $80,000); and Matthew's

*Nathaniel Barney (1792–1869), 1860s.*   *Joseph Starbuck (1774–1861), 1860s.*   *William Hadwen (1791–1862), 1850s.*

son-in-law, Thomas Macy (at $90,000). Altogether the twenty-three were worth an impressive $1,695,000. Nineteen, including Matthew, were said to have "commenced poor," which gave added importance to their achievement, and eleven, also including Matthew, were credited with some degree of "benevolence."

This was the beginning of an age of organized philanthropy in the United States, and charitable contributions were becoming as important to solid social standing as a good address, a fine house, and a respectable business. But, as the authors warned the reader, the information presented made "no great pretension to exactness." The Nantucket entries, in particular, if not inexact, suffered from a paucity of information and comments. The absence of quite a few successful and well-regarded merchants of the town, for instance, and the meager biographical data compared with entries for the mainland towns, gave the list less authority than it claimed. Nevertheless, in spite of these limitations, *Rich Men* remains a useful comparative index to the material and social achievements of a portion of the mid-century New England plutocracy. In an era of significant entrepreneurial and technical advances, Matthew and his colleagues had an important part to play, although they did not have to wait for Forbes and Greene to realize their success in the world.

To put the history in perspective, these were the same years in which Cornelius Vanderbilt (1794–1877), an exact contemporary of Matthew, was founding the family fortune, first in shipping and then in railroads, and making his name a household word. For him, outsize ambition, luck, and perseverance brought riches beyond the dreams of Croesus, but in practice, it often meant manhandling the law, national governments, and any business partners who got in the way. In comparison, Nantucket business was also international, albeit on a smaller scale, and the rewards were substantial, if less impressive, but cut-throat commercial tactics could not survive for very long among the intimate group of friends and colleagues on the island.

*The 1870s view includes New North (Steamboat), North, Straight, and South wharves, and the lighthouse on Brant Point.*

181

# 5. Down Main Street

*"Down Main Street." The Square, looking east toward Straight Wharf, circa 1870.*

In his autobiographical letter, written in April 1875, when he was eighty-four years old, Matthew confessed to being in feeble health, so that:

> for the past three weeks I have only been down along three times, as we have had a cold, bleak winter…I am now the oldest person on Main Street, except Jesse Coffin. All my old friends have gone home and I must soon follow.[1]

By "down along," he meant the short walk from his house to Market Square, the name given to that part of the street framed to the west by the Pacific Bank and to the east by the old Rotch warehouse, bought in 1861 by the Pacific Club, which architecture thereby neatly symbolized, in sturdy brick, the wealth (stored in the bank) created by the whaling industry (which operated most successfully in the Pacific Ocean).[2] Lined on both sides with shops and offices, it had long been, and still is, the social and commercial center of the town. It was the meeting place for Matthew and his friends where they gathered and shared the news, told their stories, and daily renewed the relations that bound the families of the small community together. Now that he managed only a weekly visit, it must have seemed a telling loss which foretold the coming end of a long and active life. He could, nevertheless, take some satisfaction in knowing that he had become the next oldest member of the local merchants' group. Jesse Coffin, who had spent his early life at sea aboard a whaleship, but had been retired for the last twenty-five years, died in July 1880 at 91 years and would be remembered as "a kind neighbor and a good citizen."[3] In that intimate society, even though Jesse does not appear to have been a close acquaintance, it is not surprising that Matthew knew how old he was.

Of course, there is no daily record of what those captains and shipowners talked about, but some idea of what may have interested them can be had from a letter that Matthew wrote to Henry Coffin, the son of Zenas and the brother of his first wife, Lydia, in May 1833. It is short enough to be worth quoting, since it brings us as close as we can come to the mind and thoughts of the man at forty-two years of age. The text has been left as it was written in one paragraph, but in a few cases spelling and punctuation have been corrected:

> Being something at leisure, I thought I would write a line or two believing that they will be acceptable. Your letters or journal to Eunice came to hand a few days since… We were glad to hear that your health had improved and by the tenor of your letters we have no doubt of the fact, or you could not have climbed the precipices and mountains

*Lower Main Street, circa 1860. The Rotch warehouse (center) was built in 1775 and restored after it was damaged in the Great Fire of 1846.*

as stated. I am much pleased to hear that you intended to go up the Mediterranean and through France to London. I think you will be much delighted, at least I think I should, was I in your place. From what I have heard the Mediterranean is delightful country. How much mistaken were the ancient people when they came down to the mouth of that sea, with the pillars of Hercules on each side, and said this is the *ne plus ultra*, no more beyond. I am in hopes your health will continue to improve, that you may

*The earliest known photograph of Main Street, circa 1845, before the Great Fire of 1846. Pictured to the left is part of the façade of the Pacific Bank, separated by Liberty Street from a corner of the Methodist Church (at center with single column). The other stores and buildings on the north side were all destroyed in the conflagration.*

feel able to visit the most interesting parts of Europe before your return home…I will now try to give you all the news I can think of. Our family are generally pretty well. Henry Swift lost his oldest boy with the whooping cough about 5 months since. We have added a girl to our family five weeks since and at present all well. The *Constitution* arrived the middle of last month 1230 bbl. whale oil. The *Aurora* last week all full; also the *Hero* and *Ann* both full… The *Mary* 700 bbl. in November; the *American* 1200 in December; *Catharine* 1150 bbl. November; *Phebe* 2600; *Spartan* 1100; etc. etc. The *Lydia* will be along soon. She had 2200, the *Zenas* had got round 4 and a third month at Paita 200 bbl., the *Lima* at Paita in the first month 1250, stopping a leak forward. Oil is now worth 80 cents cash. We are getting along with Commercial Wharf. We have five ships now at the wharf, and expect the *Hero* and *Ann* tomorrow. We have got our digging

*Main Street on the north side, circa 1880, with a sign for the Institution for Savings above the awning. The horses and wagons, like the motor cars today, are drawn diagonally to the curb to save space.*

machine at work and she performed admirably. We have already made water enough above the upper tier for two ships to heave out…I have got the old Cary house put up opposite Jared's store and our new meeting house is now framing to go up where it came from. Charles has nearly got his house finished and will move in in two or three months. Captain Joy in the *Charles and Henry* was spoken off St. Catharine. All well 60 days out. The *Washington* also 65 days out. The *Mariner* put into St. Catharine 60 days out having sprung the main mast. The *Phebe* lost 4 men with the scurvy, one of them John Barrett's son, William. The ship *Catharine* of Salem, Henry Paddack, master, put into Valparaiso to repair damages and while there Captain Paddack in a fit of delirium killed two clerks in the store of a merchant that was doing his business [and] afterward ran out and stabbed the governor of Juan Fernández and killed him and wounded 5 or 6 others severely. He was arrested and condemned to be shot. The American consul interfered and a new trial granted. [He] was condemned again, but [the] American [consul] interfered again and the sentence put off again for further evidence. We hope he will be spared; still it is uncertain. It is quite sickly among children. William Mitchell lost one of his twins yesterday. Sarah Barker died a month ago. William Remsen, son of Arnold, fell from the foretop of ship *Montano* a few days since and died in 8 hours after. Charles has purchased the South Friends' Meeting house for $3700, I presume for you. Judith Jones, mother of Daniel, died last week. The *Constitution* is going the same voyage again,

*Main Street on the south side, circa 1870, between Union and Orange Streets, with the array of small shops, including those of a photographer and a shoemaker.*

same captain. Captain Edwards goes in *Montano*. We are expecting *Independence* soon, as the captain stated he should be home this month. He had only 1600 bbl., last out 12 months." [From this point some parts of the letter are missing]: "Please give my respects to Captain…my letter much longer than… [un]able to think of anything more…hoping that your health…

Respectfully yours, Matthew [added at the end]: Cousin Peleg Mitchell died last winter. The Fabius arrived…Thomas & Eunice is [sic] going to Philadelphia next week…a temperance meeting, Mary C. goes with them.[4]

As we should expect, most of the references are to his family and business life. Eunice was the daughter of Zenas Coffin, Henry's sister, and the wife of Thomas Macy. Early historians named the cliffs on either side of the Straits of Gibraltar, "The Pillars of Hercules," which were said to have been once inscribed with a warning to mariners not to travel farther west, *ne plus ultra*, which irony must have appealed to Matthew.

The most likely person named Henry Swift was he who had married Henry Coffin's sister, Mary. They may well have had an infant lost to whooping cough, a common and often fatal disease in the nineteenth century. Even on Nantucket, known for its healthy climate, childhood illness and death were strikingly prevalent. In his journal for August 1817, Obed Macy reflected the general concern that "It is very sickly among the children this season, many have died of the whooping cough and other diseases."[5] In 1826, a Health Committee was appointed with a Health Officer "to remove all filth of any kind…in any of the streets, lanes, wharves, docks, or in any other place whatever within the limits of the town…whenever such filth shall in their judgment endanger the lives or the health of the inhabitants thereof."[6] It was seen to be a critical issue, and the fine for private citizens who refused to comply with the law was set at the enormous amount of $100 (or about $2,000 in today's currency).

The girl added was Judith Crosby, the fifth child of Matthew and Elizabeth and the only one to die before her father. Eighteen ships are mentioned in the space of three pages, some of which were owned by Matthew (*Washington* and *Lima*), some by Henry Coffin and his brother, Charles (*Constitution, Lydia, Zenas Coffin, Charles and Henry,* and *Independence*), and others by close friends like Paul Jones (*Mary* and *Spartan*), Jared Coffin (*Ann* and *Catharine*), and Joseph Starbuck (*Hero*). Commercial Wharf, as we have seen, was a major construction project in which Matthew and Henry were involved. The Edward Cary house on Fair Street between Ray's Court and Moors Lane, was purchased by the Society of Friends in January 1833 to clear the site for a new meeting house. The lumber was sold to Matthew for a warehouse on the south side of Commercial Wharf near Jared Coffin's store. Charles, who had almost finished his house at 78 Main Street, was Charles G. Coffin, Henry's brother and business partner.

Regarding the other references in Matthew's letter: St. Catharine, now Florianopolis, is a port on the southern coast of Brazil, which meant that the ships were still in the Atlantic Ocean. John Barrett, who lost his son, was not Matthew's neighbor in 'Sconset who also owned the house at 72 Main Street in town, but an older man, although they both had a son named William. The success of the captains responsible for his floating investments, many of whom he knew personally, was so much on his mind that the reports on their undertakings intrude at every moment in his narrative without any sense of incongruity. Indeed, this was probably just the kind of information that Henry Coffin was eager to hear. The brief life (he died at twenty-nine years) and mysterious end of Henry Paddack, therefore, was undoubtedly of interest to all his friends involved in maritime enterprise. The *Catharine* had left Salem in March 1832 and was reported burned off Hawaii in 1834. In the small island community of Nantucket, Henry's sister, Eunice, had married Obed Starbuck, the nephew of Joseph, who built the famous three brick houses on Main Street, and Matthew naturally took the side of the captain.

William Mitchell, the father of Maria, the astronomer, was cashier of the Pacific Bank and a longtime acquaintance. His twins, Eliza and Henry, who were born on September 16, 1830, lived, respectively, for three years and for seventy-two. Sarah Barker was born eight years before Matthew's father, Sylvanus, so her death at ninety-three was worth a note. The *Montano* was one of Matthew's ships, hence the remark about the unfortunate young William who died at thirty-four years.[7] Once again, the Charles in question, who bought the Friends meeting house on the corner of Main and Pleasant Streets, was Charles G. Coffin and, like Matthew, he used the materials for construction on Commercial Wharf.

Daniel Jones, a dealer in ships' supplies, had a warehouse on Straight Wharf and a house at 5 Orange Street. David N. Edwards enjoyed a long career as captain of several important whaling vessels, including the *Montano*, *Paragon*, *Harvest*, and *Nantucket*. There is a reference to another family relationship with the mention of the death of Peleg Mitchell late in 1831, the father of William Mitchell, just cited. He had another son named Peleg (Jr.), who married Mary Ann Whippey, and the Whippeys were connected to the Crosbys by the fact that Mary Ann's uncle, Benjamin, was the husband of Matthew's sister, Huldah.

The letter begins and ends with the Thomas Macys. Thomas was a staunch supporter of good causes supporting true religion, proper morals, and the popular temperance movement. There was a convention held in Philadelphia on May 24, 1833, which is where they were headed. Eunice died in 1843 and Thomas, who was nineteen years older, followed her in 1864, "a worthy and respected member of the Nantucket Monthly Meeting of Friends," but, as we learn from the family papers, a very difficult and self-centered man.

It is evident from reading the letter that Matthew's chief concern was news of the whaleships and oil cargoes that his livelihood depended on at the time. We can also infer that, while not a prolific letter-writer, he was more than willing to correspond with friends and relatives in his spare time. He had heard about some countries in Europe, but he had never been abroad and understood very little about them or their history. There are entries in his daybooks which refer to political concerns in Washington and in the country at large, and some that even provide information on events in the foreign capitals he knew something about, but they consist of general summaries gleaned from newspapers or letters with no attempt to comment on them further. But this is hardly surprising. His education and experience were more than sufficient to pave his way to success on Nantucket, and a practical mind in those circumstances was of greater value than time spent in scholarly inquiry or philosophical reflection, even if he had been able and so inclined. If we include other references in the diaries that have to do largely with money-matters, bills, loans, debts, profits, losses, and investments of one kind and another, as well as notices of the weather, crops, visitors to the island, and the births and deaths of family and friends, we can be reasonably sure that we have a good sense of the topics that made up the conversations on the Square.

As we are well aware, Matthew liked numbers. All his working life, he added up figures to document his current standing, and this concern shows up constantly in his personal papers: how many ships he had; how many barrels of oil they brought home, how many pounds of whalebone, and the current market price for all these commodities; gains and losses in stocks and bonds; a formula for the calculation of interest; the sum of loans outstanding; the cost in damages caused by the great fires on the island; the number of passengers recorded from Nantucket to Boston in 1858 (in order to determine the value of shares in the steamboat company); the distance from Nantucket to New York and the time it took to make the journey by sail or steam; export figures for the United States, Great Britain, and the West Indies. From time to time there are some oddities, like the weight of the cannons carried on the steamship *Merrimac*, or the salaries of officials in the federal government. But mostly the entries are routine, such as the years in which his friends died; the number of children he had; or the number of cords of wood needed for the winter and other expenses needed to run a household which continued to grow with the years and with his success in the business world.

With regard to the last point, we can catch a glimpse of home life in an excerpt from a set of entries for food and supplies purchased at various times during the period from March 1819 to March 1820, and from March 1835 to the end of that year. The items listed are taken from both years to illustrate the variety of goods. Specific dates are omitted and the prices, of course, varied from week to week and are copied here simply for comparative purposes. Amounts are not always given, so it is difficult to know from these figures how much a certain quantity of, say, honey, soap, or knives cost. The expected staples are noted, along with a few high-priced imports, but there is no account for seafood, which must have been often on the menu:[8]

Table 9.

**Cost of selected household staples, 1819–1820 & 1835**

| Item | Cost | Item | Cost |
|---|---|---|---|
| 1 ham | $ 1.50 | 1 barrel flour | $ 8.50 |
| honey | .50 | coffee | 2.50 |
| tea | 11.20 | 8 gallons molasses | 4.32 |
| soap | 1.50 | 1 bottle lavender water | 1.26 |
| 1 bushel corn | .80 | 1 bushel potatoes | .50 |
| beets & beans | .50 | 1 firkin butter | .18 |
| rum & gin | 3.00 | figs | 5.00 |
| 1 barrel dried apples | 3.50 | 1 goose | .60 |
| cabbage | .75 | turnips | 1.00 |
| 1 keg raisins | 8.00 | 1 keg lard | 7.00 |
| 1 barrel beef | 14.00 | 100 lbs. sugar | 22.38 |
| 3 hogs | 25.00 | 3 tons coal | 27.00 |
| knives | 7.50 | 38½ lbs. feathers | 15.20 |
| carpets | 146.00 | silverware | 24.51 |
| umbrella | 4.25 | cloth for a coat | 13.50 |
| waistcoat pattern, hosiery | 8.25 | jacket, boots, shoes, hats | 25.00 |
| book on the Indian wars | 1.25 | | |

There were other bills, of course, due from the town, from commercial firms, and from tradesmen for routine expenses of various kinds. These included taxes, business debts, costs of travel to the mainland, maintenance and repairs on the house, a blacksmith's invoice for shoeing horses and for making bolts, bars, hinges, and other iron work on Matthew's ships, the construction of a tryworks for the oil factory, allowances to his children, and a gift of silk cloth for his wife. Shopping was generally for practical purposes. Some of the clothing was made at home, but even in this relatively early period in his career, the aggregate Crosby household expenses in the two years presented here, supported by a run of successful whaling ventures, increased from about $600 in 1819–1820 to more than $5,000 in 1835, a remarkable ninefold rise. The accounts given are not complete, a few high-priced items may well have been left out, some routine expenses omitted, and Matthew is often unclear on final costs. But there seems to be no question that by wise investments, and with a good deal of luck, Matthew had achieved a comfortable living for himself and for his family.

We are concerned, of course, with market conditions that affected a minority group of the population. Not all the islanders were so fortunate, and it is useful to appreciate the social and economic differences involved. Because of its peculiar geography and growing economy, Nantucket in these years was becoming an increasingly expensive place to live. The constant grumbling heard today about the high cost of living on the island, but which in no way impedes the high-spending tourist traffic, has a long history. Already in 1824, the *Inquirer* took up the issue of rising prices, as well as that of falling quality, for household goods:

> It has become a subject of serious and general complaint, that our markets are supplied with fresh provisions in less quantity, and at rates far more exorbitant, than those of any place on the continent of North America. It is true we are forced to obtain our supplies from abroad—almost every mouthful we devour is imported; but that furnishes no apology for impositions which it is our fate to endure. Provisions, which in Boston or New York would be ordered overboard by the police, are publickly offered to our nostrils and our stomachs at prices abominably disproportionate. Our fresh provisions in general are stale, lean, and of the most inferior quality; while the most extravagant prices are demanded for them.[9]

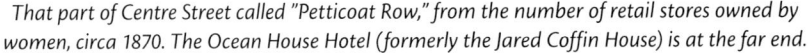

*That part of Centre Street called "Petticoat Row," from the number of retail stores owned by women, circa 1870. The Ocean House Hotel (formerly the Jared Coffin House) is at the far end.*

The editors then presented a comparison of island and mainland (Cincinnati) prices:

Table 10.

**Comparative grocery prices: Nantucket and the mainland, 1824**

|  | Nantucket | Cincinnati |
|---|---|---|
| Poultry / pound | 12½ cents | 2½ cents |
| Beef / pound | 10 cents | 3 cents |
| Pork / pound | 10 cents | 2½ cents |
| Veal /pound | 10 cents | 3 cents |
| Mutton / pound | 8 cents | 2 cents |
| Wood / cord | $ 5.50 | 75 cents |

These complaints, set out with striking comparisons in order to make a point, were undoubtedly based on realistic figures, but for the most part they were irrelevant for Nantucket, which had to be supplied by sea, whose inhabitants were always charged a premium, and for those families who had earned enough money to absorb the higher costs which they had to pay.

As Matthew prospered, and as his influence grew among his group of friends and associates, a walk down Main Street led to interests and undertakings besides whaleships, oil, and candles. In 1828, he did his duty as a surveyor of highways, and in 1834, as a member of a grand jury. But his experience as a mariner and shipowner naturally drew him to participate in the current discussions about two projects in particular that agitated the public. One was the long-debated question of the best way to deal with the sandbar that stretched across the entrance to the harbor, and the other was the feasibility of anchoring a lightship on Tuckernuck shoal.

With regard to the bar, the difficulties it caused for the whaleships and the temporary solution offered by the "camels" have already been noted. The problem had been talked about for many years. At a town meeting in 1803, it was voted to dig out the obstruction and to petition the United States Congress to share the expenses.[10] The plan was to "extend piers into the sea" in order to form a narrow channel which would then be kept open by the ebb and flow of the tides. The congressional committee that came to inspect the conditions was skeptical, and rightly so, that the tides would be so obedient, and the request for funding was denied. They were sufficiently impressed, however, by the need for some answer to the threat of long-term decline of the whaling industry to order a survey of the harbor to be made with more precise figures. The report was submitted in September, at an estimated cost of $16,000 to dredge the channel and another $38,000 to build the piers. This was evidently too expensive, and the petition was again denied.

The project languished until 1828, when a breakwater near Brant Point was proposed by the U.S. Topographical Engineers to create an artificial harbor, at a cost of between $250,000 and $898,393, depending on the size required. Such are the inscrutable machinations of governmental agencies, in this case, to reject an uncertain proposition in favor of another uncertain one costing twenty times as much. Needless to say, the latest estimate was set aside in favor of a return to the original plan, but there was still no aid forthcoming from Washington.[11]

So it fell to the Nantucket merchants and shipowners to take up the slack, and in May 1828 they organized a group of interested parties to draw new plans, to solicit subscriptions, and to carry out the work. The names of those involved are the ones we should expect: Jared Coffin, Levi Starbuck, Philip H. Folger, James Athearn, Benjamin Gardner, and Matthew Crosby as clerk of the committee.[12] Eager to proceed, they hired a crew and bought digging equipment, but, alas, it was not a job for amateurs. Costs escalated, they spent more money than they thought reasonable, and the end came before much of anything had been done.

The degree of frustration on the part of the islanders can be gauged by the outlandish proposal from a Reverend C. Rich, picked up by *Hunt's Magazine* in 1845. His plan was to cut the island in half by digging a canal two miles long from the harbor to the south shore at a cost of about $9,000. The rush of the water, he argued, would keep it deep and navigable for years to come.[13] There is no need to take the idea seriously in order to appreciate the sardonic wit or to believe in the importance of the issue behind it. In fact, it was not until the 1880s, long after the decline of the whaling industry (in support of which the work was first conceived) that the government agreed to finance a simple stone jetty; and not until the 1890s was a second, and necessary, jetty built to ensure a permanent open passage into and out of the harbor. Ironically, this late construction helped to promote the tourist trade, which was attracted to the island by the climate, but also in large part by the surviving architectural treasure which had been financed by the whaleship owners who failed to profit by it.

Marking the dangerous waters around the island also became an issue for the federal government, which was dealt with more expeditiously, and with more success, than the infamous sandbar. Matthew had a part in the negotiations concerning the need for a new lighthouse on Brant Point and a lighthouse on Tuckernuck shoal at the west end of the island. There was no argument about the utility of lamps and candles to guide mariners at sea. A tower with a light had been built on Great Point in 1785, and a new stone lighthouse, sixty feet high, replaced it in 1818. When the structure on Brant Point fell into serious disrepair by 1824, Matthew, along with Jared Coffin, George Macy, Benjamin Gardner, and a few others, urged the construction of a new building. In this, they were immediately successful. A new wooden house and tower were put up with a variety of oil lamps to insure a safe passage between the sound and the harbor.

*The lighthouse tower and keeper's house erected on Brant Point in 1856.
The brown color was changed to a more visible white in 1895.*

With regard to Tuckernuck shoal, a committee was formed in 1826 to reply to a letter of inquiry from Congressman John Read, who asked for an opinion on such a project. Once again a group of experienced captains was convened, including Zenas Coffin, David Worth, Hezekiah Barnard, Gideon Gardner, Gideon Folger, and Peter Chase, with Matthew Crosby as secretary. Various options were discussed at length, but the group determined that it was not possible to build a lighthouse there. "The tides," they said, "run about three miles per hour across said shoal and we are apprehensive it [sic] may run the sand from under the foundation an [sic] cause the building to fall." Instead, they proposed a lightship to be built and moored at the proper place, which would be of great public benefit "by saving much property and many lives."[14] The suggestion was carried through two years later, and a ship was positioned off the northeast coast of the little island. In 1852, it was moved farther to the north and named *Cross Rip*.

Lightships, buoys, and even lighthouses were subject to displacement or destruction by the elements, and because of storms, fog, shifting sands, and inadequate charts, they could never guarantee a safe passage. Vessels continued to come to grief off the coast. Closely connected to these endeavors with which Matthew was engaged, therefore, was the further concern to establish several new lifesaving stations and refuges at strategic points around the island. These latter were the so-called Humane Houses, the first of which had been erected on Great Point at Coskata as early as 1794. In 1830, Philip H. Folger launched an initiative to enlist subscribers to fund the building of ten huts, at $50 each, to provide temporary shelter for shipwrecked sailors who managed to reach the shore. They were each to be equipped with a fireplace and chimney, a supply of wood, hatchets, lanterns, candles,

*The stylish Surfside life-saving station, built in 1856, with later additions. The Humane Houses, on the other hand, were much smaller and of simpler construction.*

and matches.[15] It was a proposal which caught the interest of many of the same men, including Matthew, Joseph Starbuck, Henry Swift Charles G. and Henry Coffin, Jared Coffin, and Hadwen & Barney, who had made their fortunes from the unforgiving sea. In short, this was a local charitable undertaking that benefited greatly from their ready financial support. By the beginning of 1832, there were thirteen refuges in place, fully equipped in case of emergency.

All of these plans, whether for private gain or public benefit, or partly for both, testify to the concern and sense of responsibility of the well-to-do for the improvement of life on the island. There was an underside to daily living, of course, and in this respect, Nantucket was not much different, except in scale, from other commercial towns. Although the community had never been plagued by a high crime rate, with an increase in population from 5,617 persons in 1800 to 9,712 in 1840, before the major decline began, and a constant stream of transient workmen, its share of delinquency became noticeably greater. Other causes suggested by modern writers have ranged from the lack of authority and discipline in single-parent households, when the father was away at sea for long periods of time, to the deficient school system, which failed to keep the youngsters occupied with their lessons. Reports of juvenile gangs roaming the town at night, destroying property, intimidating elderly citizens, and injuring animals were cited by the editors of the *Inquirer* in April 1824. They called for twenty constables, "men of nerve and muscle," to augment the current force of six.[16] In fact, at the time, there was no regular and trained police force, as we understand the term, but rather watchmen, in some cases old and infirm, who made their rounds in the evening at curfew time. In 1882, Godfrey's Guide mentioned, "two night patrolmen plus a few special police, if needed."[17] Alarms were raised, but little was done. In a town where some of the rowdies were often from families known to each other, there was a natural reluctance to come down on them too heavily. In 1875, instances of crowds of youngsters who gathered nightly on the corners of Main and Orange and Centre Streets, and who blocked the sidewalks and insulted the passersby, were reported by the *Inquirer and Mirror* with nothing more than the comment that such disorder had become a nuisance and should be stopped. Equally tentative was another complaint a few years afterward, following reports of intimidation and vandalism by boys in the streets of the town, that it was "unfortunate that no one has yet been able to recognize or identify the mean rascals."[18] Now and again homeowners took to the press to air their grievances. In 1825, Elijah Pease bought space in the *Inquirer* to announce that:

*Pine Street looking south, circa 1860.*

Having been shamefully annoyed by Boys, I have lodged several complaints in the office of Josiah Hussey, Esqr. [Register of Probate and a Justice of the Peace] which will be put in operation unless the offenders behave well in the future, and in order to detect Rogues hereafter, I shall cause a watch to be kept around my house.[19]

On the other hand, when the ruffians committed serious crimes, action was often swift and certain. In 1841, the members of a gang of thieves operating in New Guinea, the black neighborhood at the south end of Pleasant Street below the old windmills, were arrested, convicted, and sentenced to the House of Correction for terms of four and six months.[20]

In the minds of many citizens, and not just those still conditioned by the Quaker legacy, crime was often thought to be aggravated by alcohol. In a seaport like Nantucket, it was not hard to find examples, and a vigorous crusade for abstinence had been launched at an early date. In 1817, a Society for the Suppression of Intemperance, and other vice and immorality, was established. The members lost no time in complaining to the selectmen that too many licenses to sell liquor had been issued. Men frequented grog shops, ruined their health, and neglected their families. It was recommended that no more than ten "proper persons" in the town be allowed to sell alcohol. Given the relatively small retail sector, this does not appear to have been a severe curtailment of the trade. But it is not surprising that the proposal was opposed by others who argued, in language that could have been heard yesterday, that restricting sales in this way infringed on their rights as individual merchants. In the customary fashion of democratic government, a committee was appointed to study the matter, the results of which were inconclusive.[21] Nevertheless, from time to time official intervention was direct and forceful, as in the case of one Daniel Russell, master mariner, in January 1825:

> The public are hereby informed that Daniel Russell of Nantucket…hath this day been placed under the guardianship of the Selectmen of the town of Nantucket and any contract or bargain of his made without the approbation of the Selectmen of the town of Nantucket will be null and void…Innholders, Retailers, and other persons are hereby forbid [sic] selling him any spirituous liquors of any kind whatsoever, as they will be dealt with therefor according to law.[22]

Temperance enthusiasts were continually overworked, as attested to by an alarmed outburst in the *Inquirer* in December 1854 deploring the "life-threatening rum-holes kept by reprobate Irishmen."[23] This was not an issue with which Matthew was directly concerned, but since it could not help to have influenced family and business relations on the island, he must have been well aware of the voices raised for and against.

Matthew's walk down Main Street would also have brought him into the circle of a number of social, charitable, musical, and literary associations organized at various times for the "improvement" of the people on the island. Quite a few of them, unable to maintain the spirit and enthusiasm which launched them, came and went within a few years. Others were soon joined together to ensure a longer survival. But they all are proof of the need felt by leading members of the community to bring Nantucket into the cultural mainstream of American life and thereby provide an answer to the perennial question that agitated the citizenry: "What shall we do during the winter?"

Matthew seems not to have been a joiner, and there is very little notice in his diaries of active participation in any one of the groups. He did subscribe to the new Atheneum, incorporated in 1834 after a merger of the Nantucket Mechanics Social Library and the Columbian Library Society. But he may have felt this was more a social obligation than an adventure into the world of books and learning. The fact that Charles G. Coffin, a son of Zenas Coffin, and David Joy, an entrepreneur in the manufacture of sperm oil candles, were the founders probably encouraged his participation. In the same way, his support of the short-lived American Art Union, established in New York City in 1840 to promote the sale of paintings by local artists and to educate the public, seems to have been motivated rather by the enthusiasm of his friends than by an abiding interest in art. Membership cards, like the ribbons on a general's chest, were important to announce to the public that you had been

*The Nantucket Atheneum, circa 1870. It was rebuilt in the Grand style after the fire of 1846.*

there, even if little was done. More to his liking, certainly, was a subscription at $4.00 per year to the Commercial Reading and News Room which was "furnished with all the principal newspapers and public journals of the day."

Nevertheless, the muse was occasionally awakened. In his diaries and letters Matthew now and then quotes with approval, but not always accurately, a few lines from the poets which were to be found in popular books of sermons and anthologies, such as those published by the Rev. Isaac Watts (London: 1801) and William Jay (Baltimore: 1833), as well as in a book called *The American Vocalist* (Boston: 1849), which he may have had in his library at home.[24] Two of these verses particularly appealed to him. One, from a tune called "Evening Shade," appears written on the back of his photographic portrait done by Freeman and again in a letter to his nieces in 1875:

> The evening shades of life have stretched themselves along,
> My three-score years are almost fled and like an evening gone.

The other, seemingly a faint echo of Psalm 133, is included in the letter to his children in 1878:

> How pleasant it is to see children and friends agree,
> Each in their [sic] proper stations move,
> And each fulfill his part with sympathizing heart,
> In all the cares of life and love.

One bit of doggerel must have touched his sense of humor since it, too, was copied twice in the daybooks:

> There are some that never hade [sic] a slice of bread
> Particularly nice and wide,
> But it fell upon the sandy floor,
> And always on the butter side.[25]

In spite of the fact that his was a practical turn of mind which found the most satisfactory investments and rewards in business life, Matthew was not indifferent to changes in fashions and modes of elegance. He lived well and in comfort at 90 Main Street with horses and carriages and silverware on the table. He enjoyed the luxury of a summer home and a working farm in 'Sconset and, for a short while, another house in New Bedford. He took trips to the mainland with members of his family when he liked; and he thought well enough of himself, and knew that others thought well enough of him, to decide in 1844, at the age of fifty-three, to have his portrait painted by William Swain. It was the socially correct thing to do. Swain (1803–1847) was a well-known and accomplished artist who lived off-island but visited frequently in the 1830s and 1840s. He had studied and exhibited abroad, and he

*Matthew Crosby at 70, 1861.*   *Matthew Crosby at 80, 1871.*   *Matthew Crosby at 82, December 1873.*

cut a prominent figure at the National Academy of Design (now The National Academy), founded in New York City in 1825. Among a large selection of paintings of Nantucket men and women left by him (or in a few cases attributed to him), there are also several of Matthew's relatives, including Benjamin F. Coffin, Charles G. Coffin, and Barker Burnell. In his own portrait, Matthew looks out at the viewer with an air of calmness and confidence, the mouth is purposeful, but not without a suggestion of good humor, and he is elegantly dressed for the occasion in a black coat and stock with white collar and pleated shirt. The result was evidently judged successful because a year later Matthew's wife, Elizabeth, had her portrait done by Swain as well. That the artist captured a good likeness of Matthew is shown by a comparison with the formal photographs taken by Josiah Freeman in 1861 when Matthew was seventy, in 1871, at age eighty, and in 1873, at age eighty-two. In spite of the lapse of time, the same positive characteristics can be discerned in the older man.

Although profits from whaling had encouraged Nantucket merchants to abandon intensive agriculture, as the industry declined, more and more captains retired and bought land and houses, and more shipowners spread their investments by taking up farming or by increasing the extent of the cropland they already had. New money, therefore, was available to fund an increase in agricultural production, and this tended to blur the distinction between the older subsistence, or homestead, farming, which had always existed at a relatively simple level, and what we might call the modern farming, which used up-to-date methods and equipment, but which was practiced at greater cost. With better feed for the animals, better seeds to plant, and better horses and cattle and hogs to breed, this use of the land was thought by some to be the means by which Nantucketers could insure themselves against want and lift themselves out of the impending economic depression.

A preliminary catalogue drawn up in 1926, which was meant to show the layout in the 1850s, listed ninety-four named farms scattered over the island. Most of them were clustered in the west around Madaket, in the rich loam of the Cato lots (the tract bounded roughly by

Vesper Lane, Atlantic Avenue, and Bartlett Road) and from Hummock Pond to the south shore, to the east along the Polpis road, and then to Quidnet and Siasconset. Matthew came to own important acreage in Cato, but to a greater extent in Siasconset, to the north of the Main Street and to the west and south near Tashama.[26] According to the memorandum written in 1910 by his son, Francis Lewis, the family members and the hired help labored to raise vegetables and fruit from June to October and to care for numerous sheep, cows, horses, pigs, and chickens.[27] There was the seasonal round of plowing, fertilizing, and seeding to be done; hay had to be cut and brought in; the cream was churned into butter; the pigs were butchered; and, with the ready assistance of the blacksmith and the saddler, the carts and tools and harnesses were repaired and kept in order.

That working the land was more than a pastime can be inferred from the detailed agricultural schedules written up by Matthew in his daybooks and by the extent and variety of the crops planted and harvested. We also know that Matthew's 'Sconset neighbors, George B. Upton, Henry Swift, and Barker Burnell, were subscribers to a report written by Henry Colman entitled *European Agriculture and Rural Economy from Personal Observation*, published in London and Boston in 1844, with a second edition in 1849. Colman (1785–1849) was a Unitarian minister who became attracted to country life and was appointed to make a survey of comparative farming techniques with the aim of improving American cultivation and production. He had already proposed an investigation into Massachusetts farming in a letter of 1837. Since Matthew's friends knew the work, it is likely that he, too, made use of the information available.[28]

The soil, which was generally said to be of poor quality on sandy Nantucket, was, in places, surprisingly good. Knowledgeable farmers made the most of the choice spots by renewing the fertility with covers of grass and clover, as well as by generous use of fish guano (not the conventional dried bird-droppings, but, appropriately, cut-up fish parts), hog manure, salt, and seaweed. Kelp (a kind of seaweed) and eelgrass that often washed ashore on the east and south side of the island, were loaded onto carts and sold to farmers. Elizabeth Coffin's stunning oil painting, "Seaweed Gatherers," finished in 1889, shows in detail the technique and the labor involved.[29] If, by chance, the fertilizers from farm and sea were thought to be insufficient, advertisements in the *Nantucket Inquirer* could be found for the widely promoted *poudrette* and *tafeu*, products made mostly from night soil "collected from the sinks and privies of New York City and free from offensive odor," and sold by the Lodi Manufacturing Company.[30]

The main crops planted in the 1850s were wheat, barley, oats, and corn, for which Matthew was getting close to, or exceeding, the average number of bushels per acre for these yields in Massachusetts.[31] Equally impressive was the variety of produce grown on the farm to feed the animals as well as to supply the family table in Siasconset and to be transported to town. The list includes potatoes, turnips, carrots, parsnips, beets (including a coarse variety for cattle feed called mangelwurzels), rutabagas, radishes, onions, squash, cabbage, beans, peas, cucumbers, asparagus, tomatoes, celery, cauliflower, parsley, cherries, pears, peaches, currants, gooseberries, watermelons, cantaloupes, and blueberries.

Since more efficient farming required better organization of field and labor, as well as new incentives to improve the harvests, there was soon a proposal to create an organization to promote these interests. The call was well timed and quickly answered, and in the spring of 1856 at the Atheneum, a group of leading businessmen founded the Nantucket Agricultural Society. The subscribers included Edward W. Gardner, George W. Macy, Francis M. Mitchell, Nathaniel Barney, and William R. Easton, who with several others, were able to raise enough capital to meet the standards set by the state to approve a charter for such an organization and, just as important, to be eligible for subsidies which were to be paid out in premiums as prizes. To promote the association and to encourage public support, a fair was held in September, the first of a long series of such entertainments-with-a-purpose to which farmers, cooks, and artists, were invited to bring examples of their best efforts and to compete for the colored ribbons. Although Matthew, as we know, was not of a nature to throw himself constantly into public

*The Nantucket Agricultural Society presented this award diploma to Phebe Coleman for her crochet work on display at the Society's exhibition held in 1856.*

*Salt haying at Joseph Folger's meadow in Quaise near Polpis Harbor, 1891.*

view or into public office, he undoubtedly took a good deal of satisfaction in his appearance at the autumn fair of 1865, where he exhibited "ten peaches raised at Siasconset, very large and handsome." In 1868, he brought pumpkins, squash, and corn. In 1870, more peaches, and his daughter, Emma, came with "a toilet set, two tidies, and a piece of worsted work."[32] Always drawn to the practical side of life, he may also have made a small contribution to the improvement of farming, since among his papers, and attributed to him, is a drawing for an automatic hog feeder, dated May 3, 1872. This was a box designed, he wrote:

> for farmers who are feeding corn to their hogs and are absent at times from home, [which] will be found convenient to put in all the corn they will want while they are absent and the hogs will help themselves when hungry and no corn will be wasted if the top is tite [sic] to keep out the wet.[33]

Whether the invention was ever patented or put into production is unknown. While the explanation of it seems clear enough, it is difficult to say exactly how it was supposed to work. If the date on the manuscript is correct, Matthew was then more than eighty years old, so that this idea may simply have been the work of an idle hour.

In spite of enthusiastic editorials in the newspaper extolling the fairs as one of the best means to encourage the economic recovery of island industry, they seem never to have been a huge success. Slowly it was becoming clear that the opportunities for reviving profitable industries on Nantucket were limited and that a return to the extraordinary productivity of the whaling days envisioned by some idealists was out of the question. Yet, the grip of the past and its glories was very strong. "Let us have a higher ambition than to make Nantucket only a watering place, or a place for summer resort," urged the editors of the *Inquirer and Mirror* in 1865, little realizing that it was precisely the growing influx of summer residents and visitors from the mainland that was to be the new industry that would assure the blossoming of new wealth in land and services. In an attempt to explain the lack of attendance at the fair, the editorial blamed, first, the steamboat company, which had neglected to arrange the usual special excursions from New Bedford that year; and, second, the officials of the fair, who had failed to hire a brass band![34] If continued success depended largely on ensuring arrangements of that kind, it is no wonder that the fair failed to develop into a strong community enterprise.

Although farming was never abandoned on the island, land for crops and cattle continued to give way to the development of new housing and roads. Better communications with ports on the mainland allowed the rapid delivery of provisions on a larger scale, and the number of people engaged with their hands in the soil, as it were, decreased with every passing year. Moreover, the tourists came for the most part during a short three- or four-month season and failed to provide a permanent structure for long-term investment. In this regard, we might leave the last word on the Nantucket agricultural revolution to Matthew. In the letter which he wrote to his children at the end of his life, ill in body but alert in mind, he added up the gains of a long and successful business career, but reminded them of the recent losses that had reduced his fortune: "At present there is not much more except our farming which dont [sic] amount to much."[35]

The style of the simple life in Siasconset naturally contributed to a round of informal gatherings and social events that delighted the newcomers and reinforced their close family and business relations. We hear of fishing excursions, picnics on the moors and at Sachacha Pond, cart rides, beach parties, elaborate balls, smaller dances, and ceremonial dinners, each of which dressed up the occasion in a particular way and proved the value of being able to leave the town for the country. A "social hop" at the Atlantic House in July 1855 brought an appreciative comment in the weekly newspaper:

> We understand that it was a very pleasant affair, and that the 'wee hours' passed by and daylight began to be neighborly before the ball closed.[36]

Little is known about the ways Matthew participated in these activities, except for one account of a dinner which he hosted for a merry group in Siasconset on October 21, 1858. It was one of those men's affairs where, fitting the occasion, partly humorous and partly serious resolutions were proposed in favor of Matthew and several other guests:

> Resolved: That Mr. Matthew Crosby, our host this evening, is always a host wherever he may be. That beginning his career in the humble capacity of cabin boy of schooner Nancy [rewritten "sloop"], he has by his ability, integrity, dignity, and force of character fought his way up against all obstacles; that whether as Captain, Merchant, Bank Director, Merchant Prince, or the happy father of 16 [rewritten over another number] children, he has at all times and in every capacity commanded the respect and esteem of his fellow citizens; that he has a brave, warm, and true heart; that he sticks to his friends and to his opinions, and is always 'ahead of the work.'[37]

The rest of the company was made up of friends and relatives, Mitchells, Barretts, Whitneys, Macys, Coffins, Gardners, and Boveys, who moved in the same small social circle. A few of them have appeared so often in this narrative that they need only a brief reminder of their relationship. Francis M. Mitchell, the son of William Mitchell, the cashier of the Pacific Bank, was the brother of Maria Mitchell, a bright young woman who was gaining a reputation in astronomy and would soon move to a professorship at Vassar College. Francis had married Ellen Mitchell, from a separate family line, but whose father, Joseph, was also on the board at the bank. John W. Barrett was the bank president and Matthew's neighbor in Siasconset. His daughter, Elisa, was the wife of John M. Bovey. Andrew Whitney's sister, Sarah, was married to Matthew Crosby Jr. and Alfred Macy, a lawyer in Nantucket and Boston, was the husband of Ann Mitchell, another sister of Francis M.

The evening unrolled in testimonials of friendship and fellowship, spiced up by references to the well-known foibles of the members. Some fun was had with Francis for his intention to leave the island paradise for Chicago in the "Wild West"; with Andrew Whitney, still a bachelor, for "not gathering in a star from the galaxy of beauty"; with the Gardners, "who may plod, but never nod"; and with a play on "sarcophagus," into which repository the ashes of all would ultimately be placed, but of which the toastmaster could hardly speak without being reminded that there was a Coffin in their midst. We can easily imagine the noise, the smiles, the laughter, the toasts, the protests, the clapping and stamping, and the endless round of lifted glasses. They went home, a few steps away, satisfied with an evening well spent, and wholly persuaded that they were in the right place with the right people at the right time.

The nearness of the surrounding sea was certainly one of the greatest attractions that drew so many people from the town to settle for a part of the season in Siasconset, and that moody "vasty deep" has one more story to tell us about the Crosby family. Just off the coast, reaching like a many-fingered hand across forty miles of the Atlantic, lie the Nantucket Shoals. They once were the hills in what is now a submerged ancient coastal plain. Hidden under the surface of the water, in some places twenty or thirty feet deep, but in others only to a depth of three or four feet, they "make this one of the most dangerous parts of the United States for the navigator."[38] Since a sailing ship of, say, 350 tons, about the size of a whaling vessel in the mid-nineteenth century, might have drawn twelve to sixteen feet with a full cargo, it was a tricky business to find a way out once you were caught within. The risk was well known, and there had been several attempts to furnish charts of the region. In 1790, Captain Paul Pinkham directed a survey from the top of the Nantucket lighthouse, which was published a year later and showed the shoals closest to the shore. It was doubtless a help, and Samuel Lambert of Salem brought out another chart in 1813, but better coverage was needed and updating was essential. A much-improved effort with a clear depiction of newly discovered hazards and accurate soundings would have to wait for the work conducted by the government office of A.D. Bache in 1851, and even then, captains came into those waters in fear and trembling.

In the decade from 1840 to 1850, there have been counted 120 ships wrecked off Nantucket, of which thirty or more came to grief on the shoals. It was just this intricate network of passages, rendered more treacherous by bad weather, that spelled the doom of the bark *Earl of Eglinton*, 519 tons, John Niven, master, on the 14th of March, 1846. We know the details of this disaster because an account was written up by the supercargo, a young man named Arthur W. Morris, and later largely confirmed by a letter from the captain to Edward K. Godfrey and printed in his handbook on Nantucket in 1882.[39]

The vessel had left Liverpool in late December 1845, bound for Boston with a load of salt, coal, sheet copper, and dry goods. On the morning of the 14th of January, the barometer was low and the wind had picked up, accompanied by rain and fog. As a precaution, the topsails were reefed and soundings constantly taken. At one point, they showed twenty fathoms, but a little later only fourteen, and then, suddenly, just over three, and the ship struck the bottom. In great haste and confusion, the yards were squared and she floated off and beat to the northwest until a depth of fourteen fathoms was reached. Visibility,

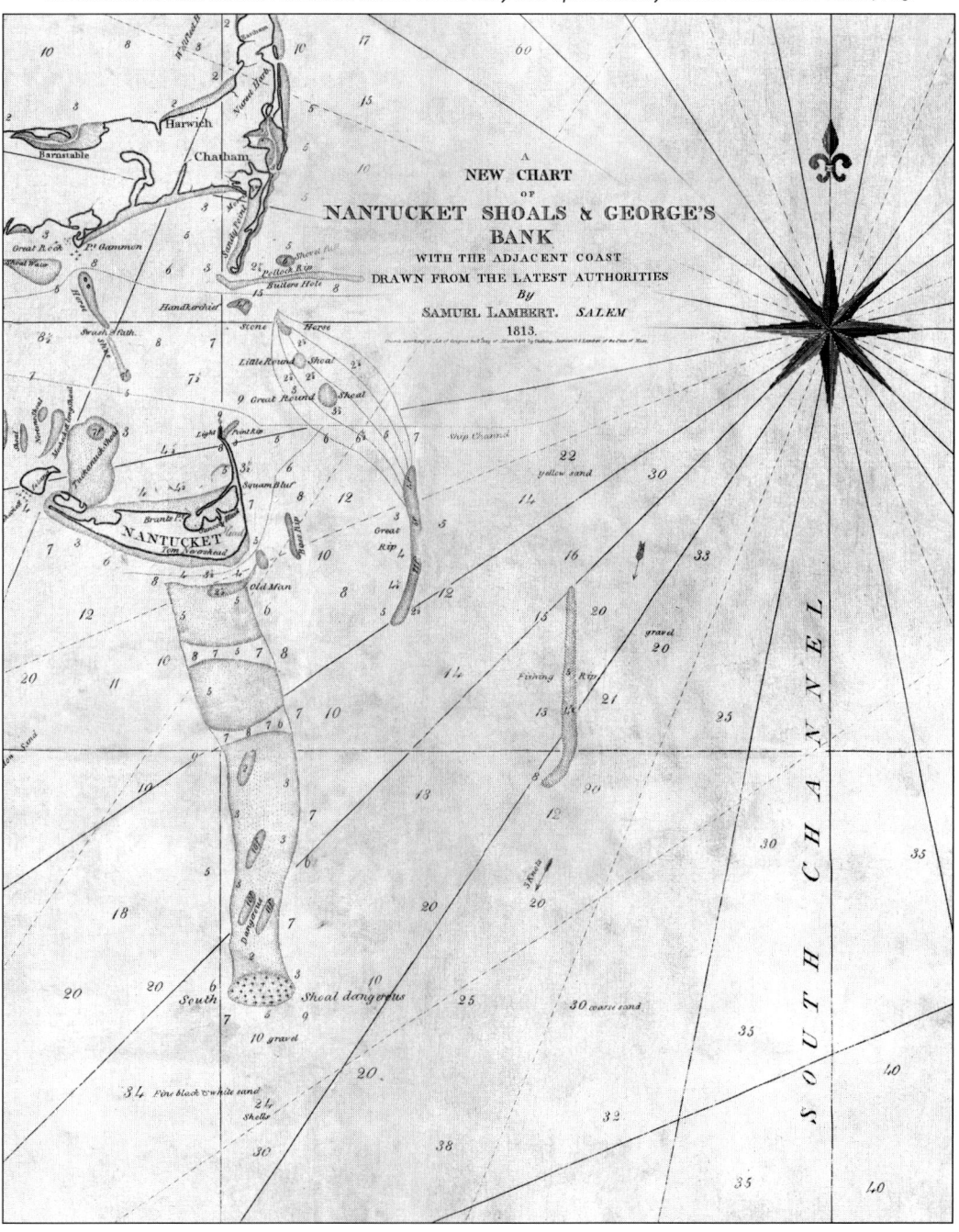

*The extensive shoals around Nantucket shown on the early chart published by Samuel Lambert in Salem, 1813.*

however, was reduced by the storm, and it was impossible to tell exactly where the vessel was. In an alarming foreboding of what was to come, the crew could see breakers wherever they looked. By now a leak in the hull was discovered and an attempt to anchor was made but without success. They continued to drift, firing guns and sending up rockets to signal a ship in distress. Then, about two o'clock in the morning, with the sea running high, they struck again with a tremendous shock which "set the masts quivering like reeds and our oaken frame tearing and groaning like a strong man in his agony."[40]

Daylight found them off the south shore of Nantucket on Old Man Shoal, far from the course for Boston. The men were exhausted, it was obvious that the pumps could not contain the leak, and as a last effort to save ship and cargo, Captain Niven decided to set sail again and to run her ashore. As they neared the coast, probably by Tom Nevers Head, a crowd of people could be seen on the beach. Help seemed at hand. But the two boats that had been lowered were splintered by the heavy surf that crashed and swept over the stern and through the cabin. Of the eight men who tried to make it to land, only two were saved by the rescuers who waded into the water. Finally, a hawser with a sling was rigged between

*The wreck of the* Shanunga *near Tom Nevers Head, June 20, 1852. Bound for Boston from New Orleans with a cargo of cotton, she came ashore in a heavy fog. The cargo was saved, but the ship could not be moved and was salvaged for $100.*

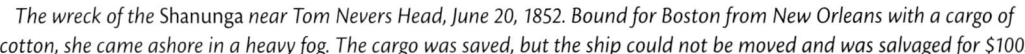

ship and shore and by this means, amid the wild fury of the waves, the rest of the crew and the captain were brought to safety. Morris was one of the first to cross, and at this point in his narrative he mentions that:

> many were the offers of coats and hats I got from the kind Yankees, and I at last accepted the loan of a coat from a gentleman who I have since learned is a Mr. Matthew Crosby, [Sr./Jr].[41]

The difficulty here is that the manuscript copy is often hard to read and, in this instance, it is uncertain whether the abbreviation, which is smudged, is "Sr." or "Jr." It could be argued that it is "Junior," because if it had been Matthew, the father, there would have been no need to write "Senior." The exception to this view is that if both Matthew Crosbys had been present at the wreck, it might have been thought useful to designate which one it was who gave Morris the coat. In 1846, Matthew, the father, was fifty-five years old and Matthew,

*The wreck of the brig* Poinsett *near Nobadeer on September 1, 1870. She was bound from Havana to Boston laden with sugar. The crew were rescued, but the vessel and cargo were a total loss.*

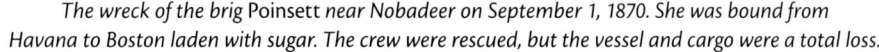

the son, was nineteen and still living on the island. Either one or both could have assisted in the rescue. In the letter dated 1881 from Captain Niven, then living in Indiana, to Godfrey, which Niven called "jottings from memory," he wrote that "The two who were saved [from the broken boats] may thank the presence of mind of Watson Burgess and Cap't. Matthew Crosby for their rescue."[42]

Godfrey follows this line and cites Matthew as "now deceased," hence the father since Matthew Jr. died in 1904. Furthermore, he identifies him "as the man who risked his life to save Cap't. Niven from drowning when he fell from the lifeline," an incident not mentioned in the account by Morris, but added by Niven without saying who the rescuer was. If, in fact, it was Matthew Sr. who strode forth as the man of the moment, he would no doubt have been slightly surprised, not to say embarrassed, by the rhapsodic end to this controversy presented by Jane G. Austin in *Nantucket Scraps*, published in Boston in 1883, which conveniently ignored the problem of the evidence:

> The hero who thus offered his life to save that of a stranger, and if 'gentleman' mean the highest development of man, let us call him 'gentleman,' was Captain Matthew Crosby, since gone to his reward, with this deed but one of many similar glittering upon his record. 'Everyone loves a lover,' may be; but, oh, every one exults in a hero, and is proud of the common ties of humanity.[43]

We do know that in 1877 Nevin paid a visit to Matthew, senior, on Nantucket, which might shift the weight a bit in his favor. Let us say that both men could have been on the beach, both could have aided the shipwrecked sailors in one way or another, and that in the end, the fact of the survival of some of those unfortunates is more important than trying to decide who should get the credit.

The captain and the crew were taken to the house of the wreck agent, Peter Ewer, on Centre Street and initially cared for there. The bodies of the drowned men were recovered, a service was held, and they were buried on the island. The drama of the disaster was followed by a legal inquiry, submission of claims, and settlement, and Matthew still had a part to play. Within the week, Captain Niven testified on oath that the wreck was due to natural causes and not because of "insufficiency of said ship or the neglect of the protestant [Captain Niven], or his officers, or any of the mariners." On April 7, a letter from Matthew Crosby, Peter H. Folger, Frederick W. Mitchell, Charles Mitchell, Charles B. Swain, and Barker Burnell confirmed that as captain he had done everything possible to save ship and cargo and had made every effort to save the crew. This was an important step to take with regard to the liability of the insurer for a commercial ship. In the case of the *Tarquin*, for example, which had sailed from Nantucket for the Pacific in 1822, and ended in a suit by the owner, Seth Paddack, against the Franklin Insurance Company, a statement from the bench made clear the legal implications:

> Where a ship is insured for a voyage, it is the duty of the owner to keep her seaworthy during the voyage, if it is in his power; and if she is rendered otherwise by damage or loss in her hull, sails, equipments, or crew, he is bound to repair or supply the damage or loss as soon as he conveniently can; and if he neglects to do so, and in consequence, a loss ensues, the underwriter will not be liable for it; but for a loss ensuing which is in no way attributable to such neglect it seems the underwriter will be responsible.[44]

A warrant for a survey of the wreck, drawn up on the 15th, named Thaddeus Coffin, shipmaster; Matthew Crosby, merchant and director of an insurance company; and Philip H. Folger, merchant and agent for New York insurance companies. The three men found it impossible to go on board because of the high surf still breaking over the stern and advised that, when the storm had died down, the cargo should be taken out and appraised and another survey made of the vessel. Four days later, they returned to find the ship heeled over, topmasts and spars and chains and anchors gone, part of the upper deck lost, the bottom stove in on one side, and what was left of the vessel breaking up.

*The wreck of the bark W.F. Marshall, bound from Hampton Roads, VA to St. John, NB. She was another vessel lost in fog that grounded on the South Shore, this time near Mioxes Pond, on March 9, 1877. The crew and passengers were brought ashore and the sails, rigging, spars, and hawsers that could be saved were stored in Matthew Crosby's warehouse on Commercial Wharf. There was hope that the ship might be refloated, but she was battered by a sudden storm and ultimately lost.*

Their recommendation was the swift removal of anything of value, which then should be disposed of at auction. The remains of the hull were to be scuttled and the timbers sold. Why they did not post a watch and why they waited four days before checking again are questions which we are left to ponder.[45]

Shipwreck on Nantucket was common enough, and in a seafaring community the response was swift and wholehearted. Crowds gathered on the shore at the sound of the first alarm to see how they might aid the stricken. Given the long history of marine disasters, the catastrophe of the *Earl of Eglinton* was in no way exceptional, except for our interest in the people involved. But there is a curious history related to the ominous burden carried by a name which, in a short space of time, was concerned with three separate misfortunes. Seven years before, in 1839, the thirteenth Earl of Eglinton, young, eager, wealthy, and imbued with romantic notions of medieval chivalry, staged an elaborate and expensive tournament with knights and ladies at his castle near Kilmarnock in Scotland. But, sad to say, the grand affair, which had attracted participants from near and far, was brought to an inglorious end by a sudden and ferocious afternoon thunderstorm which muddied the field, slowed the horses, soaked the hats and dresses, impaired the armor, and sent several thousand bedraggled people scurrying for shelter. It was the veritable shipwreck of a historical fantasy. Fourteen years after the Nantucket disaster, the large three-masted merchant vessel, also named the *Earl of Eglinton*, on her way from London to Calcutta, came ashore in a storm off the eastern coast of England near Dover and was a total loss. Surely it must have seemed the time to court the favor of a different noble ancestor.

The families on Nantucket, because of its limited resources, could never have survived without constant support from the mainland. Daily shipping, except in the worst weather, was an accepted and essential part of island life. Moreover, as we have seen, the success of the whaling industry and the increase of wealth which it brought opened up greater opportunities for the islanders and thrust them deeper into the ever-widening circles of national and international commercial and social life. Leaving the island and returning was becoming less an adventure and more a routine undertaking as the nineteenth century wore on. Schooners and sloops were always available at the wharves to carry passengers across the sound, and the early steamboats, first put into service in 1818, meant better schedules and greater comfort. The packet trade had kept Matthew in touch with the coastal towns, and he continued to travel for business and for pleasure once he had settled down as a whaleship owner. He left no consistent record of the trips he took abroad, nor is there much information on why he took them. In order to draw up even an outline itinerary, we are dependent largely on brief notes scattered among entries in his daybooks (which mostly cover his later years), on family letters, and on occasional references from other sources. While such a list doubtless omits many excursions, it does serve to show that even as he grew older his eagerness to go off-island was in no way diminished:

1839, June: An early instance is a letter from Asa S. Porter, of Solomon Porter & Co., commission agents in Hartford, to a James Brewer introducing his friends, Matthew Crosby and his lady; M. Jones, president of the Commercial Bank in Nantucket and his lady; and William Mitchell, president of the Pacific Bank, for what looks like a part social, part business, excursion.

1846, June: He wrote to his nephew, William C. Wyer, living in Ravenna, Ohio, that he and his wife had planned a trip to Niagara Falls later in the summer combined with a visit to William, but that he had had to give it up. "It is quite uncertain," he wrote, "if we ever get so far from home with our large family and other cares. Infirmity and age fast increasing. It would be quite an effort for us to leave home for any length of time."[46]

1849: four trips abroad at a cost of $200.

1855, September 6: to New Bedford with wife.

1856, May: he left for Detroit and Kalamazoo, Michigan.

1863, March 21: to New Bedford with Emma and Mary. Mary is unidentified, but likely was Matthew's eldest daughter and the wife of Benjamin F. Coffin. Emma was his youngest daughter and unmarried.

1863, November 11–21: to Boston with wife, cost $88.90.

1864, October 28–November 18: to New Bedford, cost $265.28, bought coats and pants, hat, umbrellas, gloves, knife, paid for dinner and carriages.

1865, June 7: to New Bedford with wife.

1865, July 17: to Boston with wife and Emma.

1865, October 9: to New Bedford and New York with wife, Sylvanus, and Emma, cost $408.95.

1866, December 4–25: to Detroit, self and Lydia to pick up wife and Emma. Left Detroit 17 December, arrived home 25 December. Route out: New Bedford, arrived Brooklyn 6 December, left Brooklyn 10 December, arrived Detroit 11 December. Route home: left Detroit 17 December, Syracuse, Albany, Boston, New Bedford, Nantucket. (Lydia was Matthew's daughter and the widow of Barker Burnell.)

1868, May: to New Bedford.

1870, April 22: to New Bedford, bought hat and a suit of clothes.

1870, May 7: to New Bedford with wife.

1870, November 14: to New Bedford with wife and Martha, probably Matthew's daughter, the wife of Dennis Wood.

1871, June 16: to New Bedford

1871, September 29: to New Bedford, returned October 18, route: Edgartown, Vineyard Haven, New Bedford.

1877, September 11: to New Bedford with Emma and Dennis Wood, cost $116.

1877, October 11: to New Bedford.

So many trips to New Bedford, and the fact that his daughters, Martha Wood, Susan Lowden, and Judith Ford lived there at different times, apparently convinced Matthew to buy a house and lot in the town at 82 Fourth Street (now called Purchase Street) for $4,500 in October 1856. This was a fairly high price, so it might be thought that he planned to use it often enough to justify the expense. Perhaps he did for a while, but we are ignorant of its real purpose. In any case, it did not turn out to be a profitable investment, since only a few years later, in August 1866, he sold it at a loss for $3,500.[47]

Matthew liked to go visiting, and now and again visitors came to see him. In August 1855, Joseph Gardner Swift, who had been born on the island sixty three years before, decided to relive his memories. He left by steamboat from New Bedford early in September and fell into conversation with Matthew Crosby and his wife, and a Mrs. Brayton, who were

making the same passage. Such must have been the pleasant feelings that, upon arrival, Swift writes, he was entertained by the Crosbys at a dinner party with the old Nantucket dish of corn pudding, and did not leave the island until the 17th.[48] Another acquaintance who stopped by Matthew's house came late in his life. Judge Nathan Crosby, a distant cousin, and a well-known lawyer and philanthropist in Lowell, Massachusetts, then seventy-nine years old, made the journey to Nantucket in July 1877, with his wife and daughter. Although it is not clear to what extent he and Matthew were in correspondence with each other, he brought him a copy of his book "lately finished by him of the Crosbys in America."[49] One other visitor of note was Captain Nevin of the ill-fated bark *Eglinton*, who had written to Matthew and made the journey in August 1877.[50]

*Steamboat Wharf (New North Wharf), circa 1880 with the railroad station in the foreground and the "Ladies and Gents" restaurant on the left.*

From time to time, Matthew and other, more distant members of his family, prompted by the desire to exchange news, to settle affairs, and to arrange visits at home or abroad, kept in touch by letter. Of particular interest, it seems, were the assets of the estates of deceased relatives. An early question, in 1804, which first involved Matthew's father, Sylvanus, and then spilled over into Matthew's time, concerned Lot Crosby, one of the brothers of Sylvanus. At issue was the distribution of the property of Joseph Merry, then living in Otsego County, New York, who was a relative of Lot's wife, Margaret. Sylvanus had made a journey to Albany in hopes of meeting Lot, but the latter was ill and was prevented from seeing him by "family circumstances." "My wife and I," he made a point of adding in his letter, "are sinking under a weight of infirmities into the grave." It appears that Joseph's widow had complained about Lot's share of the inheritance, and Sylvanus, playing the part of the family peacemaker, had offered to resolve the problem.[51]

Although the details remain unclear, difficulties with the same family surfaced again in 1850. This time it was Lot's son, John Crosby, almost eighty years old and "trying to make a living as a cooper" in Bergen, New York. He wrote to Matthew to say that he had heard in a roundabout way of the recent death in Nantucket of his uncle Samuel, Lot's brother, who had left some property, part of which, he thought, would descend to him:

> Now dear Sir… will you be so kind as to inform me as soon as possible about it, that I may know what to do about coming myself after it, as brother James and I may come together, and if there should be any property coming to me, I should like to have you, if you thought best, to send me something to bear my expenses, as I am needy. Respectfully yours. John X (his mark) Crosby.[52]

The letter was written out by Abner Hull Jr., Justice of the Peace in Bergen, Genesee County, who certified that "John Crosby who here made this mark is an honest, poor, hard-working man." John was well along in years and illiterate, which debilities probably account for the confusion in the letter. He did have an uncle named Samuel, who was also Matthew's uncle, but he had passed away almost thirty years before. More likely, John had heard of the death of his brother, Royal Crosby, in February 1850, confused the names, and wrote hoping that there might be something for him. There is, in fact, a letter to Matthew from Royal's widow, Dorcas, written in August 1850, in which she complains of poor health and constrained circumstances and reminds him of how often her husband had spoken of their friendship.[53] It, too, looks like a veiled plea for financial support. Although Matthew was well known for his willingness to help members of the family, in the case of these distant relatives, no letter in reply has come to hand.

By contrast, in 1829 Matthew received an invitation, free of conditions and requests for money, from his cousin, Jacob Weeks, who lived in New York near Cornwall-on-the-Hudson. Jacob may have been related to Matthew's aunt, Thankful, one of whose three husbands had been a Samuel Weeks, and he seems to have had some connection with the steamboat line on the river. He asked Matthew to address letters to him on board the *Experiment,* a new vessel which made the run to New York City twice a week. Always eager to travel abroad, Matthew proposed a visit, but his letter miscarried and Jacob did not reply until 1831. He then wrote a pleasant note in the formal Quaker style of "thee" and "thy" and "thou," mixed with the modern, asking Matthew to stay at his "humble residence" and reminding him of his island connection,

> "It would be agreeable frequently to hear from thee and my other relatives in and about Nantucket but more agreeable to see you.[54]

Of greater interest for the current news reported and the strong opinions expressed, is a long letter from Matthew's nephew by marriage, Robert Barnard, written to him in May 1843 from Macon, Georgia.[55] It is also valuable because it provides a glimpse into Matthew's ways of thinking, even though we have to glean this at second hand. Robert, who at the time was a lawyer living in the south, was the son of Frederick Barnard, the brother of Matthew's second wife, Elizabeth. Matthew had hoped for a visit and Robert wished to comply, but he suffered, he said, from lung disease and was about to retire from his practice. Nevertheless, if providing a visit would not disrupt the Crosby household, he planned to be in New York in June and would be glad to come over to the island sometime in August.

The remainder of the letter is a running commentary on the state of the Union in the form of answers to Matthew's questions about life below the Mason & Dixon line. How does it compare, he wants to know, with conditions and business practices on Nantucket? By 1843, as noted previously, Matthew was much concerned with local bank failures which, if not corrected, would destroy public confidence in the financial world. Robert admits that at one time he would have agreed, but lately he has come to see them as a blessing. The banks are "overrun with profligacy, speculation, and special legislation to favor them." They have become "merciless monsters," and one way to weed out the worst is to let them fail. Here we have what might be another recent headline in the daily press.

He is, he says, "a Whig in practice, but a Loco-Foco [a member of the radical wing of the Democratic party] in principle." But the impression we get from the letter is that he adheres more to the practice. He imagines that Matthew sees him as a portly, good-natured, easy-going gent "rioting in good liquor and turtle soup." But he is wrong. Picture, rather, he says, "a long, lantern-visaged, uneasy-looking mortal, and you have the living alderman before you." Southerners, he wants it understood, have as many problems to face in their world as do businessmen in other parts of the country.

Matthew, of course, is particularly concerned with the health of the whaling industry and he had evidently confessed to worries about a decline in future profits. Robert hardly gives him the encouraging answer he was seeking. Although he is reluctant to deliver a lecture on a subject in which he knows Matthew is an expert, his view is that no more large fortunes will be made from whaling. The number of vessels engaged has declined, the distances to sail are too great, the time spent at sea is too long, and, as necessity is the mother of invention, the genius of man has produced substitutes for whale oil in the form of gas and spirits that will be used more and more. He then turns to respond to Matthew's inquiry about his views on southern life. We are once again reminded that Matthew, like many of his fellow social leaders engaged in seagoing ventures, had far wider interests in people and places than one might expect from someone living in an island community. Moreover, from a historical perspective, this is certainly the more instructive part of the letter, providing, as it does, a few lines of personal commentary on social and economic affairs in a small corner of the world in the years just before the Civil War. It can be summarized as a lament on the deterioration of the quality of life brought about by the decline of the market in cotton and, therefore, a veiled warning to businessmen dependent on that other important commodity, whale oil. "We are in a wretched, deplorable condition," Robert wrote, "because of the loss in value of the products from field and factory." One solution, he suggested, would be to cut back the labor force, but this could not be done because slaves still had to be fed and clothed and housed, even as the market was glutted, the price of cotton fell, and their masters were in want. They had no other employment and could do nothing to earn a single dollar. England now relies on cheaper cotton from Egypt and India, and the factories in the northern states can do without exports from the South.

Such, he laments with a wink of the eye, are the blessings of slavery! "Am I in favor of emancipation," he asks, and answers:

> No, I have no interest in the matter. In fact, I am rather against it. If the abolitionists could see us in our suffering, they would remain quiet, seeing that the hand of the Almighty was sufficiently heavy upon us for the sin of this unnatural system.

It is not certain that Robert made the trip to Nantucket in the summer of 1843. If he had, he would have found himself thrust into a swarm of abolitionist activists who, in spite of violent opposition by a mob of local stalwarts, appear to have taken over popular opinion on the island. An antislavery meeting was held at the Atheneum in August 1841, sponsored by Charles G. Coffin, the son of Zenas and brother of Matthew's first wife, Lydia, among other businessmen. The following year, Stephen S. Foster (not the songwriter, but the dedicated missionary and abolitionist) gave a lecture entitled, *The Brotherhood of Thieves,* in which he indicted the American church and clergy for having failed to confront the problem. In 1843, a third meeting was followed by an announcement in the newspaper by Cyrus Peirce, the popular Nantucket educator, praising the work of the abolitionists, "who have shown up the true character of the outrageous system which is scathing the souls and bodies of thousands and blighting the prosperity of the whole land."[56] If Robert were not to be swayed by the overwhelming and soul-stirring moral problem, he surely would have been convinced by the seriousness of the economic consequences. Whether Matthew joined his friends and relatives in active support of the movement we cannot say. His instincts were charitable, but, for the most part, he preferred private support over public engagement.

One characteristic of Matthew which lent a picturesque quality to the way he expressed himself came from his long association with ships and sailors. In a chapter of his history of Nantucket, R.A. Douglas-Lithgow called attention to the habit of certain of the islanders who were given to speaking as though they were still at sea:

> the nautical expressions are so interlarded with the familiar everyday language… that they are unaware of the fact until their attention is directed to it by strangers. A Nantucketer does not pull, he always "hauls;" he does not tie or fasten anything, he "splices" it; he "rigs" and "belays, backs and fills," "gets under way," "heaves to," "comes about," and "squares away," so naturally and spontaneously that it never occurs to him that there is anything unusual in his mode of expressing himself.[57]

The habit ran in the family, so it is not surprising to read about a business deal by Matthew Crosby Jr. in 1854, when he uncharacteristically failed to move fast enough, as one in which "the authorities got to windward of us."[58] Nor is it odd to find Matthew's own description of himself at the age of eighty-four set out in similar terms:

> And now, feeling and like an old ship somewhat shaken, hauled up in a pretty sound state, spars all good, but hardly worth repairing, I have made out to finish my sheet.[59]

Like his own sturdy whaleships, he had done good service over the years and had held up remarkably well, both in mind and body. This is especially noteworthy when the average lifespan for a white male urban dweller in the United States between 1860 and 1880 was roughly calculated to be about fifty-five to sixty years. Nevertheless, by his own admission he had been:

> …much troubled during the last three winters with gout, rheumatism, or something, not having much pain; now some inflammation in ancles [sic] and feet, and a very bad cold which I have not as yet been able to get clear of.[60]

Three years later, in 1878, while he prided himself on a good memory, he still complained of poor health and about the ineffectiveness of the medicine he had been given. Among medical practitioners at the time, a correct diagnosis was often as much a problem as prescribing the right treatment. The extraordinary variety of powders, pills, syrups, and other concoctions advertised every week in the Nantucket newspapers, which promised relief from every kind of affliction, is constant proof of the desperate search for a cure among the sick. Although Matthew had to retire from the packet trade at a young age because of "health problems," we are not told what those problems were. In June 1846, he mentioned "a very severe bilious attack" that kept him confined to the house for three weeks.[61] But he was soon up and around again. Beyond that, there are no indications, aside from references to minor ailments, that he suffered in any serious way until he was well into his last decade.

When Matthew looked back over the years, as the elderly are wont to do, the accomplishments that meant the most to him were those of the practical businessman:

> I have the satisfaction in looking over the things gone past and up to the present time to say I have not been a drone in the hive, never knew anything about panics, generally using my own means, never risking other people's, always blessed with a plenty, many years with no losses in any shape… Then came failures, etc., etc. But fortunately I have a plenty left with economy and prudence to carry me through life. And I have great reason to thank God for all his blessings through a long and eventful life… I believe I can say without boasting that no person can say in this world with truth, that I ever put off a payment large or small during life. Then why should I not be more than thankful?[62]

The same sentiments are echoed in the last letter to his children written in 1878, a month before he died:

> I write this knowing my life is very uncertain. I have many things to be thankful for during a long eventfull [sic] life. I have always been blessed with property enough of my own earnings to support a large family of children and to pay every debt or obligation through my life and have spent thousands of dollars for my children that has needed my assistance. Some years since when my beloved wife was living, and then in good health, I made my will which will be found in my trunk. Myself and wife was [sic] perfectly satisfied with it, since which my property has greatly lessend by fall of real estate, lessing of bank and rail road stocks, and swindling, which has cut down my income very much, and to look back on my valuation of property from year to year will be seen on the last part of my day book, it will be noticed at this date I have much over valued my property, 1878 4 mo. 12. I dont [sic] care to open my will again, it would only add to my cares to make any alterations.
>
> If I have made anny [sic] mistake or left out any name of eather [sic] of my children, I want my administrators to correct it… as I want all to be satisfied and those of my children that need assistance, widoes [sic] and children, must be assisted by those that are able to do so keeping economy always in view… At one time before the great fire, I believe my property was worth one hundred thousand dollars, the fire took of [sic]

twenty-five thousand at least, and the last two years were manufacturing oil and candles, William and I lost at least $16,000 by the fall in price of oil and failures, and quite an amount in several bad voyages, and I ought to feel satisfied to have some property left, while many of my friends around me that was [sic] left with a large property, have nearly lost their all and their business with it. I cannot help looking at the by gons [sic], let them go. I believe it is profitable to look back and try to improve on them, to gain experiance [sic]. How much property I have seen lost by neglect and inattention. Make good use of time, especially when you have men employed and on pay, time is money. Make the best use of it.[63]

And so he did. The sentiment expressed in the letter he wrote to his nephew, William Wyer, the farmer in Ohio, in 1840, which was cited previously, can justly be said to have been Matthew's as well:

You can have the satisfaction of seeing about you an abundance of good things of your own sowing and reaping, which is, after all, the most satisfaction we can enjoy.[64]

A notice in the newspaper on May 4, 1878, announced that "Capt. Matthew Crosby, who has been sick for several days, we are glad to learn was better yesterday." But the sands had run their course and it was not to be. He passed away at 10 PM on Monday evening, May 13, 1878, aged 87 years, 1 month, 13 days.[65]

Matthew's will was presented for probate on September 2, 1878, by the executors, William H. Crosby, Matthew Crosby Jr., Charles C. Crosby, all of Nantucket, and Dennis Wood of New Bedford, the husband of his daughter, Martha. The other children, including those living in Peru, were willing to have the executors act for them in the settlement of the estate.

It is true, as Matthew said, that he had sustained considerable losses in his later years. As noted in the discussion of the legacies in Chapter 2, from a high point of over a hundred thousand dollars in the prosperous decades around mid-century, his assets had fallen to about sixty thousand dollars at the time of his death. But for a leading merchant of the island, it was still a respectable sum. The real estate was sold off and the cash was distributed to the beneficiaries. The elegant "homestead house" on Main Street, appraised for tax purposes at $2,500 in 1860, was bought by Oliver B. Hussey for a mere $1,700, and the summer house in 'Sconset, over which Matthew had lavished so much care, went to Maria L. Nichols of Cincinnati for $1,000.[66]

If we allow for the author's obligatory elevated prose, for the need to be more complimentary than critical by citing the lesser flaws in order to bring out the greater virtues, and, finally, for the liberties taken with Matthew's last thoughts and the conviction that the end is really the beginning, we can rightly say that the obituary printed in the *Inquirer and Mirror* leaves us with the portrait of a man worthy of celebration:

With the death of Matthew Crosby at the advanced age of 87 years, 1 month, and 13 days, is severed another tie which bound the present of Nantucket to her past. So, along with her declining glory, pass away those who contributed so much toward making Nantucket what it was. Mr. Crosby was a man of great force of character, indomitable energy, industry, and perseverance, and possessed of rare executive ability. Commencing his business career young and in comparative poverty, success soon began to crown his effort, and he advanced, step by step, from one post of trust and honor to another, until he at last held an enviable position among men. He was not without his faults. To have been faultless, he would have been more than human. This he was not. And the faults which he had were not of the head, neither were they of the heart, but of the temperament, and for this he was not altogether responsible. Although he was at times stern, and always uncompromising, he had a kind, warm heart and strong affection, not only for those to whom he was bound by the closest ties, but he was always ready to extend the helping hand to those in need. Plain, unostentatious, shrinking from prominence in all things, his left hand knew not the doings of his right. I quote his own words when I say that during his long and eventful life, "he lost and gave away $150,000." Quoting still further from a letter which he wrote a member of his family only a year ago, in which he referred to his approaching end, giving a short review of his life, he said, in no egotistical spirit, and, to use his own words, "not boastingly," that he had been a bank director over 45 years, and during that time a director in insurance offices, part owner, agent, and director in seven steamers, twenty-two ships, twenty-six schooners, and eleven sloops. Beside this, he was a successful packet master, an upright and successful merchant and manufacturer. And whether as packet master, ship agent, director, merchant, or man, wherever he was placed, he never swerved from the path of strict integrity, and was never guilty of a mean or dishonorable act. He never made any religious profession, but he lived a life of simple, plain honesty and purity, and he has left behind the choicest inheritance to his children which a man can leave, a name and a character unspotted and unstained by a single questionable act; a name and a memory which will long be remembered and cherished when material things shall be as naught. And what a lesson is here for our young men! Oh, that they might profit by such an example as they find in the life of such a man as was Matthew Crosby! His success in life was due to his industry, economy, and perseverance, guided by the rule of his life, which he never swerved from. In these days, when so much corruption in public and private life is coming to the surface, it is with joy and with satisfaction we can point to this Nantucket man, and say, without fear of contradiction, here was a specimen of "God's noblest work," and honest man, and now we mourn his death. Did I say, mourn? No, he will be long and sadly missed by those who knew him best, and knew him but to love. But who can mourn at the death of one who has lived and died as he did? He lived long and he lived well.

> "He liveth long who liveth well;
> All else is life but flung away;
> He liveth longest who can tell
> Of true things truly done each day."

> Thus lived him of whom we write. So I say, with our view of death, we do not mourn that he has gone. Who can tell that the visions which floated round his death bed are realized? "For now we see through a glass darkly, but then face to face; now I know in part, but then shall I know even as I am known." He was an eminently practical man, not much given to sentiment. But it did seem as he lay on his sick bed anxiously waiting to go, that he had visions of the future which we are not permitted to see; visions of that happy future which is in store for those who make good use of their God-given abilities. He, I am fully persuaded, has been granted that reunion with those who have gone before, which he so much longed for; and "Well done, thou good and faithful servant," was his greeting from Him before whom we shall all appear at last, and to whom we must render an account of our stewardship.[67]

Such was his prominence that there were two additional notices printed in the same edition of the paper. They necessarily cover much the same ground, but the first of the two adds a few more facts, enhances the appraisal of his life and work, and is interesting for what must have been public knowledge of Matthew's business gains and losses:

> Died at quarter past ten o'clock on Monday evening last, Matthew Crosby, Esq., at the ripe old age of 87 years, 1 month, and 13 days. Capt. Crosby was one of Nantucket's noblest sons. For fidelity, integrity, energy, and enterprise, he had no superior in this community. Blest with a constitution of rare power, he used it to the utmost of its indurance [sic], and what his hands found to do, he did with all his might, and has left an example of industry worthy of imitation. Having accumulated a handsome property in the coastwise business, he invested largely in whale ships and the manufacture of oil and candles, which he successfully pursued for many years, and but for the unparalleled ill success that attended the adventures of his later business life, he would have left one of the largest fortunes that was ever accumulated on this island; as it was he had more than a competency, which enabled him to pass his time as best suited him; at his country seat in the summer, and at the falling of the autumnal leaves he would repair to his more spacious mansion in town. Capt. Crosby was largely identified with the financial affairs of this place, and was for forty-two years an able and useful director in the Pacific Bank, which office he resigned in December 1874. He was twice married and has been a widower since October 3, 1876. He was the father of sixteen children, twelve of whom are now living, and in his last suffering illness, he was surrounded and his wants administered to by most of his sympathizing and loving offspring.[68]

The second is a shorter variation on the same themes and is included here for the sake of completeness:

> Death has taken from among us this week one of our oldest and most highly esteemed citizens, and one who, as a business man, was identified with all great and good enterprises in the palmy days of our activity and financial prosperity. Captain Matthew Crosby, after a brief final illness, passed peacefully away on Monday evening last, at the ripe age of 87 years, 1 month, 13 days. While he will be missed and mourned by a host of relatives and friends, we must all admit that his work here was well finished, and can unite in saying, "It is well," at the fall of the curtain upon a well-rounded life. He has left us with a shining example of purity and excellence in his private and domestic life, as well as of industry, energy, and sturdy integrity in his long business career. He has reared a numerous family of sons and daughters, nearly all of whom are still living, and his last days have been blessed with devoted love and respect of three generations of descendants.[69]

It so happened that on the day Matthew died, Monday, May 13, 1878, the Sherburne Lyceum in Nantucket held one of the popular weekly debates. This was a group recently organized with the help of Elizabeth Crosby, the wife of Matthew's son, William, "to hear questions of interest discussed in a friendly spirit." The topic for the occasion was: "Resolved, that the works of art are more to be admired than the works of nature." The vote at the close, it was reported, showed a small majority for the affirmative side.[70] The business ethic of the nineteenth century promoted the idea of the merchant who by talent, energy, ambition, and character forged ahead to occupy a position of wealth and social success, honor, and prestige. At the risk of stretching a comparison too far, we might take the coincidence of this discussion at the Lyceum, and its outcome, as a fitting comment on the life of a man who, in the small world of the island community, fashioned a noteworthy career out of his natural gifts.

In his will, Matthew directed that he was to be buried in the "Friends Burying Ground with as little expense and ostentation as is suitable." Although he had never joined the meeting, the thought that he was, nevertheless, a small part of a familiar tradition may have seemed a comfort to him in his last years. True to the Quaker view of the world, as well as to his own manner of living, he wished to leave it quietly, simply, and plainly.

The glowing tributes in the death notices were well deserved and Matthew Crosby is, indeed, a man to remember, but not, we might say, for the usual reasons. He made no name for himself in the professional world of learning, nor did he advance his career by holding important political office, or by obtaining an advantageous ecclesiastical appointment, all common avenues to notoriety and influence at the time. A reader will look in vain for mention of him in the history books, even in those that chronicle the affairs of the town and the island. Rather, he has a claim on our interest by reason of the fact that he, like so many of his friends, is so little known.

The more the past is studied and revealed in ever greater detail, the more it is apparent that satisfactory explanations for change must be sought, not in the commonly encountered abstractions such as "the State," or "the Church," or "the Party," or "the City Council," or "the Committee," or "the Ruling Class," none of which ever did anything by itself, but rather in the thoughts and actions of the individual men and women who were involved. Whatever was done, we should remember, was done by someone, or by some few, somewhere at some time. Their decisions and efforts often go unnoticed, but how they acted form the bedrock of the historical process. If they can be brought out of the shadows and given a place in our memory, part of the debt of the living to the dead is paid. In the case of Matthew and his fellow businessmen, it was they who, through diligence and perseverance, were the force which succeeded in raising a small and insignificant island to enduring prominence. When we see them going about their daily work, we see ourselves, like them, creatures of habit and routine, moved by moments of success and failure, joy and sorrow, and we may, therefore, appreciate to a keener degree the significance of their achievement.

*The Hadwen-Satler house, 96 Main Street, circa 1870.*

OCEAN HOUSE.

SHERBURNE HOUSE.

BIRD'S EYE
NAN
STATE O
LOOKI

1. Athenæum—Museum.
2. Pacific Nat. Bank.
3. Academy.
4. Coffin School.
5. Old Mill, Built 1746.
6. Oldest House, Built 1686.
7. Soldiers' Monument.
8. Asylum.
9. Brant Point Light House.
10. North (Congregational) Church.
11. South (Unitarian) "
12. Methodist Episcopal "
13. Baptist "
14. Friends' "
15. Pleasant St. Baptist "
16. Catholic "
17. Episcopal "
18. U. S. Life Saving Station.
19. Fair Grounds.
20. Water Works Reservoir.
21. Bug Light Houses.

PUB. BY J.J. STONER, MADISON, WIS.

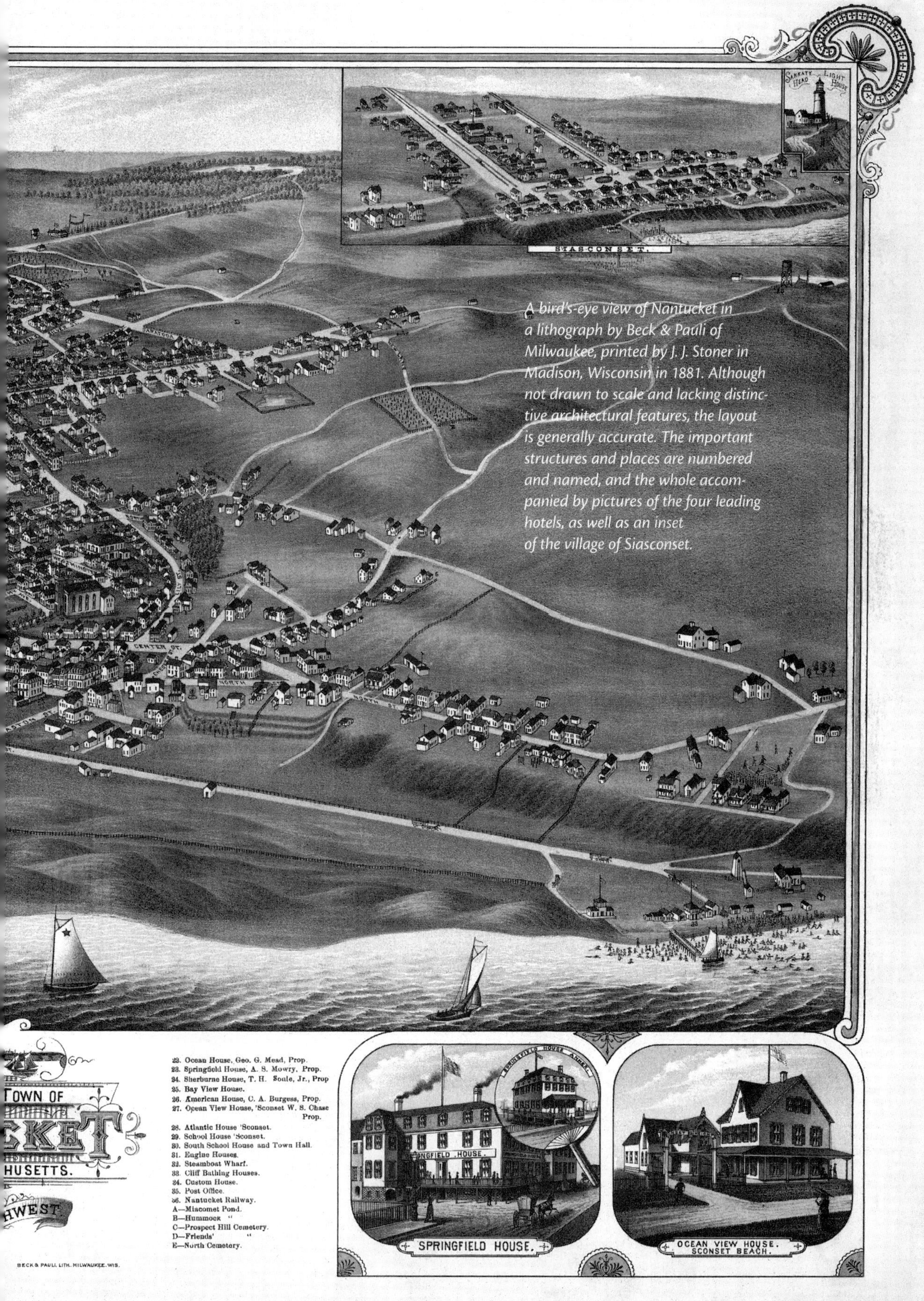

A bird's-eye view of Nantucket in a lithograph by Beck & Pauli of Milwaukee, printed by J. J. Stoner in Madison, Wisconsin in 1881. Although not drawn to scale and lacking distinctive architectural features, the layout is generally accurate. The important structures and places are numbered and named, and the whole accompanied by pictures of the four leading hotels, as well as an inset of the village of Siasconset.

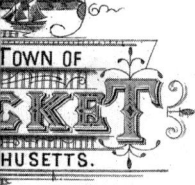

22. Ocean House, Geo. G. Mead, Prop.
23. Springfield House, A. S. Mowry, Prop.
24. Sherburne House, T. H. Soule, Jr., Prop
25. Bay View House.
26. American House, C. A. Burgess, Prop.
27. Ocean View House, 'Sconset W. S. Chase Prop.
28. Atlantic House 'Sconset.
29. School House 'Sconset.
30. South School House and Town Hall.
31. Engine House.
32. Steamboat Wharf.
33. Cliff Bathing Houses.
34. Custom House.
35. Post Office.
36. Nantucket Railway.
A—Miacomet Pond.
B—Hummock "
C—Prospect Hill Cemetery.
D—Friends' "
E—North Cemetery.

BECK & PAULI LITH. MILWAUKEE, WIS.

# Appendix I

### Vessels in which Matthew Crosby owned an interest, circa 1816–1871

| Ships, Brigs, Barks | Schooners | Sloops |
|---|---|---|
| American | Abbie Bradford | Amy |
| Amy | Arial | Betsey |
| Bohio | C. C. Davis | Fame |
| Constitution | C. D. Stacy | Galen |
| Edward | Charlotte Brown | Jule Ann |
| Independence | Colonel Simeons | Martha |
| Islander | Conveyance | Nancy |
| Lexington | D. D. Gyer | New Packet |
| Lima | Daniel Webster | Patriot |
| Loper | Ellen H. Gott | Senator |
| Mariner | George H. Rogers | Success |
| Mary | J. L. Hammond | Union |
| Montano | James Freeman | |
| Nantucket | Madison | **Steamboats** |
| Navigator | Nathaniel Chase | |
| Plowboy | Northern Belle | Eagle's Wing |
| R. L. Barstow | Oliver Cromwell | Helen Augusta |
| Sarah | Onward | Martha's Vineyard |
| Sea Ranger | Passport | Massachusetts |
| Susan | Queen of the Cape | Monohansett |
| Tylestone | Sarah Jane | Telegraph |
| Washington | Sylvester | |
| Zenas Coffin | Titmouse | |
| | Vestal | |
| | White Foam | |

# Appendix II – Genealogical Charts

1. Simon Crosby "the emigrant" (circa 1608–1639) ⚭ Anne Brigham (circa 1606–1675)
2. Thomas Crosby (circa 1634–circa 1721) ⚭ Sarah (Fitch?)
3. Simon Crosby (1665–circa 1717) ⚭ Mary Nickerson (1668–1746)
4. John Crosby (1701–1750?) ⚭ Sarah Luce (1715–circa 1752)
   children:   Thankful (1735–1802)
               Lot (1738–1818)
               John (1740–1807)
               Samuel (1743–circa 1820)
               Sylvanus Crosby (1747–1817)
5. Sylvanus Crosby ⚭ Huldah Pease (1750–1833)
   children:   Anna (1771–1797) ⚭ Sylvanus Ewer (1767–1836)
               Sylvanus Jr. (1773–1794)
               Huldah (1776–1853) ⚭ Benjamin Whippey Jr. (1775–1837)
               Mary ( Polly) (1778–1837) ⚭ Owen Wyer (1774–1836)
               William (1782–1799)
               Betsey (1785–1853) ⚭ John Clisby (? –1807)
               **Matthew (1791–1878)**
6. **Matthew Crosby** (first marriage) ⚭ Lydia Coffin (1793–1823)
   children:   William H. (1813–1896) ⚭ Elizabeth C. Pinkham (1816–1897)
               Mary (1816–1878) ⚭ Benjamin F. Coffin (1813–1889)
               Ann (1818–1904) ⚭ George C. Macy (1814–1895)
               Lydia (1820–1900) ⚭ Barker Burnell Jr. (1819–1861)
7. **Matthew Crosby** (second marriage) ⚭ Elizabeth Barnard Powell (1800–1876)
   children:   Martha (1826–1899) ⚭ Dennis Wood ( ? –1878)
               Matthew Jr. (1827–1904) ⚭ Sarah C. Whitney (1827– ? )
               Sylvanus (1829–1894) ⚭ Castora Tizón ( ? –1879)
               Elizabeth B. (1831–1912) ⚭ William C. Gardner ( 1829– ? )
               Judith (1833–1865) ⚭ James Ford Jr. (1833– ? )
               Susan (1835–1919) ⚭ Andrew Lowden ( 1830–1874)
               Charles C. (1836–1905) ⚭ Ellen M. Easton (1839–1901)
               Emma (1839–1892)
               Francis L. (1840–1912) ⚭ Mercedes Tizón (1850–1891)
8. Micajah Coffin (1739–1827) ⚭ Abigail Coleman (1735–1807)
   children:   Isaiah (1757–1813)
               Gilbert (1759–1843)
               Zenas (1764–1828)
9. Zenas Coffin ⚭ Abial Gardner (1764–1856)
   children:   Eunice (1788–1843) ⚭ Thomas Macy (1787–1864)
               Lydia (1793–1823) ⚭ **Matthew Crosby (1791–1878)**
               Mary (1799–1827) ⚭ Henry Swift (1793–1862)
               Charles G. (1801–1882) ⚭ Elisa McArthur (1799–1857)
               Frederic (1804–1817)
               Henry (1807–1900) ⚭ Elisa Starbuck (1811–1903)

# Notes

### ABBREVIATIONS USED IN NOTES

      DB = Deed Book, Nantucket County Records
    NHA = Nantucket Historical Association
NHA MSS = Nantucket Historical Association, manuscript collections
    WSL = *Whalemen's Shipping List and Merchants' Transcript* (New Bedford: 1843–1914)

### INTRODUCTION

1. John Greenleaf Whittier, *The Exiles* (1841).
2. J. Hector St. John de Crèvecoeur, *Letters from an American Farmer*, p. 116.
3. *Ibid.* p. 51.
4. *Ibid.* p. 175.
5. PRO MS. (London): Co. 5/154, pt. II, fol. 238.
6. See, for example, the account in Edward Byers, *The Nation of Nantucket*, pp. 153–158.
7. Obed Macy, *History of Nantucket*, p. 80.
8. As concisely defined by an elegantly balanced sentence in *Webster's International Dictionary*, 2nd. ed. (1955), p. 2253.
9. A Letter from the Hon. Thomas Pickering…to James Sullivan, Governor of Massachusetts (Boston: Greenough & Stebbins, 1808), p. 8.
10. Obed Macy, *Journal*, NHA MSS. 96, folder 2.
11. *Ibid.*
12. *Ibid.*
13. *Niles Register*, June 1, 1833, p. 224.
14. *WSL*, December 18, 1849.
15. *Inquirer and Mirror*, Saturday, December 8, 1866.
16. *WSL*, February 4, 1873.
17. Samuel Adams Drake, *Nooks and Corners of the New England Coast*, p. 330. R. R. Minturn, "Nantucket," *The Lakeside Monthly* 10 (1873), pp. 140–144.
18. Josiah Quincy, "Account of a Journey," in Everett U. Crosby, *Nantucket in Print*, pp. 112–120.
19. D. H. Strother, "A Summer in New England," *Harper's New Monthly Magazine* 21, November 1860, pp. 745–763.
20. Henry M Baird, "Nantucket," *Scribner's Monthly*, vol. 6, August 1873, pp. 385–399.
21. *Visitors' Guide to Martha's Vineyard*, p. 10.
22. Edward K. Godfrey, *The Island of Nantucket*, pp. 268–269.
23. A comprehensive list of the developments is given in Henry B. Worth, *Nantucket Lands and Landowners* (NHA, 1904), vol. 2, no. 4, pp. 213–216.
24. The political tract of Peter Folger, the grandfather of Benjamin Franklin, is reproduced in Everett U. Crosby, *Nantucket in Print*, pp. 19–36.

### CHAPTER 1

1. Walter Folger, "A Topographical Description of Nantucket in 1791," *Collections of the Massachusetts Historical Society*, 3 (1794).
2. *The First Census of the United States taken in the Year 1790* (Washington, D.C. 1908). The two males were his sons, Sylvanus Jr. (1773–1794), who died at sea, and William (1782–1799), who died of Yellow Fever in New York City.
3. DB 13, pp. 44, 91. DB 15, p. 151. DB 16, p. 219. DB 17, p. 167. DB 20, pp. 93,171. DB 24, p. 86.

4. Log of the *Asia*, NHA, MS. 226, #3. Also online: *Journal of the Whaleship Asia*, and in print edited by Rod Dickson as *The Cruise of the Nantucket Ships Asia and Alliance* (Perth: 2007). Edouard A. Stackpole, in *The Sea Hunters* (New York: Lippincott, 1953), alleged that the manuscript was "hidden for over one hundred and sixty years…and then discovered." But, in fact, it was known long before and there is a note about it by Benjamin Sharp in the Proceedings of the NHA, July 22, 1915, pp. 33–37.
5. Rod Dickson, *op. cit.*
6. Obed Macy, *Journal*, NHA MSS. 96, #2.
7. Alexander Starbuck, *The History of Nantucket*, pp. 294–295.
8. Nantucket Probate Records, Book 6, pp. 115–116.
9. Arthur H. Gardner, *Wrecks around Nantucket* (Nantucket: 1877 and later editions).
10. NHA MSS. 4, folder 1.
11. Proceedings of the NHA, July 22, 1914, pp. 21–22. A similar permit issued for the sloop *Polly*, owned by Zenas Coffin, was included by Obed Macy in his *Journal* for August 1814.
12. NHA MSS., folder 1.
13. *Inquirer and Mirror*, January 18, 1868.
14. John Lambert, *Travels through Lower Canada and the United States of North America in the Years 1806, 1807, and 1808*, vol. II, pp. 155–156.
15. Paul E. Cohen & Robert T. Augustyn, *Manhattan in Maps*, pp. 66–69, 106–109.
16. NHA MSS. 10, Account book 262. Consumer Price Index Conversion Table. The very general estimates for the purchasing power of the dollar are based on the CPI updated to 2016. Minutes of the Common Council of New York City: 1784–1831, vol. xi (New York: 1917), p. 159.
17. NHA MSS. 342
18. *The Naval War of 1812*, William S. Dudley, ed., vol. II, p. 162.
19. Autobiography of James Jenkins Written for his Grandchildren, p. 10.
20. NHA Accession no. 1996.0016.011

# Chapter 2

1. *Papers of Benjamin Franklin*, vol. 15 (New Haven: Yale, 1972), 182–185.
2. NHA MSS. 96.
3. Alexander Starbuck, *History of the American Whale Fishery*, pp. 177–178.
4. Barney Genealogical Record under "Clisby," but an unverified reference.
5. For a brief note on Zenas, see Will Gardner, *The Coffin Saga*, pp. 158–195.
6. Micajah Coffin attained some notice in 1808 when he accused a fellow member in the House of being a thief, was sued for his pains, and lost. The affair brought up the delicate question of how free is free speech and was called by Josh Chafetz, in *Democracy's Privileged Few*, p. 93, "the most important early American case on the free-speech privilege…"
7. Nantucket Probate Records, vol. 12, pp. 376–379, 389–391, 422–433; vol. 13, pp. 144–146, 160–161; vol. 14, pp. 109–115.
8. *Nantucket Inquirer*, July 2, 1828.
9. It seems that a son, Frederick G. Coffin, was born in 1796, but died two years later. A second son, also named Frederick G. Coffin, was born in 1804, but drowned in 1817.
10. NHA MSS. 51–52: Minutes of the monthly meetings, vol. 2, February 25, 1813; and vol. 3, p. 329.
11. Henry B. Worth Collection, NHA MSS. 35, box 4, book 7, p. 84; book 9, p. 143. NHA MSS. 51: A Record of Births, Deaths, Receptions, Disownments, and Remains…in the Society of Friends on the Island of Nantucket (December 27, 1838). Allen Coffin, "The courts of Nantucket. The law and the lawyer from an early period," NHA *Proceedings*, July 1907.
12. Printed in the *Island Review*, May 25, 1878.
13. On the other hand, at a party in Siaconset on October 21, 1858, it was recalled that he had 16 children, but the number was changed from an earlier one which is now illegible, This is printed as "fourteen" in B. Tyler, *A Walk Down Main Street*, p. 57.
14. NHA MSS. 4, folder 1.

15. *Ibid.*
16. Nantucket Probate Records, vol. 12, pp. 376 & 393.
17. NHA MSS. 4, folder 1.
18. *Reports of Cases Argued and Determined in the Supreme Judicial Court of Massachusetts,* Charles Allen, ed. (Boston: 1865), vol. I, pp. 354–358.
19. NHA MSS. 334, folders 13–14.
20. Florence B. Anderson, *Through the Hawse Hole,* pp. 211–213. "A Nantucketer Remembers. From the Commonplace Book of Elizabeth Plaskett Bennett," Florence B. Anderson, ed., pp. 3–11.
21. Harry B. Turner, "Vanished Treasures," NHA *Proceedings,* July 20, 1916, pp. 44–45. The notice of the arrival of the *Henry Astor* in the *Inquirer and Mirror* for May 23, 1844, was laconic to the point of travesty: "Reports nothing new. Captain Pinkham died at Perambuco April 17. His remains to be embalmed and sent to Boston." See also Nathaniel H. Bishop, *A Thousand Miles' Walk Across South America,* p. 275.
22. NHA *Proceedings,* July 21, 1909, pp. 39–40.
23. NHA MSS. 150, folder 6.
24. Nantucket Probate Records, file 389, p. 23 (June 24, 1889).
25. NHA MSS. 4, folder 2.
26. Asa Bunker, *Letter Book,* NHA MSS. 3, folder 20. There is a point of confusion in Bunker's report which appears to make Matthew Crosby the debtor to George C. Macy, rather than the other way around. The context, however, supports the allegation that Macy borrowed from Crosby.
27. DB 54, p. 203.
28. *The Congressional Globe,* 28th Congress, 1st session, December 14,1843, pp. 36–37.
29. *Ibid.*
30. Asa Bunker, *Letter Book,* NHA MSS. 3, folder 20.
31. *The Trial of Barker Burnell, Late Cashier of the M & M Bank in Nantucket,* Court of Common Pleas, June term 1847 (Boston: B. Mussey, 1847), p. 8.
32. *Ibid.* p. 19.
33. *Daily Warder,* August 12 September 1, and 12, 1846.
34. NHA MSS. 332, folder 10.
35. Jethro C. Brock, *A Correct List of Persons Belonging to Nantucket Now in California, or On Their Way There.* DB 57, p. 163.
36. NHA MSS. 335, folder 969, diary d.
37. *Ibid.*
38. *Nantucket Inquirer,* June 18, 1847.
39. *Bankers' Magazine and State Financial Register* (Baltimore: 1847), vol. 1, July 1846, p. 124.
40. Alexander Starbuck, *History of the American Whale Fishery,* pp. 426–578. *Catalogue of Nantucket Whalers* (Nantucket: Hussey & Robinson, 1876), pp. 38–48. *Hunt's Magazine,* vol. 42 (1860), p. 627. Joseph Grinnell, *Speech on the Tariff,* House of Representatives, May 1, 1844 (Washington, D.C. 1844).
41. NHA MSS. 334, folder 23.
42. Connecticut Historical Society, Hartford: Tracy Family Papers, folder 5, Ms. 89778.
43. Francis Lewis Crosby, autobiographical letter, NHA MSS. 4, folder 11. A personal letter from Guillermo Crosby in Lima, Peru, November 22, 1967, in possession of the author.
44. There is a notice by André Aubuchon in *Historic Nantucket,* April 1978, pp. 28–29; July 1978, pp. 20–27; October 1978, pp. 20–27.
45. *Inquirer and Mirror,* June 6, 1885. Harvard Class of 1877, 40th Reunion Book, June 1917.
46. *Nantucket Inquirer,* July 2, 1856.
47. Francis Lewis Crosby, autobiographical letter, NHA, MSS. 4, folder 11. Internacional 14.com/en/crosby.
48. *Inquirer and Mirror,* November 1 & October 4, 1879; June 7, 1890; January 5, 1895. A little later, Charles applied for a license "to build a pile bulkhead for the protection of his wharf in Nantucket harbor." It was granted on June 27, 1898.
49. *Inquirer and Mirror,* March 6, 1875. See also, *American Series of Popular Biographies,* Massachusetts edition, pp. 256–257; and NHA *Proceedings,* 1905.
50. *Inquirer and Mirror,* June 6, 1896 & April 20, 1889. Henry S. Wyer, *Sea-Girt Nantucket,* prints an advertisement.

51. Obituary of Dennis Wood in the *New Bedford Republican Standard*. September 12, 1878. Wood & Nye Records in the New Bedford Whaling Museum Library, MS. 66.
52. NHA *Proceedings*, July 18, 1906, p. 24.
53. Records of Deaths in the Town of Dedham, Mass., Don G. Hill, ed. (Dedham: 1895).
54. NHA MSS. 4, folder 1.
55. Nantucket Probate Records, July 10, 1879.
56. NHA MSS. 150, folder 6.
57. John Adams, *A Defence of the Constitutions of the Government of the United States of America* (Boston: 1788), vol. 1, chapter 1.
58. Fifth Annual Report of the State Board of Health, Lunacy, and Charity of Massachusetts. Supplement on Public Health. (Boston: Wright & Potter, 1884), pp. 190–209.
59. DB 27, pp. 364–366.
60. Asa Bunker, *Letter Book*, NHA, MSS. 3, folder 20.
61. Florence B. Anderson, *Through the Hawse Hole*, pp. 202–212.
62. *Inquirer and Mirror*, February 14, 1874.
63. NHA MSS. 302, folder 3.

# Chapter 3

1. Herman Melville, *Moby-Dick, or the Whale* (New York: W. W. Norton, 1967), chapter 16.
2. William M. Davis, *Nimrod of the Sea*, pp. 22–23.
3. These are general figures which can be relied upon to demonstrate the rise and fall over a long stretch of time, but which are not precise for specific years. Useful sources include *WSL*, with annual summaries of the whaling industry; Alexander Starbuck, *History of the American Whale Fishery*, pp. 318 et seq.; Obed Macy, *History of Nantucket*, p. 214; Clifford Ashley, *The Yankee Whaler*, p. 23; Samuel Jenks in the *Nantucket Inquirer*, October 4, 1828 & February 21, 1829; John P. Bigelow, *Statistical Tables for Massachusetts* (Boston: 1838); A. Howard Clark, "The Whale Fishery" in *The Fisheries and Fishing Industries of the United States*, vol. II (Washington, D.C.:1887); *Hunt's Magazine*, 3 (1840) & 42 (1860); and the National Maritime Digital Library, American Offshore Whaling Voyages, Judith N. Lund, ed. et al.
4. The word "ship" in general use refers to any large seagoing vessel, but among seamen it means one with three masts, all of which are square-rigged. A bark also has three masts, but it is rigged with square sails only on the first two, while the mizzenmast has a fore-and-aft sail. A brig has two masts, both square-rigged. A schooner has two masts and is generally rigged with fore-and-aft sails on both. A sloop has one mast with a fore-and-aft sail. For illustrations, see *The Seaman's Friend* by R. H. Dana Jr., plate IV. "Tonnage," at the time, usually meant carrying capacity.
5. Obed Macy, *op. cit.* p. 215. Speech of Mr. Grinnell of Massachusetts on the Tariff, May 1, 1844 (Washington, D.C.: 1844)., p. 10.
6. Grinnell, *op. cit.* pp. 10–11.
7. *Ibid.* The calculation of just how much money was made, however, is an ongoing problem. A vigorous statistical wrestling bout with regard to the profits from a whaling voyage is on exhibit in chapter 11 of the book *In Pursuit of Leviathan*, by Lance E. Davis, et al.
8. Walter Tower, *The History of the American Whale Fishery*, p. 72. That seafaring was a gamble with the weather and the whales has been down-played from time to time, but the argument remains unconvincing. See, for example, George W. Shuster, "Productivity and the decline of American sperm whaling," *Boston College Environmental Affairs Law Review*, vol. 2 (1972), 345–357.
9. *A Whaling Voyage in the Bark* Willis: *1849–1858*, Thomas Perkins, ed. (Boston : 1924), p. 8.
10. To simplify the statistics for the purposes of this review, only sperm oil, the most valued oil cargo, is considered. Whale oil and bone, if any, are omitted, although by the 1840s and 1850s more and more ships hunted the right whale and other species. See also A. Howard Clark, "The Whale Fishery," in *Fisheries and Fishing Industries*. II, Part XV, p. 170, and Lance E. Davis, et al., *In Pursuit of Leviathan*, pp. 131–135.
11. NHA MSS. 10, folder 232.

12. Lance E. Davis, et al., *In Pursuit of Leviathan*, pp. 133–135. The figure of 5000 sperm whales a year was proposed by Gregory Cushman in *Guano and the Opening of the Pacific World*, p. 40.
13. Henry T. Cheever, *The Whale and its Captors*, pp. 153–156.
14. *The New Bedford Mercury*, February 15, 1823, and printed in Edouard Stackpole, *The Sea Hunters*, pp. 409–410.
15. William M. Davis, *Nimrod of the Sea*, p. 365. The date of the voyage is purposely omitted in the narrative, but the encounter likely took place in August 1837. This was the year and the month when the *Chelsea*, the *Washington*, and the *Ocean*, also from Nantucket, could have been together near the Galapagos. Lee Bay was identified by Herman Melville in the fourth sketch of *The Encantadas* (1856).
16. John B. Moore, *History and Digest of the International Arbitrations to which the United States has been a Party* (Washington, D.C.: 1898), vol. II, pp. 1615–1629. The mixed Commission was composed of two members from Peru and two from the United States with a fifth added as umpire in case of a deadlock. The group began deliberations in July 1863 and was dissolved the following November.
17. National Archives, Records of the Department of State, Domestic Letters, 46, pp. 14 & 88.
18. *New York Times*, December 12, 1863.
19. Nuku Hiva (Nukaheira): *WSL*, April 3, 1849. Pitcairn: Herbert Ford, *Pitcairn Island as a Port of Call*. Juan Fernández: *WSL*, July 3 & August 7, 1849. Paita: *WSL*, August 28, 1849. Oahu: *WSL*, November 20, 1849, and a notice in the *Polynesian*, August 18, 1849.
20. *WSL*, December 18, 1849.
21. *Nantucket Inquirer*, September 19, 1849. *WSL*, October 30 & December 18, 1849, and February 26, March 26, April 2, April 9, & May 14, 1850.
22. NHA MSS. 150, folder 6: certificate of Registration for the *Washington* and bill of sale, September 5, 1849. Benjamin Coffin sailed on the *Akbar*, William Worth, captain (*Nantucket Inquirer* September 8, 1849).
23. NHA MSS. 10, AB 232. NHA, MSS. 4, folder 2.
24. *New York Times*, December 26, 1861. Herman Melville, "The Stone Fleet" in *Battle Pieces and Aspects of the War* (New York: Harper, 1866).
25. Alexander Starbuck, *History of the American Whale Fishery*, pp. 462–463. Rosendo Melo, *Historia de la Marina del Perú*, I, p. 217.
26. Alexander Starbuck, *op. cit.*, pp. 528–529.
27. The half-hull model of the *Navigator*, dated to about 1841, is in the collections of the NHA, accession no. 1897.0395.001. For Captain Palmer and his wife, see Herbert Ford, *Pitcairn Island as a Port of Call*.
28. Useful notes on the problem of the dates and persons confused in Melville's accounts can be found in Hershel Parker, *Melville* (Baltimore: JHU, 1996), vol. I, pp. 192–199; Wilson Heflin, *Herman Melville's Whaling Years* (Nashville: Vanderbilt, 2004); and Thomas F. Heffernan, *Stove by a Whale* (Middletown: Wesleyan, 1981).
29. The signboard and the tiller of the *Lima* are in the NHA collections, accession no. 1908.0019.001.
30. *Inquirer and Mirror*, May 23, 1868. Samuel Smiles, *Self-Help*, p. 403.
31. For the *Bohio*, see Paul H. Silverstone, *Civil War Navies: 1855–1883*, p. 104, and *WSL*, April 28, 1868.
32. *Inquirer and Mirror*, July 11, 1868, and *WSL*, May 26, 1868.
33. *WSL*, February 20, 1872.
34. Alexander Starbuck, *History of the American Whale Fishery*, pp. 540–541 & 590–591.
35. *Nantucket Weekly Mirror*, February 15, 1862.
36. *Otago Daily Times*, June 20, 1873, and *Inquirer and Mirror*, March 15, 1873.
37. NHA MSS. 10, AB 232.
38. NHA MSS. 15, folder 38.
39. NHA MSS. 10, AB 232.
40. Ibid.

## Chapter 4

1. NHA MSS. 10, AB 72
2. Wharfage and Dockage Fees: NHA MSS. 12, box 1.
3. *Inquirer and Mirror*, March 4, 1876.
4. NHA MSS. 96, Journal 2.

5. *Nantucket Inquirer*, October 25, 1823.
6. *Ibid.* June 6, 1838.
7. *Ibid.*
8. *Ibid.* June 16, 1838. The destruction of the candle factories, warehouses, and oil stores is corroborated by Jane F. Russell (1816–1842) in a letter to her brother dated June 3, 1838 (NHA, MSS. 172, folder 10).
9. *Ibid.* June 2, 1838.
10. *Ibid.* June 16, 1838.
11. John Warner Barber, *Historical Collections* (Worcester, Mass: Dorr, Howland, 1840), p. 44.
12. *Nantucket Inquirer*, July 24, 1846, and the *Daily Warder*, September 1, 1846.
13. Christopher C. Hussey, *Talks about Old Nantucket*, p. 62.
14. *Nantucket Inquirer*, 2 July 28, 1847.
15. NHA MSS. 4, folder 4, ledger d.
16. DB 33, p. 293; DB 32, p. 594; DB 39, pp. 509,523; DB 57, p. 310; DB 60, p. 508.
17. Proprietors' Records, 1808–1887, p. 19. See also Louise S. Baker, *Eunice Hussey* (Nantucket: 1938), p. 82.
18. DB 39, p. 45.
19. A. Judd Northrup, *'Sconset Cottage Life. A Summer*, p. 38.
20. Obed Macy, *The History of Nantucket*, pp. 260–261.
21. NHA MSS. 4, folder 2 and MSS. 335, folder 969. The name is given as "Pendleton" in B. Tyler, *Main Street 'Sconset* (Nantucket: 2012), p. 61, but "Pendexter" clearly appears in the contract. Moreover, in the 1840 census for Nantucket we find "Charles Pendexter (Jr.), son of Charles Pendexter, carpenter, and Susan, born December 26, 1844." There also exists a receipt for a house built by Charles Pendexter for Paul Folger, January 26, 1841 (NHA, MSS. 282, folder 3).
22. NHA MSS. 4, folder 11.
23. DB 65, p. 88. For the quotation, see John Quincy Adams, *Diary*, no. 40 for September 17, 1835, p. 531.
24. NHA MSS. 4, folder 4.
25. *Nantucket Inquirer*, July 30, 1855.
26. *Ibid.* July 20, 1855
27. The advocates of the new road may have been encouraged to act by the state law of 1846, chapter 203, which ruled that roads were to be laid out, not by "ancient right," but by an established legal proceeding. See Frances R. Karttunen, *A History of Nantucket Roads and Ways* (2008).
28. NHA MSS. 4, folder 6.
29. *Inquirer and Mirror*, December 18, 1915.
30. NHA MSS. 10, folder 232.
31. NHA MSS. 4, folder 2.
32. Pacific National Bank archives: minutes of the directors' meetings.
33. Elmo P. Hohman, *The American Whaleman*, p. 279.
34. NHA MSS. 335, folder 982.
35. *The Private and Special Statutes of the Commonwealth of Massachusetts*, vol. 8 (Boston: 1848), p. 31.
36. *Laws Relating to Inland Fisheries in Massachusetts: 1623–1886* (Boston: 1887), p. 302. NHA MSS. 10, folder 301. *Niles Register*, August 24, 1833, p. 420.
37. *Nantucket Inquirer*, October 23, 1854.
38. NHA MSS. 266–267.
39. See chapters 2 and 3
40. In the light of present-day agitation over credit-rating agencies, the historical commentary is of particular interest. See Scott A. Sandage, *Born Losers. A History of Failure in America* (Cambridge, Mass: Harvard, 2005). Ralph W. Hidy, "Credit rating before Dun and Bradstreet," *Bulletin of Business History* 13 (1939), 81–88. James D. Norris, *R. G. Dun & Co. 1841–1900. The Development of Credit-Reporting in the Nineteenth Century* (Westport, Conn: Greenwood, 1978). Bertram Wyatt-Brown, *Lewis Tappan and the Evangelical War against Slavery* (Cleveland, Ohio: Case Western reserve, 1969). William Yates Chinn, *The Mercantile Agencies Against Commerce* (Chicago: Charles H. Kerr, 1896). P. R. Earling, *Whom to Trust. A Practical Treatise on Mercantile Credits* (Chicago: Rand, McNally, 1890). James H. Madison, "The Evolution of commercial credit-reporting agencies in nineteenth-century America," *Business History Review* 48 (1974), 164–186.

41. NHA MSS. 3, folder 21
42. *Nantucket Inquirer*, January 8, 1855.
43. William Yates Chinn, *The Mercantile Agencies Against Commerce*, p. 132.
44. NHA MSS. 3, folders 21–22.
45. NHA MSS. 4, folder 11.
46. NHA MSS. 3, folders 21–22.
47. Ibid.
48. Ibid.
49. NHA MSS. 332, folder 10.
50. Elmo P. Hohman, *The American Whaleman*, pp. 327–328.
51. *The Rich Men of Massachusetts*, pp. 221–222.

# Chapter 5

1. The letter was printed in the *New Bedford Mercury*, May 20, 1878, and again in the *Island Review*, May 25, 1878.
2. For "down along," see *The Nantucket Scrap Basket*, William F. Macy & Roland B. Hussey, pp. 129–130; and the *Nantucket Inquirer*, July 7, 1845.
3. *Inquirer and Mirror*, July 31, 1880.
4. NHA MSS. 334, folder 23.
5. NHA MSS. 96, Journal 3.
6. *Nantucket Inquirer*, May 13, 1826.
7. The entry in The Barney Genealogical Record has his death by drowning after a boat overturned in the harbor.
8. NHA MSS. 10, AB 232, 266.
9. *Nantucket Inquirer*, March 22, 1824.
10. NHA Town Meeting Reports: 1784–1822, pp. 175–178.
11. *Nantucket Inquirer*, February 16, 1828, and October 18, 1828.
12. NHA MSS. 4, folder 8.
13. *Hunt's Magazine and Commercial Review*, vol. 13, August 1845, p. 191.
14. NHA MSS. 4, folder 7.
15. *Nantucket Inquirer*, February 23, 1839.
16. Ibid., April 19, 1824.
17. Edward K. Godfrey, *The Island of Nantucket*, p. 257.
18. *Inquirer and Mirror*, October 16, 1875, and April 5, 1879.
19. *Nantucket Inquirer*, January 3, 1825.
20. Ibid., March 13, 1841.
21. NHA MSS. 96, Journal 3, October 1817.
22. *Nantucket Inquirer*, January 3, 1825.
23. Ibid., December 22, 1854.
24. *An Arrangement of the Psalms, Hymns, and Spiritual Songs of the Rev. Isaac Watts*, John Rippon, ed. (London: 1801). *Short Discourses to be Read in Families*, William Jay, ed. (Baltimore: 1833).
25. NHA MSS. 335, folder 969, Daybooks b and e.
26. NHA MSS. 92. In Siasconset, Matthew used the Mitchell lot, Chase lot, Potehee lots, Gibbs lot, Hill lot, Fisher lot, and Wigwam lots. He also farmed a portion of the 600-acre Bloomingdale Farm north of Main street, owned by Levi Coffin, a grandson of Zenas Coffin.
27. NHA MSS. 4, folder 11.
28. Henry Colman, *European Agriculture and the Rural Economy from Personal Observation*, 2nd ed. (Boston: Little & Brown, 1849). Also by Colman: *Letter to the Farmers of Massachusetts on the Subject of an Agricultural Survey of the State* (Boston: 1837) and *First Report on the Agriculture of Massachusetts* (Boston: 1838).
29. Elizabeth R. Coffin (1850–1930), *Seaweed Gatherers* (1889), now in the Coffin School, Nantucket.
30. *Nantucket Inquirer*, April 14, 1856. Tafeu was another patented product, said to double the production of a farm in the first year! See *The Cultivator* (Albany, N.Y.), vol. 5 (May 1857), 135; the *American Agriculturist* (N.Y.), vol. 19 (January 1860), 135; *The Country Gentleman's Magazine* vol. 4 (London 1870), 415.

31. *Hunt's Magazine & Commercial Review*, vol. 31, 1854. See also the optimistic note by W.W. McIntosh in E.K. Godfrey's, *The Island of Nantucket*: "Rye, oats, and barley do well, and I think with proper selection of seed and soil and proper cultivation, we may raise as good an average yield of wheat as is raised in any of the wheat states east of the Mississippi," p. 9.
32. *Inquirer and Mirror*, September 30, 1865; October 3, 1868; September 27, 1870.
33. NHA MSS. 4, folder 3.
34. *Inquirer and Mirror*, September 30, 1865.
35. NHA MSS. 4, folder 3.
36. *Nantucket Inquirer*, July 23, 1855.
37. NHA MSS. 4, folder 1.
38. *United States Coast Pilot 2* (2015), p. 162, which was a modern phrasing of the comment appended to the chart by Paul Pinkham in 1790: "…these dangerous shoals which are a terror to navigators."
39. NHA MSS. 316, folder 1. Edward K. Godfrey, *The Island of Nantucket*, pp. 350–356.
40. NHA MSS. 316, folder 1.
41. *Ibid.*, the word must be "hats," although the author does not cross the "t" as he usually does.
42. Edward K. Godfrey, *The Island of Nantucket*, pp. 350–356. Watson Burgess was a local fisherman of modest means who was thirty-eight years old at the time.
43. Jane Austin, *Nantucket Scraps*, pp. 270–271.
44. *Reports of Cases in the Supreme Judicial Court of Massachusetts*, vol. XI (Boston: 1833), p. 227.
45. NHA MSS. 15, folder 51.
46. NHA MSS. 332, folder 10.
47. Register of Deeds, New Bedford, Mass., DB 33, p. 23.
48. *Memoirs of Gen. Joseph Gardner Swift*, Harrison Ellery, ed. (1890).
49. NHA, MSS. 4, folder 4. The book in question was *A Crosby Family. Josiah Crosby, Sarah Fitch, and their Descendants*, by Nathan Crosby (Lowell, Mass: Stone, Huse & Co., 1877). Nathan's line was descended from Simon Crosby Jr. (the son of Simon, the Emigrant) who married Rachel Brackett and settled in Billerica, Massachusetts.
50. NHA MSS. 4, folder 5.
51. *Ibid.*
52. *Ibid.*
53. *Ibid.*
54. *Ibid.*
55. NHA MSS. 4, folder 2.
56. *Nantucket Inquirer*, August 12, 1843.
57. R. A. Douglas-Lithgow, *Nantucket. A History*, p. 296. The list was enlarged by William F. Macy and Roland B. Hussey in *The Nantucket Scrap Basket*, chapter II.
58. Tracy Family Papers, Connecticut Historical Society, Hartford, Conn., MS. 89778, folder 5.
59. *Island Review*, May 25, 1878. "To finish my sheet," was a common expression by writers of the period to refer to the completion of a letter, or by typesetters in reading pages for printing.
60. *Ibid.*
61. NHA MSS. 332, folder 10.
62. *Island Review*, May 25, 1878.
63. NHA MSS. 4, folder 1.
64. *Journal of Timothy W. Riddell*, July 1871–November 1882, Town Clerk's Office, Nantucket, Mass. See also the *Inquirer and Mirror*, May 4 & May 18, 1878, and the *WSL* May 21, 1878.
65. DB 65, pp. 491–493. DB 66, p. 474.
66. *Inquirer and Mirror*, May 18, 1878.
67. *Ibid.*
68. *Ibid.*
69. *Ibid.*
70. For the Lyceum debates in general, see *Ibid.*, November 24, December 1, December 15, 1877.

# Bibliography

Agler, Raymond B., "William Swain, portrait painter," *The Magazine Antiques*, July, 1981, 124–133.

Albion, Robert G., *The Rise of New York Port: 1815–1860* (Boston: Northeastern University Press, 1939; Rp. 1984).

*America and the Sea. A Literary History*, Haskell Springer, ed. (Athens, Georgia: University of Georgia Press, 1995).

*American Offshore Whaling Voyages. A Database*, Judith N. Lund, ed. et al. (National Maritime Digital Library, 2008).

*American Series of Popular Biographies* (Boston: Graves & Steinbarger, 1901).

*American Vessels Captured by the British during the Revolution and the War of 1812* (Salem, Mass: Essex Institute, 1911).

Anderson, Florence B., *Through the Hawse Hole. The True Story of a Nantucket Whaling Captain* (New York: Macmillan, 1932).

Anderson, Florence B., "A Nantucketer remembers. From the commonplace book of Elizabeth Plaskett Bennett," *Old Time New England*, vol. 42, no. 1 (1951), 3–11.

Arthur, Brian, *How Britain Won the War of 1812. The Royal Navy's Blockades of the United States: 1812–1815* (Woodbridge: Boydell, 2011).

Ashley, Clifford W., *The Yankee Whaler* (Boston: Houghton Mifflin, 1926; 2d. ed. 1938).

Austin, Jane, *Nantucket Scraps* (Boston: James Osgood, 1883).

*Autobiography of James Jenkins Written for his Grandchildren* (Oshkosh, Wisconsin: 1889).

Baird, Henry M., "Nantucket," *Scribner's Monthly*, vol. 6, no. 4 (August, 1873), 385–399.

Baker, Louise S., *Eunice Hussey* (Nantucket: 1938).

Balliett, Blue, "The mysterious ledger of Asa G. Bunker," *Historic Nantucket* (July, 1979), 10–15.

Barber, John Warner, *Historical Collections…relating to the History and Antiquities of every Town in Massachusetts…*(Worcester: Dorr, Howland, 1841).

Barrett, Walter, *The Old Merchants of New York City* (New York: Carleton, 1863).

Baxley, H. Willis, *What I Saw on the West Coast of South and North America and at the Hawaiian Islands* (New York: Appleton, 1865).

Bidwell, Percy Wells, *Rural Economy in New England at the Beginning of the Nineteenth Century* (New Haven: Connecticut Academy of Arts & Sciences, 1916).

Bigelow, John P., *Statistical Tables for Massachusetts* (Boston: 1838).

Bishop, Nathaniel H., *A Thousand Miles Walk across South America* (Boston: Lee & Shepard, 1870).

Black, John D., *The Rural Economy of New England* (Cambridge, Mass: Harvard University Press, 1950).

Blanchard, Dorothy C. A., *Nantucket Landfall* (New York: Dodd, Mead, 1956).

Bliss, William Root, *Quaint Nantucket* (Boston: Houghton Mifflin, 1896).

Bliss, William Root, *September Days on Nantucket* (Boston: Houghton Mifflin, 1902).

Brandt, Karl, *Whale Oil. An Economic Analysis* (Stanford: Stanford University Press, 1940).

Briggs, L. Vernon, *History of Shipbuilding on North River, Plymouth County, Massachusetts* (Boston: Coburn, 1889).

Brock, Jethro C., *A List of Persons from Nantucket now in California or on their Way there…*(Nantucket: Hussey & Robinson, 1849).

Browne, J. Ross, *Etchings of a Whaling Cruise* (London: John Murray, 1846).

Byers, Edward, *The Nation of Nantucket. Society and Politics in an Early American Commercial Center: 1660–1820* (Boston: Northeastern University Press, 1987).

*Catalogue of Nantucket Whalers. Voyages from 1815 to 1870* (Nantucket: Hussey & Robinson, 1876).

*Centennial Catalogue of the Nantucket Historical Association* (Nantucket: I & M Press, 1895).

Chafetz, Josh, *Democracy's Privileged Few. Legislature, Privilege, and Democratic Norms in the British and American Constitutions* (New Haven: Yale University Press, 2007).

Chatterton, E. Keble, *Whalers and Whaling. The Story of the Whaling Ships up to the Present Day* (Philadelphia: J. B. Lippincott, 1926).

Cheever, Henry T., *The Whale and its Captors* (New York: Harper, 1850).

Church, Albert Cook, *Whale Ships and Whaling* (New York: W.W. Norton, 1938).

Church, Ella Rodman, "A Glimpse of Nantucket," *The Southern Magazine*, vol. 16 (1875), 389–396.

Claflin, James W., *Historic Nantucket Lightships: New South Shoal, 1854–1896* (Worcester, Mass: 2005).

Clark, A. Howard, "History and present condition of the fishery," in "The Whale Fishery," vol. II, part XV, pp. 3–218, of *The Fisheries and Fishing Industries of the United States*, , George B. Goode, ed. (Washington, D.C: 1887).

Cohen, Paul E. & Robert T. Augustyn, *Manhattan in Maps* (New York: Rizzoli, 1997).

Cook, R. H., *Historical Notes of the Island of Nantucket and Tourist's Guide* (Nantucket: 1871).

Creighton, Margaret S., *Dogwatch and Liberty Days. Seafaring Life in the Nineteenth Century* (Salem, Mass: Peabody Museum, 1982).

Creighton, Margaret S., *Rites and Passages. The Experience of American Whaling: 1830–1870* (Cambridge: CUP, 1995).

Crèvecoeur, Hector St. John de, *Letters from an American Farmer* (London: Thomas Davies, 1782).

Crosby, Everett U., *Ninety-Five Percent Perfect. The Older Residences on Nantucket* (Nantucket: Tetaukimmo Press, 1937; 2d ed. 1944; 3d ed. 1953).

Crosby, Everett U., *Nantucket's Changing Prosperity and Future Probabilities* (Nantucket: Tetaukimmo Press, 1939).

Crosby, Everett U., *Nantucket in Print* (Nantucket: Tetaukimmo Press, 1946).

Crosby, Nathan, *A Crosby Family. Josiah Crosby, Sarah Fitch, and their Descendants* (Lowell, Mass: Stone, Huse, 1877).

Cushman, Gregory T., *Guano and the Opening of the Pacific World. A Global Ecological History* (Cambridge: CUP, 2013).

Dana, Richard H., *The Seaman's Friend* (Boston: Little, Brown, & Loring, 1842).

Davis, Lance E., Robert E. Gallman, Teresa D. Hutchins, "Productivity in American whaling. The New Bedford fleet in the nineteenth century," in *Markets in History*, David W. Galenson, ed. (Cambridge: CUP, 1989), 97–147.

Davis, Lance E. & Robert E. Gallman, "American whaling: 1820–1900. Dominance and decline," in *Whaling and History. Perspectives on the Evolution of the Industry*, Bjorn L. Basberg, ed. (Sandefjord: 1993), 55–65.

Davis, Lance E., Robert E. Gallman, Karin Gleiter, *In Pursuit of Leviathan. Technology, Institutions, Productivity, and Profits in American Whaling: 1816–1906* (Chicago: University of Chicago Press, 1997).

Davis, William M., *Nimrod of the Sea, or the American Whaleman* (New York: Harper, 1874).

Davison, Robert A., *Isaac Hicks, New York Merchant and Quaker: 1767–1820* (Cambridge, Mass: Harvard University Press, 1964).

De Kay, James T., *The Battle of Stonington* (Annapolis, Maryland: Naval Institute Press, 1990).

Dodge, Ernest S., *New England and the South Seas* (Cambridge, Mass: Harvard University Press, 1965).

Dolin, Eric Jay, *Leviathan. The History of Whaling in America* (New York: W. W. Norton, 2007).

Douglas-Lithgow, R. A., *Nantucket, a History* (New York: G.P. Putnam, 1914).

Dow, George Francis, *Whale Ships and Whaling* (Salem, Mass: Marine Research Society, 1925).

Drake, Samuel A., *Nooks and Corners of the New England Coast* (New York: Harper, 1876).

Drake, William B., "Nantucket," *Lippincott's Magazine*, vol. 2 (Philadelphia: 1868), 283–292.

Druett, Joan, *Petticoat Whalers. Whaling Wives at Sea: 1820–1920* (Hanover, New Hampshire: University Press of New England, 2001).

Dudley, Myron C., *Churches and Pastors of Nantucket, Mass.* (Boston: David Clapp, 1902).

Duprey, Kenneth, *Old Houses on Nantucket* (New York: Architectural Book Publishing Co., 1959; Rp.1965).

Ellis, James H., *A Ruinous and Unhappy War. New England and the War of 1812* (New York: Algora, 2009).

Ellis, Leonard B., *History of New Bedford and its Vicinity: 1602–1892* (Syracuse: D. Mason, 1892).

Farnham, Joseph E. C., *Brief Historical Data and Memories of My Boyhood Days in Nantucket* (Providence, R.I: 1923).

Ferguson, Henry L., *Fishers Island, New York: 1614–1925* (Harrison, N. Y: 1974).

Findlay, Alexander G., *A Directory for the Navigation of the Pacific Ocean*, 2 vols. (London: R.H.Laurie, 1851).

Folger, Isaac, *Handbook of Nantucket, Containing a Brief Historical Sketch of the Island with Notes of Interest to Summer Visitors* (Nantucket: Island Review, 1874).

Folger, Walter, "A topographical description of Nantucket in 1791," *Massachusetts Historical Society Collections*, series 1, vol. 3 (1794), 153–155.

Ford, Herbert, *Pitcairn Island as a Port of Call. A Record: 1790–2010* (Jefferson, N.C: McFarland, 2012).

Forman, Henry C., *Early Nantucket and its Whale Houses* (New York: Hastings House, 1966).

Foulke, Roy A., *The Sinews of American Commerce* (New York: Dun & Bradstreet, 1941).

Fowlkes, George A., *A Mirror of Nantucket. An Architectural History of the Island: 1686–1850* (Plainfield, N.J: 1959).

Furniss, William, *Rip Raps, or Drift Thoughts Wide Apart* (New York: De Witt & Lent, 1871),

Gardner, Arthur H., *Wrecks around Nantucket* (Nantucket: 1877; rev. ed. 1915; & later eds.).

Gardner, Will, *The Coffin Saga* (Cambridge, Mass: Riverside Press, 1949).

Garland, Catherine A., *Nantucket Journeys. Exploring the Island, its Architecture, and its Past* (Camden, Maine: Down East Books, 1988).

Gibbons, Marianna, "Old Nantucket," *Lippincott's Magazine*, old series, vol. 28 (Philadelphia: 1881), 303–310.

Godfrey, Edward K., *The Island of Nantucket. What It Was and What It Is* (Boston: Lee & Shepard, 1882).

Goldenberg, Joseph A., "The Royal Navy's blockade in New England waters: 1812–1815," *International History Review* 6 (1984), 424–439.

Grinnell, Joseph, "Speech on the tariff with statistical tables of the whale industry of the United States," U.S. House of Representatives, 1 May, 1844 (Washington, D.C: Gales & Seaton, 1844).

Guba, Emil T. *The Great Nantucket Bank Robbery Conspiracy and Solemn Aftermath* (Waltham, Mass: 1973).

Guthorn, Peter J., *United States Coastal Charts: 1783–1861* (Exton, Pa: Shiffer. 1984).

*Hand-Book of the Island of Nantucket* (Nantucket: I.H.Folger, 1878).

Hart, Francis Russell, *The New England Whale-Fisheries* (Cambridge: CUP, 1924).

Hart, Joseph C., *Miriam Coffin, or the Whale-Fishermen. A Tale*, 2 vols. in 1 (New York: G. & C. & H. Carvill, 1834).

Hawes, Charles, B., *Whaling* (New York: Doubleday, Page, 1924).

Hedges, James B., *The Browns of Providence Plantations: Colonial Years* (Cambridge, Mass: Harvard University Press, 1952).

Heffernan, Thomas F., *Stove by a Whale. Owen Chase and the* Essex (Middletown, Conn: Wesleyan University Press, 1981).

Heflin, Wilson, *Herman Melville's Whaling Years* (Nashville, Tenn: Vanderbilt University Press, 2004).

Hickey, Donald R., *The War of 1812: A Short History* (Urbana, Illinois: University of Illinois Press, 2012).

Hinchman, Lydia S., *Early Settlers of Nantucket, their Associates and Descendants* (Philadelphia: J. B. Lippincott, 1896; 2d ed. Philadelphia: Ferris & Leach, 1901; 3d ed. Philadelphia: W. A. Henry, 1926).

*Historical Whaling Records*, Michael F. Tillman, ed., et al. Reports of the International Whaling Commission, Special Issue, no. 5 (Cambridge: 1983).

Hohman, Elmo P., *The American Whaleman. A Study of Life and Labor in the Whaling Industry* (New York: Longmans, Green, 1928).

Horsman, Reginald, "Nantucket's peace treaty with England in 1814," *New England Quarterly*, vol. 54 (June 1981), 180–198.

Hough, Franklin B., *Papers Relating to the Island of Nantucket* (Albany: 1856).

"Huntsmen of the sea," *Harper's New Monthly Magazine*, 49 (October, 1874), 650–662.

Hussey, Christopher, *Talks about Old Nantucket* (Nantucket: 1901).

Hussey, Roland B., *The Evolution of Siasconset* (Nantucket: 1912).

"The Island of Nantucket," *The Merchant's Magazine and Commercial Review*, vol. 17 (New York: 1847), 368–377.

Jay, William, *Short Discourses to be Read in Families*, 2 vols. (Hartford, Conn: Oliver D. Cooke, 1807).

Jefferson, Thomas, "Report on the American Fisheries, 1 February, 1791," in *The Papers of Thomas Jefferson*, vol. 19 (Princeton: Princeton University Press, 1974), 206–236.

Jenks, Samuel H., "Compendium of the American Whale Fishery," *Hunt's Merchants' Magazine*, vol. 3 (New York: 1840), 172–173.

Johnson, Harry & Frederick S. Lightfoot, *Maritime New York in Nineteenth-Century Photographs* (New York: Dover, 1980).

*Journal of Captain Edmund Gardner of Nantucket and New Bedford*, John M. Bullard, ed. (New Bedford: 1958).

Karttunen, Frances R., "A history of roads and ways in Nantucket county." (Nantucket: 2008).

Karttunen, Frances R., *The Other Islanders. People who Pulled Nantucket's Oars* (New Bedford: Spinner Publications, 2005).

Kendall, Edward A., *Travels Through the Northern Parts of the United States in the Years 1807 and 1808*, 3 vols. (New York: I. Riley, 1809).

*Kendall Whaling Museum Prints*, M.V. & Dorothy Brewington, ed. (Sharon, Mass: Kendall Museum, 1969).

Kert, Faye M., *Privateering. Patriots, and Profits in the War of 1812* (Baltimore: Johns Hopkins Press, 2015).

Kittredge, Henry C., *Shipmasters of Cape Cod* (New York: Houghton Mifflin, 1935; Rp. Hyannis, Mass: 1963).

Kugler, Richard C., "The penetration of the Pacific by American whalemen in the nineteenth century," in *The Opening of the Pacific. Image and Reality* (London: National Maritime Museum, 1971).

Lambert, John, *Travels Through Lower Canada and the United States of North America in the Years 1806, 1807, and 1808*, 3 vols. (London: Richard Phillips, 1810; 3d ed. 2 vols. London: 1816).

Lancaster, Clay, *The Architecture of Historic Nantucket* (New York: McGraw-Hill, 1972).

Lang, J. Christopher, *Building with Nantucket in Mind. Guidelines for Protecting the Historic Architecture and Landscape of Nantucket Island* (Nantucket: Historic District Commission, 1978; 2d ed. 1992).

Lanman, James H.,"The American whale fishery," *Hunt's Merchant's Magazine*, vol. 3 (1840), 361–394.

Lauer, Jack, "From rumor to written record. Credit reporting and the invention of financial identity in nineteenth-century America," *Technology and Culture*, 49 (April, 2008), 301–324.

Leach, Robert J. & Peter Gow, *Quaker Nantucket* (Nantucket: Mill Hill, 1997).

Leavitt, John F., *The Charles W. Morgan* (Mystic, Conn: Mystic Seaport, 1973).

Leavitt, John F., *Wake of the Coasters* (Middletown, Conn: Wesleyan University Press, 1970; 2d ed. Mystic Conn: Mystic Seaport, 1984).

*Life in New Bedford a Hundred Years Ago. The Diary of Joseph R. Anthony*, Zephaniah W. Pease, ed. (New Bedford: Old Dartmouth Historical Society, 1922).

Lipartito, Kenneth, "Mediating reputation. Credit reporting systems in American history," *Business History Review* 87 (2013), 655–677.

*Loan Exhibition of Heirlooms…at the Charles G. Coffin Mansion, Main Street*, 7–18 August, 1935 (Nantucket: 1935).

Lofstrom, William L., *Paita, Outpost of Europe. The Impact of the New England Whaling Fleet on the Socio-Economic Development of Northern Peru: 1832–1865* (Mystic, Conn: Mystic Seaport, 1996).

Logue, Barbara J., "In pursuit of property. Disease and death in a Massachusetts commercial port: 1660–1850," *Journal of Social History* 25/2 (1991), 309–343.

Lovelace, C. S., *A Nantucket Enclave. Monomoy Heights: 1852–2005* (Nantucket: Mill Hill, 2005).

Lund, Judith N., *Whaling Masters and Whaling Voyages Sailing from American Ports* (New Bedford: New Bedford Whaling Museum, 2001).

Macy, Clinton T., *The History of the Episcopal Church on Nantucket Island* (Nantucket: I & M, 1939).

Macy, Obed, *The History of Nantucket* (Boston: Hilliard, Gray & Co., 1835; 2 ed. continued to 1880 by William C. Macy, Mansfield, Mass: Macy & Pratt, 1880).

Macy, William F., *The Story of Old Nantucket* (Nantucket: 1915; 2 ed. Boston: Houghton Mifflin, 1928).

Macy, William F. and Roland B. Hussey, *The Nantucket Scrap Basket* (Nantucket: 1916).

Macy, William H., *There She Blows! The Log of the Arethusa* (Boston: Lee & Shepard, 1877).

Marti, Donald B., "The Reverend Henry Colman's agricultural ministry," *Agricultural History* 51 (July 1977), 524–539.

McMorris, Debra A., *Town Farms and Country Commons. Farming on Nantucket* (Nantucket: Mill Hill, 2010).

Melo, Rosendo, *Historia de la Marina del Perú*, 2 vols. (Lima: Southwell, 1907–1911).

Melville, Herman, *Moby-Dick, or the Whale* (New York: W.W. Norton, 1967).

Melville, Herman, "The Stone fleet," in *Battle Pieces and Aspects of the War* (New York: Harper, 1866).

*Memoirs of General Joseph Gardner Swift,* Harrison Ellery, ed. (Worcester, Mass: 1890).

Mendell, Charles S., "Shipbuilders of Mattapoisett," *Old Dartmouth Historical Sketches*, no. 66, (New Bedford: 1937).

Millet, Samuel, *A Whaling Voyage in the Bark 'Willis': 1849–1850*, Thomas Perkins, ed. (Boston: 1924).

Minturn, R.R., "Nantucket," *The Lakeside Monthly* 10 (1873), 140–144.

Morison, Samuel E., *The Maritime History of Massachusetts: 1783–1860* (Cambridge, Mass: Riverside Press, 1921; rev. ed. 1961).

Moss, Roger W., *Lighting for Historic Buildings. A Guide to Selecting Reproductions* (Washington, D.C: Preservation Trust, 1988).

*Nantucket Argument Settlers* (Nantucket: I & M Press, 1917; rev. eds. 1920, 1924, 1926, 1936, 1943, 1946, 1959, 1966, 1994).

*Nantucket Signals. Private Signal Flags, Owners' Flags, and House Flags of Nantucket Whalers,* Donald E. Ridley, ed. (New Bedford: New Bedford Whaling Museum, 2004).

*Naval War of 1812, The. A Documentary History,* William S. Dudley, ed., 3 vols. (Washington, D.C: Government Printing Office, 1992).

Nevens, William, *Forty Years at Sea, or a Narrative of the Adventures of William Nevens* (Portland, Maine: Dunston, Fenley, & Co., 1846).

*New England and the Sea*, Robert B. Albion, ed. et al. (Mystic, Conn: Mystic Seaport, 1972; rev. ed. 1994).

Nordhoff, Charles, "Cape Cod, Nantucket, and the Vineyard," *Harper's New Monthly Magazine* 51 (1875), 52–66.

Nordhoff, Charles, *Whaling and Fishing* (New York: Dodd, Mead, 1895).

Northrup, A. Judd, *'Sconset Cottage Life* (Syracuse: C.W. Bardeen, 1881; 2d ed. 1901).

"Notes on Nantucket, August 1, 1807," *Massachusetts Historical Society Collections*, III (Boston: 1815), 19–38.

Olmsted, Francis A., *Incidents of a Whaling Voyage* (New York: D. Appleton, 1841).

Rapaport, Diane, *New England Court Records. A Research Guide for Genealogists and Historians* (Burlington, Mass: Quill Pen, 2006).

*Rich Men of Massachusetts, The* (Boston: Fetridge & Co., 1851).

Robinson, John & George F. Dow, *The Sailing Ships of New England: 1607–1907* (Salem, Mass: 1922: Rp. Westminster, Maryland: 1953).

Rodgers, Daniel T., *The Work-Ethic in Industrial America: 1850–1920* (Chicago: University of Chicago Press, 1978).

Rotch, William, *Memorandum Written by William Rotch in the Eightieth Year of his Age* (Boston: Houghton Mifflin, 1916).

Sandage, Scott A., *Born Losers. A History of Failure in America* (Cambridge, Mass: Harvard University Press, 2005).

Scammon, Charles M., *The Marine Mammals of the Northwestern Coast of North America, together with an account of the American whale fishery* (New York: G.P. Putnam's Sons, 1874).

Schweinfurth, J. A., "The early dwellings of Nantucket," *White Pines Series of Architectural Monographs*, vol. 3, no. 6, December 1917 (New York: 1917).

Scoresby, William, "The whale fishery," *North American Review*, vol. 38 (1834), 84–115.

Sharp, Benjamin, "The log of the Asia," *NHA Proceedings* (July 22, 1915), 35–37.

Sheldon, Frank, "Nantucket," *Atlantic Monthly*, 17 (1866), 296–302.

Sherman, Stuart C., *The Voice of the Whaleman* (Providence, RI: Providence Public Library, 1965).

Shuster, George W., "Productivity and the decline of American sperm whaling," *Boston College Environmental Affairs Law Review*, vol. 2 (1972), 345–357.

Silverstone, Paul H., *Civil War Navies: 1855–1883* (New York: Routledge, 2006).

Smiles, Samuel, *Self-Help* (London: John Murray, 1908).

*The South Sea Whaler. An Annotated Bibliography,* Honore Forster, ed. (Sharon, Mass: Kendall Whaling Museum, 1985).

Spears, John R., *The Story of the New England Whalers* (New York: Macmillan, 1922).

Sprague, Stuart S., "The Whaling Ports. A Study of Ninety Years of Rivalry: 1784–1875," *American Neptune* (April 1973), 120–130.

*Spun Yarn from Old Nantucket,* Henry S. Wyer, ed. (Nantucket: I & M Press, 1914).

Stackpole, Edouard, *The Sea Hunters* (New York: Lippincott, 1953).

Starbuck, Alexander, *The History of Nantucket* ((Boston: Goodspeed, 1924).

Starbuck, Alexander, *History of the American Whale Fishery from its Earliest Inception to the Year 1876* (Waltham, Mass: 1878).

Starbuck, Mary Eliza, *My Home and I. A Chronicle of Nantucket* (Boston: Houghton Mifflin, 1929).

"Statistical view of the whale fishery of the United States in 1841," *Hunt's Magazine*, vol. 6 (1842), 187–188.

Stevens, William Oliver, *Nantucket, The Far-Away Island* (New York: Dodd Mead, 1947).

Stroher, D. H., "A summer in New England," *Harper's New Monthly Magazine*, vol. 21 (November 1860), 745–763.

Tower, Walter S., *A History of the American Whale Fishery* (Philadelphia: University of Pennsylvania Press, 1907).

*Trial of Bunker Burnell, Late Cashier of the M. & M. Bank in Nantucket, The,* Court of Common Pleas, June Term, 1847 (Boston: B. B. Mussey, 1847).

Turner, Harry B., *The Story of the Island Steamers* (Nantucket: I & M Press, 1910).

Tyler, Betsy, *A Walk Down Main Street* (Nantucket: Preservation Trust, 2006).

Tyler, Betsy, *Main Street, 'Sconset. The Houses and their Histories* (Nantucket: Preservation Trust, 2012).

*Underhill's, The Old Houses on 'Sconset Bank,* Henry C. Forman, ed. (Nantucket: Myacomet Press, 1961).

*United States Coast Pilot* 2 (Washington, D.C: 2015).

Verrill, A. Hyatt, *The Real Story of the Whaler. Whaling Past and Present* (New York: D. Appleton, 1916).

Vickers, Daniel, "Nantucket whalemen in the deep-sea fishery. The changing anatomy of an early American labor force," *Journal of American History* 72 (1985), 277–296.

*Visitor's Guide to Martha's Vineyard* (Vineyard Grove, Mass: Packard, Stedman, 1876).

Watts, Isaac, *An Arrangement of the Psalms, Hymns, and Spiritual Songs of the Rev. Isaac Watts,* John Rippon, ed. (London: 1801).

*Whale Fishery of New England,* State Street Bank & Trust Co. (New Bedford: Reynolds DeWalt, 1968).

Whitecar, William B., *Four Years Aboard the Whaleship* (Philadelphia: J.B. Lippincott, 1860).

Whittier, John Greenleaf, "The Exiles," in *The Complete Poetical Works of John Greenleaf Whittier* (Boston: Houghton Mifflin, 1895), pp. 14–17.

Worth, Henry B., *Nantucket Lands and Landowners* (Nantucket: 1904).

Wright, Helen, *Sweeper in the Sky. The Life of Maria Mitchell, First Woman Astronomer in America* (Nantucket: Maria Mitchell Association, 1959).

Wyer, Henry S., *Sea-Girt Nantucket* (Nantucket: 1902, 2 ed. 1906).

# Index

## A

abolitionists 173, 218–219
*Abstracts of Whaling Voyages* 96
Adams, John 100
Adams, John Quincy 80, 161
Adams, Orison 174
Adams, Orrin F. 108
Adams, Zenas 135
Adirondacks 157
Africa 34
agriculture. *See farming and agriculture*
Albany, NY 213, 216
Allen, Joseph 105
*American Coast Pilot, The* 44
American Trading Company 93
*American Vocalist, The* 200
Andrews, Thomas S. 132
Appongansett, MA 54–55
architectural styles 23, 75, 81–82, 100, 103–111, 159, 183, 194, 199, 227
Arctic Ocean 122
Argand burner 168
Ashmead, Albert S. 139
Associated Press 94
Athearn, James 137, 146–148, 165–168, 194
Atheneum 107, 199, 203, 218
Atlantic House hotel 159, 161, 205
*Atlantic Neptune, The* 44, 63
Atlantic Ocean 15, 23, 34, 48, 78, 122, 135, 167, 189, 206
Atlantic Pump Company 161
Austin, Jane G. 210
Australia 34, 36–37, 66
Azores Islands 49

## B

Bache, A.D. 206
Bailey, Capt. Stephen 125–127
Baird, Henry M. 26
Baltimore, MD 47, 171–173
*Bankers' Magazine and State Financial Register, The* 87
banks / banking 68, 81–84, 96, 116, 141, 164–168, 171–173, 217
Bank of Commerce, Boston 172
Citizen's Bank, Nantucket 83
Commercial Bank, Boston 172
Commercial Bank, Nantucket 138, 213
Granite Bank, Boston 172
Manufacturers and Mechanics Bank, Nantucket 81, 83, 86–87
Mechanics National Bank, New Bedford 172
Nantucket Bank 22, 82–83
Nantucket Institution for Savings 83, 186
National Banks 82
Pacific Bank, Nantucket 74, 82, 103, 111, 138, 148, 159, 164–165, 183, 185, 189, 205, 213, 223
Phoenix Bank, Nantucket 83, 164
Webster National Bank, Boston 172
Barbadoes Islands 14
Barber, John Warner 141
Baring Company, London / Boston 173
Barker & Athearn 165
Barker, Josiah 22
Barker, Sarah 187, 189
Barnard, Alice 106
Barnard, Cromwell 91
Barnard, Emily T. 97
Barnard, Frederick 217
Barnard, Hezekiah 167, 195
Barnard, Jonathan 91
Barnard, Robert 217–220
Barnard, Shulbael 72
Barney, Daniel 153
Barney, Elizabeth 69
Barney family 41, 88, 101
Barney, Jacob 54
Barney, Nathaniel 70, 110, 178–179, 203
Barnstable County 99
Barrett, Elisa (Mrs. John M. Bovey) 205
Barrett Family 158, 205
Barrett, John W. 110, 159, 161, 164, 187, 189, 205
Barrett, William 187
Barstow, John & Elijah 122
Bates, Sen. Isaac C. 80
Bedford, MA 97
Bergen, NY 216
Bermuda Islands 59
Biddle, Cmdr. 91
Birch, Thomas 113
Black Point 62
blockade 40–41, 46–48, 57, 59, 133
Block Island, RI 43, 51, 58–61
Blunt, Edmund 44
Boston Belting Company 93, 139
Boston, MA 11–12, 22, 27, 33, 36, 39–40, 80–84, 90–93, 137, 139, 141, 145, 149, 164–165, 171–174, 190–192, 202, 205–210, 213
Bovey family 205
Bovey, John M. 205
Bowen, William H. 163
Brant Point 53, 65, 181, 194–195
Brant Point lighthouse 53, 181
Brayton, Mrs. 214
Brazil 11, 75, 189
Brenton Reef, RI 40, 47–48
Brewer, James 213
British 11–16, 39–54, 57–62, 130
Brooklyn, NY 77, 97, 172, 213
Brooklyn Water Loan bond 172
*Brotherhood of Thieves, The* 218
Brown, S.E. 141
Buchanan, Secretary of State James 126
Bufford & Company 149
Bunker, Asa 79, 81, 85, 104, 128–129, 173–179
Bunker, Callott & Company 91
Bunker, Capt. George 90
Bunker family 41, 158
Bunker, Jesse 67
Burgess, Watson 210
Burke, Edmund 80
Burnell, Barker II 88
Burnell, Barker Jr. 75, 80–88, 98, 106, 159, 163–166, 173, 201–202, 210, 213, 229
    Barker Burnell affair 82–88, 164
Burnell, Barker Sr. 75, 80
Burnell, Deborah Barker 87–88
Burnell family 86, 88, 158
Burnell, Jonathan 87
Burnell, Mary 88
Burying Grounds 103
Butler, John 34
Butler, William 34
Buzzards Bay 42–43, 58

## C

Cabot, John 7
Cahoone, John 44
Calcutta, India 212
Calder, T.W. 150
Caldwell, Train & Company, Melbourne 90
California 33, 77, 80, 88, 127–128, 154
Callao, Peru 90–93, 125–127, 134
camels, the 16, 18, 67, 193
Canada 40, 46–47
Canary Islands 34
candles / candlemaking 9, 40, 47, 49, 54, 71–76, 86, 89, 101–102, 108, 110, 116, 138–139, 142, 144, 146, 151, 168–171, 175, 193–196, 199, 221, 223
Canton, China 90
Cape Cod 11, 57, 94, 169
Cape Cod Steamboat Company 94, 170
Cape Horn 13
Cape of Good Hope 14, 34
Carronade Ironworks 49
Cartwright, Charles W. 55
Cary, Edward, house 188
Castino, Raymond 54
Cato lots 72, 88, 201–202
charities and public service 11, 22, 33, 68, 74, 107, 148, 161, 178–179, 195–196, 198, 219
Charleston, SC 91, 129, 133
Chase, Capt. Owen 131–132
Chase, Eunice 132
Chase, Gilbert 52
Chase, Joseph C. 167
Chase, Oliver 91
Chase, Peter 55, 195
Cheever, Rev. Henry T. 124
Chesebrough, Ephraim 45
Chicago, IL 206
Childs, Capt. 51, 58
Chile 88, 93, 125, 137
Chincha Islands, Peru 93
Chinn, William Yates 174
Choate, Rufus 86
churches
    Baptist 101
    Congregational 101
    Congregational Unitarian 101
    Episcopal 101
    Methodist 101, 185
Cincinnati, OH 172, 193, 221
Clapp, Henry 17
Clark, George S. 131
Clasby, Sarah 72
Cleveland, OH 173, 175
Clifford, J. H., District Attorney 84
Clisby, Benjamin 91
Clisby, John 34, 67, 91, 229
coastal trade. *See packet boats and trade*
Coatue 27, 65
Cochrane, Adm. Alexander 42, 47, 59
Coffin, Abial Gardner (Mrs. Zenas Coffin) 68, 72–74, 73, 74, 104, 143, 229
Coffin, Benjamin F. 75, 77, 99, 105–106, 128, 147, 201, 213, 229
    Benjamin F. Coffin house 105
Coffin, Capt. Bartlett 34
Coffin, Capt. Barzillai 133
Coffin, Capt. Benjamin F. 76
Coffin, Capt. Elijah 34
Coffin, Charles G. 68, 71–74, 76, 85, 104, 139, 143–144, 159, 188–189, 196, 199, 201, 218, 229
Coffin, Elisa McArthur 229
Coffin, Elizabeth 202

244

Coffin, Eunice (Mrs. Thomas Macy) 68, 72, 184, 188–189, 229
Coffin family 22, 41, 70, 74, 103, 103–104, 205–206
Coffin, Frederic 229
Coffin, George C. 128
Coffin, Gilbert 57, 104, 143
Coffin, Henry 27, 68, 72–76, 78, 85, 90, 104, 139, 143–144, 159, 184, 188–189, 196, 229
Coffin, Isaiah 75, 102
Coffin, Jared 75–76, 99, 110, 131, 143, 188, 192, 194, 196
 Jared Coffin House 131, 192
 Jared Coffin's store 188
Coffin, Jared II 77–78
Coffin, Jesse 183–184
Coffin, Lydia. *See Crosby, Lydia Coffin (Mrs. Matthew Crosby)*
Coffin, Marianna (Mrs. Frederic Worth) 77–79, 99
Coffin, Mary Crosby. *See Crosby, Mary (Mrs. Benjamin F. Coffin)*
Coffin, Mary (Mrs. Henry Swift) 72, 143, 229
Coffin, Micajah 68, 75, 104, 229
Coffin, Rowland M. 156
Coffin, Thaddeus 211
Coffin, Tristram 8
Coffin, William B. 76, 143
Coffin, William Jr. 17
Coffin, William S. 77–78
Coffin, Zenas 42, 54, 56, 67–76, 81, 85, 88, 90, 98, 101, 104–106, 120, 122, 130, 142–143, 177, 184, 186, 188, 195, 199, 218, 228–229
 Zenas Coffin house 72
Coit, Cmdr. William 48
Coleman, Abigail (Mrs. Micajah Coffin) 229
Coleman, Hezekiah 50
Coleman, Joseph G. 34, 40
Coleman, Phebe 203
Coleman, Silas 50, 56
Colesworthy, Henry 75
Colman, Henry 202
Colt revolvers 90, 126
Columbian Library Society 199
*commenda* 118
Commercial Reading and News Room 200
Commercial Wharf 74, 76, 89, 94, 142–150, 175, 186–189, 211
 reconstruction of 143–145
Congressional Record 126
Continental Congress 12
Cornwall-on-the-Hudson, NY 216
Coskata 152, 195
Cottle, Barzillai 50
cotton 20, 40, 44, 89, 208, 218
counting house 88, 137
Crèvecoeur, Michel Guillaume Jean de 10–11, 22

Crosby, Anna (Mrs. Sylvanus Ewer) 34, 66, 67, 229
Crosby, Ann G. (Mrs. George C. Macy) 70, 72, 75, 78–79, 105, 150, 229
Crosby, Betsey (Mrs. John Clisby) 40, 67, 91, 228, 229
Crosby, Castora Tizón 93, 229
Crosby, Charles C. 70, 90, 93–100, 132, 139, 142–143, 167, 187, 229
Crosby & Company, Sylvanus 90–93
Crosby, Daniel 33
Crosby, Dorcas 216
Crosby, Elizabeth B. (Mrs. William C. Gardner) 70, 96–98, 108, 229
Crosby, Elizabeth B. Powell 70, 74, 88, 91, 95, 98, 104, 188, 201, 217, 224
Crosby, Elizabeth C. Pinkham 75, 91, 94, 97, 106–107
Crosby, Ellen M. Easton 94, 229
Crosby, Emma L. 70, 88, 97–98, 204, 213, 229
Crosby family 68, 93, 101, 150, 158, 189, 206, 209, 215
Crosby, Francis L. 36, 70, 91–93, 98, 100, 160, 175, 202, 206, 229
Crosby, Gilbert 229
Crosby, Huldah (Mrs. Benjamin Whippey Jr.) 34, 40, 67, 87, 189, 229
Crosby, Huldah Pease (Mrs. Sylvanus Crosby) 34, 66, 229
Crosby, Isaiah 229
Crosby, John 33, 229
Crosby, John I 229
Crosby, John, of NY 216
Crosby, Judge Nathan 215
Crosby, Judith C. (Mrs. James Ford Jr.) 70, 89, 96, 188, 214, 229
Crosby, Lot 216, 229
Crosby, Lydia Coffin (Mrs. Matthew Crosby) 62, 69–75, 78–80, 98, 100, 103, 229
Crosby, Lydia (Mrs. Barker Burnell Jr.) 72–75, 73, 80, 87–89
Crosby, Margaret 216
Crosby, Martha (Mrs. Dennis Wood) 89, 96, 98, 214, 221
Crosby, Mary E. "Polly" (Mrs. Owen Wyer) 34, 40, 67, 67–68, 95, 229
Crosby, Mary (Mrs. Benjamin F. Coffin) 68–77, 88, 99, 105, 128, 188, 213, 229
Crosby, Matthew, house 103–104, 160
Crosby, Matthew Jr. 70, 74, 89–92, 97–98, 126–130, 134, 143–144, 175, 205, 210, 219, 221, 229
Crosby, Matthew Lewis 91
Crosby, Mercedes Tizón 229

Crosby, Nathaniel 33
Crosby, Royal 216
Crosby, Samuel 216, 229
Crosby, Sarah C. Whitney 90, 97, 205, 229
Crosby, Sarah Luce 33, 229
Crosby, Simon 33, 229
Crosby & Son 139
Crosby, Susan B. (Mrs. Andrew Lowden) 70, 89, 96–98, 100, 214, 229
Crosby's warehouse 211
Crosby's Wharf 94, 142
Crosby, Sylvanus 33–42, 39, 47, 54, 66–67, 124, 144, 189, 216, 229
Crosby, Sylvanus II 70, 90–91, 92, 93, 98, 100, 129, 135, 213, 229
Crosby, Sylvanus Jr. 34, 66, 229
Crosby, Thankful 216, 229
Crosby, Thomas 33, 229
Crosby, William 229
Crosby, William H. 62, 66, 70–74, 91, 97–98, 106, 108–109, 128–131, 143, 147, 150, 162, 167, 173, 221, 229
 William Crosby house 106–107, 110
Cross Rip 51, 195
Cuba 91, 209
Curtis, J. O 131

**D**

Dagget, Silvanus 52
Dartmouth, MA 53–54
Davis, Capt. Henry W. 134
Davis, Moses 55
De Berdt, Dennis 11
Decatur, Capt. Stephen 49–51, 59
Declaration of Independence 107
Dedham, MA 96–97
Delaware 42, 173
Democratic Party 217
Derbyshire, England 8
Des Barres, Joseph F.W. 44, 63
Detroit, MI 88, 171, 213
Devon, England 8
Dickson, Rod 34
Dorset, England 8
doubloons 61
Douglas-Lithgow, R.A. 219
Dover, England 212
Drake, Samuel Adams 20
Dukes County, MA 99
Dun and Bradstreet 173
Duxbury, MA 15

**E**

Easton, William R. 75, 90, 94, 203
East River, NY 43, 45
Edgartown, MA 16, 34, 53, 129, 130, 213. *See also Martha's Vineyard*
 Cape Poge 51, 53
 Chappaquiddick Island 54
 Waqua (Wasque Point) 53–54

Edwards, Capt. David N. 188–189
Eglinton, Earl of 212
Elizabeth Islands 8, 43, 55
 Quicks Hole 43
Elkins, George B. 161
Ellis, F. A. 27
embargo 12–13, 43, 46, 50–54
Engine Company John B. Chace No. 4 95
England / English 8–29, 12, 33, 35, 38, 43, 50, 118, 153, 171, 212. *See also British*
Essex (Pettipaug), CT 59
Europe 11, 22, 78, 171, 186, 190
Ewer, Ferdinand C. 154
Ewer, Peter 210
Ewer, Sylvanus 34, 66

**F**

factories 9, 16, 101, 108, 142–143, 146, 148, 218
Fairhaven, MA 53, 131, 134–135
Fall River, MA 53–54
Falmouth, MA 41, 52, 54, 57–58. *See also Woods Hole, MA*
farming and agriculture 9, 13, 18, 27, 81, 103, 160, 177, 200–205
Farmington, MA 34
Falkirk, Scotland 49
fires 83, 108, 144–151, 170, 190, 220
 fire of 1799 66–69, 144, 229
 fire of 1812 145
 fire of 1836 146–148, 150, 165
 fire of 1838 1, 76, 146–148
 Great Fire of 1846 83, 86, 148–151, 184–185, 199, 220
 reconstruction 150
firewards 145
Fisher, John 132
Fishers Island, NY 51, 62–63
fishing boats
 *Maria*, sloop 57
 *Mary E. Crosby*, schooner 95
fishing industry 8–13, 20, 57, 89, 120–124, 135, 144, 151, 157, 161, 167–168, 205
 cod fishery 9, 12, 116, 167
 mackerel fishery 167–168
Florida 46
Folger family 75, 103, 158
Folger, Gideon 195
Folger, Isaac 144
Folger, Joseph 203
Folger, Peter 8, 29, 67, 210
Folger, Philip H. 143, 146–147, 159, 161, 194–195, 211
Folger, Walter 31–32, 104, 110
Forbes, Abner 178
Ford, James 96, 229
Fort McHenry 47
Fosdick, Nicoll 44
Foster, Stephen S. 218
France / French 12–14, 31, 35, 45–46, 52, 76, 108, 113, 147, 171, 185

Franklin, Benjamin 66
Franklin Schoolhouse Association 161
Fredericksburg, VA 41
Freeman, Josiah 200–201, 228
French & Coffin 76
French, W.S. 147
Friends Burying Ground 224
Friends Meeting House 76, 187
Friends School, Providence 74, 93

## G

Galapagos Islands 125
Gardner, Arthur H. 41
Gardner, Benjamin 70, 72, 194
Gardner, Edward W. 97, 138, 203
Gardner family 41, 70, 158, 205–206
Gardner, Gideon 47, 195
Gardner, H. Marshall 86
Gardner, John 8
Gardner, Richard 34
Gardner, Simeon 59, 61, 63
Gardner, Simon 55
Gardner, Thomas 71
Gardner, William C. 90, 97, 143, 159, 229
Gardner, Zenas 52
Garneray, Ambroise L. 135
Gay Head, MA 39
Gelston, Samuel 51, 61
Genesee County, NY 216
Georgia 78, 217
Gifford, R. Swain 13
Godfrey, Edward K. 27, 197, 206, 210
gold 11, 18, 61, 77, 80, 95, 127
Gorges, Sir Ferdinando 8
Grant, Ulysses S. 174
Grassy Island 54, 57
Great Britain 14, 45, 51, 190. *See also England / English*
Great Point 41, 194–195
Greene, David R. 96
Greene, J.W. 178
Greenwich, RI 57
Grinnell, Rep. Joseph 126
Groton Long Point, CT 49, 51, 63
guano 91, 93, 202
Gulf Stream 23
guns 37–38, 48–51, 59, 90, 208

## H

Hadwen & Barney 90, 101, 138, 151, 196
Hadwen-Satler house 225
Hadwen, William 90, 101, 109–110, 138, 151, 159, 178–179, 196, 225
Halifax, NS 48, 60, 61
Hammatt, William 22
Hampton Roads, VA 211
Hancock, John 11
Hanover, MA 122
Hardy, Sir Thomas 49, 51

*Harper's New Monthly* 26
*Harper's Weekly* 129
Hartford, CT 90, 213
Harvard University 22, 33, 91
Hassler, Ferdinand R., chart 45
Havana, Cuba 91, 209
Hawaii 113, 123, 127, 189
Head of Plains, Nantucket 152
Health Committee 188
Hell Gate, NY 43, 45, 49
Hispaniola Island 39
hog feeder, design for 204
Hohman, Elmo 166
Horse Shoe Shoal 41
Hotham, Adm. Henry 42, 58–59, 63
House of Correction 198
Howland, Capt. 48
Howland, Isaac 9, 139
Howland, Sarah 97
Howland's Ferry Bridge 52–55
Hull, Abner Jr. 216
Hulsart, C.B. iv, 113
Humane Houses 195–196
Hummock Pond 202
Huntington, CT 43
*Hunt's Magazine* 194
Hussey, Benjamin M. 150
Hussey, Capt. 22
Hussey, Christopher 8
Hussey family 74, 158
Hussey, Josiah 72, 198
Hussey, Oliver 221
Hussey, Phebe 69
Hussey, Timothy 167
Hussey, Valentine 73, 146–147
Hyannis, MA 170–171

## I

Indiana 210
Indians 8–11
Indian territories 46
Inott family 70
insurance companies
Commerical Insurance Company of Nantucket 90, 138, 167
Franklin Insurance Co. 210
Howard Insurance Co, 167
Marine Board of Underwriters 94
Mutual Insurance Company of New York 138
Phoenix Insurance Co. 167
Union Insurance Co. 167
insurance industry 45, 77–78, 96, 108, 116, 119, 128–130, 133, 138, 141, 150, 166–167, 171, 211, 222
investing / investors 7, 8, 13, 16, 22, 27, 33–34, 65–69, 75–76, 80–85, 91, 96–100, 115–123, 128–130, 133–136, 141–143, 152, 156, 161, 164–167, 170–177, 189–191, 200–201, 204, 214, 223

## J

James, Joseph 147
Jay, William 200
Jefferson, Thomas 13, 168
Jenks, Samuel H. Jr 148, 149
Jenner, Edward 38
Johnson, Eastman 28
Jones, Daniel 146, 147, 187, 189
Jones, Judith 7
Jones, Paul 188
Jones, Sally 103
José Somontes & Son, commission merchants, Peru 130
Josiah Macy & Son, New York 90
journals, logbooks and diaries 34, 36–39, 43, 46–47, 56–57, 62–63, 75, 108, 114, 124–125, 128, 158, 184, 188, 190, 199–200
 logbook of the ship *Asia* 38, 46
 Matthew Crosby's journal 46–47, 56–57, 63–64
 Obed Macy's Journal 39
Joy, Capt. David 48, 187, 199
Juan Fernández Islands, Chile 125, 187

## K

Kalamazoo 213
Kelley, Henry A. 139
Kelley, James S. 169
Kerguélen Islands 34
kerosene 94, 169
King Charles I 8
King Henry VII 7
King James I 8

## L

Ladies and Gents restaurant 215
Ladies Howard Society 107
Lake Erie 52
Lambert, John 43
Lambert, Samuel 206–207
lamps 150, 168, 169, 194
letters 22, 46, 62, 70, 91, 94, 108, 126–127, 174, 184, 190, 200, 212, 217
*Letters from an American Farmer* 10
Lewis & Tappan, Boston 90
lifesaving stations 195–196
lighthouses 49, 63, 150, 181, 194–195, 206
lightships 63, 195
Lima, Peru 88, 126–127
Lincoln, Abraham 174
liquor 50, 198, 217
Liverpool, England 40, 48, 78, 206
Loco-Foco Party 217
logbooks. *See journals, logbooks and diaries*
London, England 9–12, 15, 40, 118, 173, 185, 202, 212

Long Island, NY 40
Long Island Sound 43–49, 52, 62, 141
Long Shoal 51
Lowden, Andrew 96, 97, 98, 229
Lowden, Matthew Crosby 96
Lowden, Robert 94
Lowell family 103
Lowell, MA 215

## M

Macy, Alfred 139, 205
Macy, Daniel, house 152
Macy family 70, 80, 101, 189, 205
Macy, George C. 78–79, 105, 150, 173, 194, 229
Macy, George W. 27, 86, 203
Macy, Gorham 79, 150
Macy, Isaac 110
Macy, Joseph B. 133, 135, 167
Macy, Mary (Mrs. Valentine Hussey 73
Macy, Obed 12, 14–15, 39, 47, 66, 144, 158, 188
 *History of Nantucket* 12, 158
 Obed Macy's Journal 39
Macy, Oliver C. 98
Macy, Rowland Hussey 80
Macy, Sylvanus 105
Macy, Thomas 8, 69, 72, 73, 74, 105, 179, 188, 189, 229
Madagascar 34, 38
Madaket 27, 152, 201
Maine 8, 47, 157
Manchester, NH 93
manufacturing 18, 20, 22, 90, 151, 168–169, 199, 221, 223
 boot and shoe 22, 151
 brass 151
 silk 22, 151
 straw 22
 woolens 151
maps and charts 10, 17, 44–45, 63, 75–76, 139, 142, 149, 154, 195, 206–207
 Coffin town map of Nantucket 1834 76
 Damerum map of Long Island, 1815 44
 Ewer map of Nantucket, 1869 154–155
 Jenks map of section destroyed by 1846 fire 149
 Ratzer map of New York 44
 Walling (Henry F.) map of Nantucket 1858 99, 139, 159
Marcy, Secretary of State William L., 126–127
Marquesas Islands 127
Martha's Vineyard 8, 26, 33–34, 34, 40, 43, 51–54, 59, 94, 129–130, 130, 169–170, 213, 228. *See also Edgartown, MA*
Mason Dixon Line 217
Massachusetts Bay Colony 8
Massachusetts General Court 80

Massachusetts House of Representatives 68, 80
Massachusetts Senate 80, 84
Massachusetts State bond 172
Mattapoisett, MA 120, 125, 135
Maverick, Peter Jr. 44
Mayhew, Thomas 8
McArthur, Elisa (Mrs. Charles G. Coffin) 229
Medford, MA 131
Melbourne, Australia 90
Melville, Herman 7, 31, 113–114, 129–132
Mercantile Agency of New York 173–174
Merry, Joseph 216
Miacomet 27
Michigan 172–173, 213
Minneapolis, MN 33
Minturn, R.R. 20
Mioxes Pond 211
Mitchell, Aaron 151
Mitchell, Ann (Mrs. Alfred Macy) 73, 205
Mitchell, Charles 210
Mitchell, Eliza and Henry 189
Mitchell, Ellen 205
Mitchell family 22, 205
Mitchell, Francis M. 203, 205
Mitchell, Frederick W. 52, 110, 159–161, 210
Mitchell, Joseph 205
Mitchell, Maria 70, 205
Mitchell, Obed 151
Mitchell, Peleg 188–189
Mitchell, Peleg Jr. 189
Mitchell, William 164, 187–189, 205, 213
*Moby-Dick* 7, 31, 130, 132
Moore, Thomas 145
Moors End house 76, 110
Morris, Arthur W. 206
Morris, William W. 126
Morton, Andrew 83
Mt. Hope Cemetery 88
Muskeget 8, 53–54

**N**

Nantucket Agricultural Society 203
Nantucket and Cape Cod Steamboat Co. 94, 170
Nantucket Cordage Co. 90
Nantucket County 99
Nantucket Fishing Co. 94, 167
Nantucket Historical Association 62, 88, 94, 96, 132, 151
Nantucket Improvement and Industrial Association 27
Nantucket Looms 86
Nantucket Mechanics Social Library 199
Nantucket Monthly Meeting of Friends 189
Nantucket Shoals 41, 45, 63, 68, 206–207
    Old Man Shoal 208

Nantucket Steamboat Company 169, 170
Nantucket Surf-Side Co. 27
Nantucket Whaling Museum 151
Nantucket Women's Suffrage Association 108
Napoleon Bonaparte 46
National Academy of Design 201
Naushon Island 54–55, 55, 60. *See also* Tarpaulin Cove
neutrality 5, 12–15, 22, 40, 42, 45
New Bedford City bond 172
New Bedford Cordage Company 89
New Bedford, MA 13, 16, 18, 40, 48–49, 52–54, 57–60, 66–67, 83–85, 89–90, 96–97, 117, 120, 130, 134–135, 139, 169–172, 200, 204, 213–214, 221
    Acushnet River 54
    Clarks Cove 52–53
    Rural Cemetery 96
New Haven, CT 40, 171
New Jersey 157
New London, CT 16, 42, 48–51, 58–59, 63, 125
Newman, Emma M. (Mrs. Barker Burnell II) 88
New North Wharf 65, 142, 181, 215
New Orleans, LA 40, 47, 208
Newport Neck 40
Newport, RI 40, 41, 43, 48, 52, 54, 55, 58, 59, 157
newspapers 18, 68, 84, 135, 146–148, 154, 162, 176, 204–205, 218, 221
    *Inquirer and Mirror* 27, 42, 68, 75, 87, 133, 144–148, 162, 169, 174, 192, 196–198, 202–203, 221
    *Nantucket Gazette* 43
    *Nantucket Mirror* 85
    *New Bedford Mercury* 57, 59, 61
    *New York Evening Post* 43
    *Poulson's American Daily Advertiser* 48
    *Whalemen's Shipping List* 16, 19, 127–128
New York, NY 13, 34, 39–45, 49–50, 58–60, 66–70, 78, 80, 88, 90, 93–97, 107, 134, 138–141, 145, 154, 165, 169–173, 190, 192, 199, 201–202, 211, 213, 216–217
    Manhattan 43, 146
New York City bond 172
New Yorkers 157
New Zealand 135
Niagara Falls, NY 213
Nichols, Maria L. 221
Nickerson, Mary 33, 229
Nickol Bay, Australia 66

Niles Register 16
Niven, Capt. John 206–210, 215
Nobadeer / Nobadeer Pond 27, 209
Nobska Point 55, 57
No-Headed Hill 34
Norfolk, England 8
Northeast Auctions 131
North River 122
Northrup, A. Judd 157
North Wharf 34, 65, 181
Nova Scotia 13, 47, 60, 61
Nuku Hiva, Marquesas Islands 127
Nye, Parkin & Company, Canton 90
Nye, Willard 96

**O**

Oahu, Hawaii 123, 127
Oak Bluffs, MA 94
    East Chop 51
Ocean House Hotel 75–76, 192
Ohio 67, 75, 87, 98, 177, 213, 221
Oil Creek, PA 18
Old North Cemetery 67
Old North Wharf 65, 142
Old South Wharf 94–95, 142, 145
Otsego County, NY 216
Our Island Home 163

**P**

Pacific Ocean 13, 15, 74, 75, 111, 115, 116, 122, 124, 127, 128, 132, 134, 135, 164, 183, 185, 205, 210, 223
packet boats and trade 35, 39–45, 48, 51–55, 57, 67–69, 72, 78, 88, 100, 122, 141, 212, 220, 222
    *Amy*, sloop 42, 58
    *Earl*, sloop 54, 55, 212
    *Experiment*, sloop 42
    *Factor* 45
    *Fame*, sloop 42
    *Lily* 51
    mail packet 41, 51–54, 57–58
    *Mary*, sloop of Sag Harbor 41
    *Nancy*, schooner 205
    *Nancy*, sloop 42
    *New Packet*, sloop 41, 42, 45, 47, 49, 69, 228
    *Omega* 45
    *Paragon*, sloop 59
    *Patriot*, sloop 42–46, 69, 72
    *Ranger*, sloop 41
    *Rose*, sloop 40
    *Sally*, sloop 40
    *Solon*, schooner of Fredericksburg 41
    *Sophronia* 45
    *Success*, sloop 42
    *Susannah*, schooner 41
    *Young Hero* 67
Paddack, Capt. Henry 187, 189
Paddack, Peter 57

Paddack, Seth 210
Paita, Peru 91, 127, 130, 134, 186
Palmer, Capt. George 130
Palmer, Cook, & Company, San Francisco 90
Palmer, Eliza 131
Panama 91, 134
Parker, Robert and Love 86
Parker's Point (Juniper Point) 54, 57
Parliament 80
passenger ships
    Black Ball transatlantic line 40
    *Falcon* 88
    *Great Eastern* 78
    *Queen Mary*, HMS 78
    Red Star, transatlantic line 40
    *Rising Star* 134
    *Savannah* 78
    *Susan and Ellen* 33
Peirce, Cyrus 218
Pendexter, Charles 159–160
Pennsylvania 18, 20, 173
Perry, Cmdr. Oliver H. 52
Perth, Australia 37
Peru 74, 75, 81, 88–95, 126–127, 129–130, 175, 221
Peruvian Claims Commission 126
petroleum 18, 169
Petticoat Row 192
Pewabic Mining Company 172–173
Phelon, Capt. Henry 138, 176
Philadelphia, PA 48, 58, 66, 139, 172–173, 188–189
Phillipine Islands 90
Pickering, Sen. Timothy 14
Pimnys Point 143
Pinkham, Alexander 91
Pinkham, Capt. Paul 206
Pinkham, Capt. Seth 75
Pinkham family 41, 108
Pinkham, Helen 97
Pinkham, Mary B. (Mrs. Henry Plaskett) 106
Pisco, Peru 93
Pitcairn Island 127, 131
Pitman, R.B. 163
Plainfield, Nantucket 161
Plaskett, Elizabeth Crosby 106–109
Plaskett, Henry 106
Plum Island, NY 63
poetry / poets 8, 35, 96, 114, 129, 200
Point Judith, RI 39, 48, 58, 61
Polpis / Polpis Harbor 202, 203
population of Nantucket 9, 11, 15, 21, 89, 103, 123, 153, 157, 191, 196
Porter, Asa S. 213
Portland, ME 40–41
Portsmouth, RI 40, 53, 131
Portugal 47, 157
Potter, Thomas 139

247

Poughkeepsie, NY 70
Powell, Caleb 70
Powell, Phebe (Mrs. Oliver C. Macy) 70
privateers 12, 35, 41, 59. *See also warships*
Prospect Hill Cemetery 88
Providence, RI 40, 45, 47, 52, 74, 91, 172
Purdy, John 45

**Q**

Quaise 8, 153, 164, 203
Quakers / Quakerism 8, 12, 22, 32, 69, 70, 100, 107, 110, 168, 188, 198, 217, 224
Quidnet 163, 202
Quincy, Josiah 22

**R**

Race, the 43, 49, 58, 63
railroads 28, 40, 42, 91, 141, 171, 179, 215
  Boston & Albany Railroad 172
  Boston and Providence Railroad 172
  Boston and Worcester Railroad 172
  Burlington and Missouri River Railroad 172
  Cambridge Horse 172
  Delaware & Hudson Canal and Railway Company 173
  Eastern Railroad 172
  Kennebec and Androscoggin Railroad 172
  Michigan Central Railroad 172
  Nantucket Railroad 171
  New Bedford & Taunton Railroad 172
  Old Colony Railroad Company 94
  Philadelphia, Wilmington, and Baltimore Railroad 172
Randel, John 45
Ravenna, Ohio 67, 87, 98, 213
Rawson, Joseph 52
Ray, Captain 45
Read, Rep. John 195
real estate 28, 34, 68–69, 100, 133, 141–142, 151–152, 156, 163–165, 220–221
Recife, Brazil 75
Register of Deeds 174
Remsen, Arnold 187
Remsen, William 187
Rhode Island 53, 74
*Rich Men of Massachusetts, The* 178–179
Rich, Rev. C. 194
Riker's Island 43
Rio de Janeiro, Brazil 131
Robinson, Capt. 45
Robinson, Charles H. 27, 58–59
Robinson, Edward M. 139
Robinson, William 50

Rockwell, Norman 93
Rodgers, Cmdr. John 52
Rogers, Capt. Jonah 41
ropewalk 146
Rotch, Joseph 11
Rotch warehouse 183–184
Rotch, William 11, 69, 90
Rotch, William Jr. 69
Russell, Benjamin 13, 137
Russell, Daniel 55, 198
Russell & Sturgis, Manila 90

**S**

Sachacha / Sachacha Pond 161, 205
Sag Harbor, NY 16, 41, 62, 127
Saint John, NB 211
Saint Thomas, VI 14
Sakonnet Point, RI 63
Sakonnet River 53
Sakonnet Rocks 48, 58
Salem, MA 187, 189, 206–207
Sampson & Tappan 139
San Diego, CA 88
Sandwich, MA 81, 87
San Francisco, CA 88, 90–91, 130
Sankaty Head 161
Sansom, Joseph 7
Santiago, Chile 88
Saybrook, CT 43, 50
schools 36, 74, 93, 161, 196
Scotland 49, 121, 212
*Scribner's Monthly* 26
Seaman's Bethel 130
Shaw, Judge Lemuel 132
sheep / sheep commons 9, 11, 13, 40, 152–156, 202
Sherburne, Nantucket 7, 27, 31, 34, 224
  Sherburn Bluffs 27
  Sherburne Lyceum 224
Shimmo shore 31
ship chandlers 9, 90, 93–94
shipwrecks 41, 195, 206–212
  *Earl of Eglinton*, bark 206–212, 215
  *Earl of Eglinton*, merchant ship 212
  mail packet 41
  *Poinsett*, brig 209
  *Ranger*, sloop 41
  *Shanunga*, ship 208
  *Solon*, schooner 41
  *Susannah*, schooner 41
  *Tarquin*, ship 210
  *W.F. Marshall*, bark 211
Siasconset / 'Sconset 27–28, 94, 100, 111, 152, 156–164, 171, 175, 189, 200–206, 221, 227
slavery 218
Slocum, Squire 54
smallpox 35, 38
Smiles, Samuel 133
Smith, Henry 75
Smith's Point 41
Smooth Hummocks, Nantucket 152

Society of Friends. *See Quakers / Quakerism*
Solomon Porter & Company, Hartford 213
Somerset, MA 54–57
Sorosis Society 107
South America 88, 91
Southampton, England 78
South Beach 142, 151, 153
Southeast Pasture, Nantucket 152
South Shore 28, 211
South Wharf 72, 143, 168, 181
Spain 35, 47, 92
spermaceti 9, 16, 71
sperm oil / whale oil 9, 11, 13, 16, 18, 20, 54, 71, 75, 89, 94, 113, 115, 119–123, 127–131, 135–138, 146, 150, 168, 176–177, 199
Squam / Squam Pond 41, 152
Squash Meadow Shoal 51
Starbuck, Edward 8
Starbuck, E. F. 145–146
Starbuck, Elisa (Mrs. Henry Coffin) 229
Starbuck, Eliza (Mrs. Nathaniel Barney) 110
Starbuck, Eunice (Mrs. William Hadwen) 110
Starbuck family 101, 109–110, 158
Starbuck, George 109
Starbuck houses 109, 143
Starbuck, Joseph 69, 101–104, 109–110, 143–144, 178–179, 188, 196
Starbuck, Levi 143, 165, 194
Starbuck, Mary Swain 110 110
Starbuck, Matthew 109
Starbuck, Obed 189
Starbuck, Simeon 143
Starbuck, William 109
State Board of Health 102
steamboat ferries 18, 27, 63, 78, 94, 169, 190, 204, 214, 217
  *Atlantic* 63
  *Eagle* 51, 169, 228
  *Eagle's Wing* 170
  *Massachusetts* 8–9, 68, 111, 132, 170
  *Monohansett* 170, 228
  *Sankaty* 161
  *Telegraph* 18, 170, 228
Steamboat Wharf 65, 142, 215
Stirling, William, Earl of 8
Stone Fleet, the 129
Stonington, CT 16, 47–49, 58–59, 63
Straight Wharf 34, 114, 142–145, 150, 181, 183, 189
streets, squares, and neighborhoods
  Atlantic Avenue 202
  Bartlett Road 202
  Broad Street 76, 101, 152
  Broadway 156

  Candle Street 143
  Centre Street 23, 34, 101, 150, 165, 192, 210
  Cliff Road 24
  Cliff, the 27–28
  Creeks, the 141
  Dover Street 156
  Easton Street 24
  Easy Street 171
  Fair Street 76, 101, 108, 110, 188
  Federal Street 101, 152
  Fourth Street, New Bedford 214
  Gay Street 151
  India Street 34, 78
  Liberty Street 152, 185
  Lily Street 21, 34
  Lyon Street 79
  Main Street 76–77, 81, 86, 101–106, 109–111, 142–143, 145–148, 159–161, 165, 183–189, 193, 198, 200–202, 221, 225
  Market Square 82, 145, 183, 190
  Milestone Road 162
  Mill Street 102, 110
  Moors Lane 188
  Morey Lane 159, 163
  New Dollar Lane 102, 104
  New Guinea 198
  Newtown, Nantucket 156
  North Shore Hill 24
  Orange Street 29, 81, 86, 101, 106, 163–164, 187, 189
  Pearl Street 34, 146
  Pine Street 72, 79–80, 88, 101, 104–105, 197
  Pleasant Street 76, 88, 101–110, 150, 198
  Polpis Road 202
  Quince Street 152
  Ray's Court 101, 188
  Summer Street 72, 101
  Surfside 28, 171, 196
  Traders Lane 101, 103, 138, 152
  Union Street 146, 165, 187
  Vesper Lane 202
  Wall Street 146
  Washington Street 142, 146
  Whale Street 94–95, 132, 143
Strother, D.H. 26
Surrey, England 8
Swain, Alfred 27
Swain, Capt. Reuben 122, 125
Swain, Charles B. 210
Swain, Mary G. 110
Swain, William ii, 70, 77, 81, 130, 200–201
Swift family 101
Swift, Henry 72, 105, 130, 143, 186, 188, 196, 202, 229
Swift, Joseph Gardner 214
Swift, Mary 72
Swift, Sarah 72
Sylvia, Peter 95
Syracuse, NY 213

## T

Tanner, Benjamin 7
Tappan, Lewis 173, 175
Tarpaulin Cove 54–61
Tarr farm, PA 18
Tashama 202
temperance movement 107, 188–189, 198
Thain, David 84
Tiverton, RI 53
    Old Stone Bridge 53
Tom Nevers Head 208
Tourtellot, S. D. 27
Town Meeting 145, 147, 162–163, 193
Tracy, John Ripley 90–91
Tribunal of the Consulado 126
Trot's Hills, Nantucket 152
Tuckernuck 8, 193, 194, 195
Tumbes, Peru 130
Tupper, James 10
Turner, Harry B. 75

## U

Union army 18
Union Coal in Pennsylvania 172–173
Unitarian Church 65, 95, 101, 114, 202
United Fire Society, The 145
United States bond 172
United States Navigation Act 41
Universalist Church 101
Upton, George B. 139, 202
US Congress 12, 51, 75, 86, 193
US Department of Commerce and Labor 78
US House of Representatives 80
US Topographical Engineers 194

## V

Van Beest, Albert, artist 13
Vanderbilt, Cornelius 179
Vassar College 205
Veazie, W. and J. 27
Vermont State bond 172
Vineyard Haven, MA 59, 213
    Holmes Hole 58–59
Vineyard Sound 43, 55
Virginia 211

## W

Warren, Adm. Sir John B. 51
wars / battles
    American Civil War 25, 122, 129, 133, 218
    American Revolutionary War 12–14, 48
    Battle of Lexington 12
    French Revolution, 1789 13
    War of 1812 14–15, 35, 41, 45–46, 62, 178
    Word War I / Great War 171
warships
    *Borer*, HMS brig 51
    *Dispatch*, HMS sloop-of-war 58–59, 63
    *Eagle*, US schooner 50, 51
    *Endymion*, HMS frigate 58–59, 63
    *Hornet*, US sloop-of-war 49
    *Liverpool Packet*, HMS privateer 48
    *Lunenberg*, HMS privateer 59–61
    *Macedonian*, US frigate 49
    *Merrimac* 190
    *Nimrod*, HMS, bark 55, 57
    *Nymph*, HMS, frigate 57
    *Orpheus*, HMS frigate 47–49
    *Pactolus*, HMS frigate 58
    *Paledeus*, HMS sloop-of-war 59, 61
    *President*, US frigate 52, 59
    *Ramillies*, HMS frigate 47–51, 59
    *Retaliation*, HMS, privateer 57, 60
    *Superb 74*, HMS frigate 42, 51, 58–59, 63
    *Terror*, frigate 59
    *Two Friends*, sloop 54, 57
    *United States*, US frigate 12–14, 41, 49–50, 93, 206
Washington, DC 46, 171, 190, 194
Washington, George 13, 31
Washington House hotel 146, 165
Watch Hill, RI 62
Watertown, MA 8
Watts, Rev. Isaac 200
Weeks, Jacob 216
Weir, Robert Jr. 125
Wesco house lots 152
West, Capt. Joseph 40
Western Union Telegraph Co. 94
West Indies 14, 34, 40, 47, 190
West Island, Fairhaven 52–53
West, Paul 52
Westport, MA 16, 54, 58
    Cestawso Ledge 58
whalemen 11, 18, 31, 36, 129, 131
whale oil 9, 11, 12–20, 26, 35, 36, 40–42, 49, 52, 54, 57, 68, 71–76, 81, 86, 89–90, 96–97, 101, 108, 110, 113–116, 119–131, 134–143, 146–147, 150–152, 157, 165, 168–170, 175–178, 186, 189–194, 199, 202, 218, 221–223
*Whales, Grand Ball given by the*, cartoon 20
whale oil. *See* sperm oil / whale oil
whaling 7, 9, 11–17, 20, 22, 26–28, 35–40, 47, 62, 65–68, 71, 74–77, 80, 82, 85, 88–93, 96, 100, 106, 113–139, 141, 144, 150–151, 163–170, 176–178, 183, 189–194, 201, 204, 206, 212, 217–218
whaling ships 12–16, 20, 34–35, 66–67, 72–78, 81, 89–91, 106, 116–134, 138, 151, 164, 170, 176–177, 184, 189, 193–194, 212, 219
    *Acushnet*, ship 54, 114, 131–132
    *Adam*, ship, of London 15
    *Alexander Coffin*, ship 67
    *Alliance*, ship 34, 37
    *Alligator*, ship 14
    *American*, ship 73, 74, 128–129, 133, 176
    *Amy*, bark 20, 26, 228
    *Ann*, ship 186–187
    *Asia*, ship 34–39, 46, 124
    *Beaver*, ship 116
    *Bohio*, bark 20, 133–135, 228
    *Brothers*, ship 67
    *Catharine*, ship 75, 121, 186–189
    *Charles and Henry*, ship 120–122, 178, 187–188
    *Charles Carroll*, ship 93, 118, 131–132, 177
    *Chelsea*, ship 114, 125
    *Christopher Mitchell*, ship 130
    *Clara Bell*, bark 125
    *Clarkson*, ship 137
    *Commerce*, ship 67
    *Constitution*, ship 31, 72, 186–188, 228
    *Criterion*, ship 52
    *Daniel Webster*, ship 75
    *Dauphin*, ship 75
    *Enterprise*, ship 67, 81
    *Essex*, ship 131–132
    *Eunice H. Adams*, brig 20
    *Fabius*, ship 121–122, 188
    *Fame*, ship 14
    *Franklin*, ship 81
    *Galen*, ship 75
    *Ganges*, ship 81
    *Harvest*, ship 189
    *Henry Astor*, ship 75, 81
    *Henry Clay*, ship 81
    *Hero*, ship 67, 186–188
    *Hope*, ship 14
    *Independence*, ship 72, 188–189
    *Islander*, bark 134–135, 228
    *Joseph Starbuck*, ship 106, 121
    *Leo*, brig 14
    *Lima*, ship 54, 90, 126–127, 130–132, 186, 188, 228
    *Loper*, ship 121, 228
    *Lydia*, ship 52, 72, 103, 104, 105, 106, 121, 163, 165, 184, 186, 188, 213, 218, 229
    *Manilla*, brig 14
    *Maria*, ship 121
    *Mariner*, ship 19, 74, 130, 175–177, 187, 228
    *Maro*, ship 121
    *Mary*, ship 127, 188
    *Montano*, ship 75, 121, 187, 188, 189, 228
    *Mount Hope*, schooner 14
    *Mount Vernon*, ship 81
    *Nantucket*, ship 81, 130, 189
    *Navigator*, ship 19, 74, 81, 85, 130–131, 175–177, 228
    *Neptune*, schooner 63, 138
    *Oak*, bark 20
    *Ocean*, brig 14
    *Ohio*, ship 75
    *Orion*, ship 81
    *Paragon*, ship 189
    *Pequod*, fictional ship 113
    *Persia*, ship 126
    *Peru*, ship 121–122
    *Peruvian*, ship 81
    *Phebe*, ship 187
    *Phoenix*, ship 72
    *Planter*, ship 75
    *Ploughboy*, ship 138
    *President*, ship 54
    *Ranger*, ship 14
    *Reaper*, ship 76
    *Renown*, ship 15
    *R. L. Barstow*, bark 20, 135, 228
    *Romulus*, ship 127
    *Sarah*, ship 75, 121–122
    *Scotland*, ship 121
    *Sea Ranger*, bark 67, 228
    *Sophia Somontes*, ship 130
    *Spartan*, ship 188
    *Spermo*, ship 132
    *Thomas*, ship 76
    *Three Brothers*, ship 121, 138
    *Washington*, ship 19, 72, 74, 77, 81, 90, 122, 123–128, 131, 165, 176–177, 187–188
    *Willis*, bark 120
    *Zenas Coffin*, ship 72, 121
Whig Party 217
Whippey, Benjamin Jr. 34, 67, 189, 229
Whippey, James 67
Whippey, Mary Ann 189
Whippey, Zebulon 67
Whitney, Andrew 90–91, 205–206
Whitney, Daniel 90
Whitney, Elizabeth 97
Whittier, John Greenleaf 8
Wiltshire, England 8
Wing, Abraham 81, 85
Withington family 58–59
Wood and Nye Company 96
Wood, Dennis 96, 98, 213, 221, 229
Woods Hole, MA 43, 51–57, 171
Worcester, MA 27, 172
Worth, David 195
W.R. Grace Company 93
Wyer, Owen 34, 40, 52, 67–68, 229
Wyer, William 67–68, 87–88, 98, 177, 213, 221

## Y

yellow fever 66, 91
Yorkshire, England 33

249

# Illustration Credits

*All photographs and artwork in this book are credited to the source from which they were obtained. If possible, the artist is identified in the caption accompanying the image. In the references below, the letters "a," "b," "c," following a page number refer to the image's location as it appears on the page, in order, from left to right, top to bottom.*

**Nantucket Historical Association:** *ii; 18; 21; 23; 24; 31; 32; 38; 56; 62; 65; 70; 72; 76a; 76b; 77a; 77b; 79; 81; 82; 85; 92; 94; 95a; 95b; 96a; 96b; 96c; 97; 101; 102; 103; 104; 105; 106a; 106b; 107; 111; 114; 126; 133; 134; 141; 142; 143; 145; 151; 153; 156; 157; 160; 161; 162; 164; 169; 171; 179a; 179b; 179c; 183; 184; 185; 186; 187; 192; 197; 199; 201a; 201b; 201c; 203a; 203b; 209; 211; 214; 225*

**Spinner Publications Archives:** *Cover; 7; 13; 19; 43a; 43b; 43c; 48; 53; 55; 57; 59; 61; 99; 109; 117; 128; 129; 130; 135; 136; 158; 168; 170; 180; 195; 196; 207*

**Library of Congress / National Archives:** *2; 10; 17; 28; 44; 63; 139; 149; 154; 159; 226*

**New Bedford Whaling Museum:** *15; 60; 113; 120; 125; 131*

**Private Collection:** *118; 132; 208*

# About the Author

Everett U. Crosby is Emeritus Professor of History and Chairman of the Medieval Studies Program at the University of Virginia. Born in Philadelphia, he was educated at the Germantown Friends School, Yale University (B.A. in history) and the Johns Hopkins University (Ph.D).

Although his research and publications have dealt largely with medieval Europe, the history of Nantucket—a unique off-shore community with a richly variegated past—has always been of interest as a subject for further study. He can claim a long acquaintance with the island, inasmuch as he first disembarked from the steamer *Naushon* in 1934, and members of his family have been summer, as well as year-round, residents for more than a hundred years.